D0085201

THE RUSSIAN LANGUAGE TODAY

MODERN LANGUAGES AND LITERATURE

Languages Editor

R. AUTY, M.A., DR.PHIL.

*Professor of the Comparative Philology of the Slavonic
Languages in the University of London*

The
Russian Language
Today

SYSTEM AND ANOMALY

DENNIS WARD

Professor of Russian in the University of Edinburgh

HUTCHINSON UNIVERSITY LIBRARY

LONDON

HUTCHINSON & CO. (*Publishers*) LTD
178–202 Great Portland Street, London, W.1

London Melbourne Sydney
Auckland Bombay Toronto
Johannesburg New York

★

First published 1965

This book has been set in Times New Roman type face. It has been printed in Great Britain by William Clowes and Sons, Limited, London and Beccles, and bound by them

to
R.H.S.
who gave me my first lessons in Russian

Contents

Preface

When Professor Jopson, formerly Modern languages editor of the Hutchinson University Library, asked me to write a book on Russian for the series I was, and still am, rather alarmed at being associated with the distinguished scholars who had contributed earlier volumes to the series. This book is therefore offered to the reader in all modesty.

Since it is impossible to describe the whole of a language exhaustively in a small book, the scope of this book is very limited. I have dealt only with certain aspects of Russian, but I have tried to keep in mind the word 'today' in the title. I wanted above all to capture recent or present-day developments—some of them only incipient or potential. For that reason all but a few of the examples from Russian authors and periodicals are taken from matter written in the last thirty or so years. A great many of them are from two or three works written in the last decade or so and from recent numbers of a few periodicals.

Where it seemed necessary, I have treated a subject at some length. For instance, the declension of substantives is described in detail to provide a background against which to describe changes that have taken place recently or are taking place now, and, since the most obvious and largest number of changes in a language occur in vocabulary, two entire chapters are devoted to word-formation. Another thing which I have tried to do is to devise, for such things as the 'negative genitive', the short form of the adjective, the verbs of motion, etc., statements which are 'fundamental', i.e. which explain the basic meaning, from which all, or nearly all, other meanings derive logically. I do not expect that everybody will agree with my formulations, but perhaps they will at least stimulate others to produce more accurate formulations. In one or two places I have referred to or set out what other writers have said on these subjects. I hope that these writers will understand that my remarks are not made in any spirit of carping criticism but are made simply to illustrate the nature of the problem. In the first section of Chapter 4, 'Syntax and Parts of Speech', I have done no more than indicate by example a method of analysis of Russian syntax. Here again, I hope that my efforts will stimulate others to analyse Russian syntax on these lines or on other, more promising lines.

In writing this book I have made constant use of B. O. Unbegaun's *Russian Grammar*, the 'Academy Grammar', F. M. Borras and R. F. Christian's *Russian Syntax*, and *Современный русский язык* by Ye. M. Galkina-Fedoruk, M. V. Gorshkova and N. M. Shansky. Where necessary, I have requoted some examples from these books, and I want here to express my thanks to Professor Unbegaun and Messrs Borras and Christian for the examples which I have borrowed from their works.

Mr J. Forsyth, of the Department of Russian, University of Aberdeen, read and commented on the first version of the chapter on stress and the section 'Verbs of Motion' in Chapter 10. He also discussed the latter with me at length in conversation and correspondence. With Dr W. A. Morison, of the B.B.C., I have discussed in letters several features of Russian grammar and have received his kind permission to quote from some of his letters to me. Several colleagues in the University of Edinburgh gave me assistance. Professor

W. E. J. Farvis (Electrical Engineering) verified the accuracy of the footnote on p. 145. Dr A. K. Warder (Sanskrit) furnished me with some notes on reduplication. Professor David Abercrombie (Phonetics) gave me advice on phonetic terminology and transcription. Dr M. A. K. Halliday (English Language and General Linguistics) discussed with me problems of the analysis of Russian clause and sentence structure. Dr J. Ellis (English Language and General Linguistics) discussed this and other topics with me in conversation and in many letters and also allowed me to see a résumé of his doctoral dissertation on compound nouns. Of my colleagues in the Department of Russian, Dr Militsa Greene and Miss E. Vosnesenky have acted, sometimes unwittingly, as informants on usage in their native language, and Mr R. McWhirter has frequently stimulated my interest in Russian grammar with questions on particular problems. Miss Irene Andrew, Secretary-Typist in the Department of Russian, typed several chapters from a manuscript which was not always distinguished by legibility. And two of my children sorted the typescript into top copy and carbons. It is a pleasure to have this opportunity of expressing my gratitude to all these people. Finally, I want to thank my publishers for their patience in waiting for a typescript which, for various reasons, I have presented over a year later than I had promised. Originally I had marked stress only in the chapters where stress was relevant to the argument. The present editor of this series, Professor Robert Auty, of the University of London, rightly suggested that it would be helpful to students to mark stress throughout, and I have accordingly marked 'lexical' stress on all words of more than one syllable. This has meant a short further delay before the book could be printed.

DENNIS WARD

Table of
Phonetic Symbols

Note: ˈ signifies that the following syllable is stressed
ː signifies that the preceding vowel is long

	as in	similar to
i	[ˈivə] и́ва	i in [iːv] *eve*
ɨ	[bɨl] был	———
ɪ	[ɪˈvan] Ива́н	in [hɪt] *hit*
ɪ̯	[bɪ̯ˈla] была́	———
e	[ˈeti̯] э́ти	e in Fr. [le] *les*
ε	[ˈεtə] э́то	ε in [gεt] *get*
a	[ˈatəm] а́том	a in Fr. [la] *la*
æ	[s̢æt̢] сядь	æ in [sæt] *sat*
ɑ	[znɑl] знал	ɑ in [pɑːm] *palm*
ʌ	[gʌˈda] года́	ʌ in [kʌp] *cup*
ə	[ˈgodə] го́да	ə in [ˈsoudə] *soda*
o	[kot] кот	ɔ in [kɔːt] *caught*
ö	[ˈt̢öt̢ə] тётя	———
u	[um] ум	u in Gmn. [tux] *Tuch*
ü	[t̢ül̢] тюль	———
i̯	[boi̯] бой	———
p	[pot] пот	p in [pɔːt] *port*
p̢	[p̢os] пёс	———
b	[bak] бак	b in [bul] *bull*
b̢	[ˈb̢odrə] бёдра	———
m	[mosk] мозг	m in [mout] *moat*
m̢	[m̢ot] мёд	———
f	[ˈfarə] фа́ра	f in [fæt] *fat*
f̢	[ˈf̢εskə] фе́ска	———
v	[vas] вас	v in [væn] *van*
v̢	[v̢æs̢] вязь	———

13

t	[ton] тон	t in Fr. [ta] *ta*
ţ	[ţɛ] те	———
d	[da] да	d in Fr. [dam] *dame*
ḍ	[ˈḍɛlə] дéло	———
n	[no] но	n in Fr. [nu] *noue*
ņ	[ˈņɛbə] нéбо	———
s	[son] сон	s in [sʌn] *son*
ş	[ˈşolə] сёла	———
z	[za] за	z in [ˈjuːzə] *user*
ʐ	[ˈʐornə] зёрна	———
r	[rof] ров	r in Ital. [daˈra] *darà*
ŗ	[ŗof] рёв	———
l	[luk] лук	l in [wulf] *wolf*
ļ	[ļuk] люк	———
k	[kot] кот	k in [kɔːt] *caught*
ķ	[ķɛm] кем	———
g	[got] год	g in [gud] *good*
g̦	[nʌˈg̦ɛ] ногé	———
x	[xam] хам	x in Gmn. [ax] *ach*
χ	[dʌˈχɛ] дохé	———
ts	[bats] бац	ts in [buːts] *boots*
tʃ	[tʃas] час	tʃ in [tʃæt] *chat*
ʒ	[ʒok] жёг	———
ʓ	[ˈvoʒʒɪ] вóжжи	ʒ in [ˈlɛʒə] *leisure*
ʃ	[ʃol] шёл	———
ʆ	[ˈʆʆotka] щётка	ʆ in [ʆɪp] *ship*
ɣ	[ˈboɣə] бóга	———
ɦ	(see Chap. 2)	———
h	(English [hɪt] *hit*)	
j	[juk] юг	j in [jɛs] *yes*
dz	[ʌˈţɛdz bɨ] отéц бы	dz in [ædz] *adze*

Abbreviations

Authors' names

A. N. Tol.	А. Н. Толсто́й
Arb.	А. Арбу́зов
Bab.	И. Ба́бель
Babaev.	С. Бабае́вский
Chekh.	А. Че́хов
Chuk.	К. Чуко́вский
Ehr.	И. Эренбу́рг
Fad.	А. Фаде́ев
Fur.	В. Фу́рманов
G. Nik.	Г. Никола́ева
Gog.	Н. Го́голь
Gor.	М. Го́рький
Kat.	В. Ката́ев
Kav.	В. Каве́рин
Klen.	А. Клёнов
Leon.	Л. Лео́нов
Lerm.	Ю. Ле́рмонтов
Nekr.	В. Некра́сов
N. Ostr.	Н. Остро́вский
Pan.	В. Пано́ва
Paust.	К. Паусто́вский
Piln.	Б. Пильня́к
Pol.	Б. Полево́й
Prish.	М. При́швин
Rom.	П. Ро́манов
Shol.	М. Шо́лохов

| Zoshch. | М. Зóщенко |
| Zur. | Л. Зýров |

Periodicals

Izv.	*Извéстия*
Kom.Pr.	*Комсомóльская прáвда*
Krok.	*Крокодíл*
Sov. Sojuz	*Совéтский сою́з*

Introduction
Russian in the Soviet epoch

A living language is continually changing, even in a small community. Usually, linguistic changes take place so slowly that it is only by looking back over at least several decades that one can detect changes. The most obvious changes in the language of a large, sophisticated community occur in the field of vocabulary, for in such a community new words are constantly being created and old words discarded. Changes take place in pronunciation too, and there may be quite obvious, though small, differences in the pronunciation of speakers from different generations. Fundamental changes in the *phonetic system* of a language, however, usually accumulate gradually over many decades or even centuries. Fundamental changes in the grammar of a language are also slow-working, so that the grammar may appear to remain unchanged for a long period of time. Yet grammatical changes are going on all the time as speakers discard one grammatical structure or explore the furthermost limits of another grammatical structure and sometimes extend its limits. Some 'changes', both in vocabulary and, to a smaller extent, in grammar, are not in fact changes in the language as a whole but cases of transference of an item or structure from one style to another. Thus, a word which was formerly regarded as 'colloquial', or 'dialect', or even 'slang' may come to be accepted by the 'literary language', the boundaries of which are in any case indefinite.

A change which, in retrospect, seems to have been quite sudden has usually occupied several years. For example, before 1917 there were, at most, a few score 'stump-com-pounds', such as штабарм for штаб áрмии, линкóр for линéйный корáбль (see Chapter 6), in Russian, but within a few years after the Revolution several hundred such words had been created. This increase in stump-compounds might therefore be described as a sudden change. The only sphere in which linguistic changes can take place overnight, so to speak, is that of orthography, if orthographical changes are to be recognized as linguistic changes. Such a change took place in Russian in 1917–1918 (see Chapter 3), when certain modifications to the orthography were decreed. One of those modifications meant in fact a grammatical change for, whereas её had previously been only the genitive of онá (and then not in the sense of 'hers' or 'its'), it now took on the function of accusative as well.

It is in periods of social and political upheaval that, generally speaking, linguistic changes take place most rapidly, and here again it is in the field of vocabulary that the most obvious changes occur. New institutions, new offices, new concepts and new artifacts demand new words. The period of the French Revolution is one example of a period when rapid changes in vocabulary occurred in a European language. The Second World War and the follow-ing years have been another such period of change, on a smaller scale, for several European languages, and that not merely in the field of vocabulary. The language of states-men's speeches is, by and large, much less 'formal' today than it was before 1939, and it would be difficult to imagine a statesman of the pre-war period using such an expression as, 'You've never had it so good'!

The period since the Russian Revolution has been one of vast social, political and economic upheaval in Russia. The entire structure of society is fundamentally different from what it was fifty years ago. The organs of government, both national and local, are new. Industry has been developed on an enormous scale, the structure of the agricultural community has been changed, education and literacy have been brought to millions. Yet in most respects the Russian language remains fundamentally the same. A very slight change in the phonetic system may be observed (Chapters 1 and 2), some small changes in grammar have taken place, certain processes of word-formation have ceased to operate and others have been productive in greater or smaller degree. The principal change has been in the increase in vocabulary and this is no more than one would expect. It would be a strange language indeed which did not reflect great social and political changes in its vocabulary.

The linguist whose task is merely to describe a language should not in general make any value-judgments about features of that language. The most he can allow himself is a comment that a particular structure is 'uneconomical' and even this presupposes a comparison with another language or with another structure in the same language. Judgments of the aesthetic qualities of the language of a particular author are the work of the linguist who is dealing with style. To make those judgments the linguist must have certain criteria, of which some at least will be quite arbitrary. Judgments of the aesthetic qualities of a language as a whole, in so far as they are possible, are suspect, for the only criteria applicable are completely arbitrary. If we say that Russian is a 'clumsy' language, then we can only mean that it does not express things in the same way as some other language (presumably our own) and we have arbitrarily taken that other language as our yardstick. All we are saying really is that Russian is not the same as another language. If we say that Russian has been 'spoilt' or 'sullied' in the last half-century, then we have decided, again quite arbitrarily, that Russian of fifty years ago was somehow 'better'. In fact, all we mean is that Russian is not the same as it was.

The authors of *Русский язык при советах*, Andrei and Tatyana Fesenko, frequently give the impression that this is the way their thoughts run: since 1917 there has been a fall from grace and Russian is no longer the beautiful language it once was. The greater part of their book, however, merely records that many new words have been created, that many words have been given new meanings and that some authors use colloquial, dialect and even slang words in their works. A. and T. Fesenko see the origins of the Soviet language (*sci.* vocabulary and phraseology of Russian in the Soviet epoch) in the First World War: 'There is no doubt that it was on the battlefields of the First World War that there sprang up the shoots of the new language, which soon almost overran the language of the classics, created over the centuries by the careful selection and cultivation of linguistic material.'[1] Stump-compounds and initial words, which had made their appearance earlier, became more common during the war. Meanwhile, in the rear, the seeds of 'politicization' of the language were sown. 'Politicization' meant the use of bureaucratic jargon and, in particular, the proliferation of words of foreign origin which denoted new social, political and economic ideas and which were common in the language of one-time *émigré* revolutionaries. Later, with the development of industry, another factor began to affect the Russian vocabulary: 'technicization'—the spread of technical jargon.

Soviet authors and critics have complained not infrequently of the 'impoverishment' or 'sullying' of the language. K. Chukovsky, who has been well known for half a century not only as a writer of children's verse and a collector of linguistic curiosities but also as one who is concerned for the 'purity' of the Russian language, says[2] that people

1 *Русский язык при советах*, p. 16.
2 'О соразмерности и сообразности', *Новый мир*, 1961, no. 5. See also his *Живой как жизнь*, chap. 2.

who write to him about Russian in the Soviet epoch fall into several categories. Some consider that it is inordinate borrowing of foreign words which Russian is suffering from, others demand that the language should be cleansed of vulgarisms. A third category feels that the language is sullied with dialect words, but others 'are indignant because we are too strict with regard to the provincial dialects'. A fifth category wants the language to be more elegant, while a sixth category attacks 'such stump-compounds as Облупрпромпродтовары, Ивгосшвейтрикотажупр, Ургторрудметпромсоюз, etc., and even such as Детгиз, диамат, биофак do not escape censure'. But many of the diseases which Russian suffers from 'turn out, when you look closely into the matter, to be non-existent, imaginary, invented'.[1] And yet, Chukovsky goes on, there is one disease which the language must be saved from—and the sooner the better. 'This disease emaciates the language, because of this disease the language loses its expressiveness, its colour, flexibility and precision. . . . This disease is known as the bureaucratic sickness. Its main symptom is a gravitation to the stereotyped words of the soulless jargon of the bureaucrats.'[2]

The criticism of stylistic abuse can certainly be levelled at bureacrats and journalists, though *Известия* and *Комсомольская правда* under the editorship of Mr Adzhubei, have recently moved somewhat away from the 'soulless jargon of the bureaucrats'. The Soviet cult of 'gigantomania' —the exaggeration of potentialities and achievements (to say nothing of failures and crimes)—has been responsible for some of the worst abuses in bureaucratic-journalistic jargon, for the ordinary and even the downright insignificant can be given massive proportions if it is set on the built-up heels of polysyllabic words and draped in the camouflage of grammatical complexity.

1 K. Chukovsky, *op. cit.*, p. 223.
2 K. Chukovsky, *op. cit.*, p. 223.

Russian is not the only language which suffers from 'gobbledegook'. This and other 'diseases' which have attacked Russian have attacked other European languages too, though they have attacked Russian on a larger scale. We must bear in mind, however, that present-day means of communication lead not only to the rapid spread of linguistic diseases but also to the rapid cure of those diseases. The problems raised by the vast influx of foreign words in the time of Peter the Great were not settled until a century later, but the contemporary language has already gone a long way in discarding unnecessary foreign words. The ponderosities of the Slavonic style afflicted the literary language for centuries: the contemporary literary language can hardly be said to be suffering any longer from the enormities of bureaucratic jargon. And if authors occasionally mine for linguistic material in slang and dialect, this need be no bad thing: the uncultured, crude, racy, sometimes downright vulgar language of Avvakum in his *Житие* was worth the whole of the rest of the seventeenth century.

It is not in literature that the grosser linguistic abuses have been committed. In general, Soviet authors have used political and technical jargon sparingly: sometimes for satirical purposes (as earlier writers satirized linguistic gallomania or slavomania) but usually for the very good reason that they were describing contemporary life (an author can hardly be castigated for using such words as антéнна, фéйдинг, корòтковòлновый, etc., if he is writing about radio reception). The Soviet epoch in fact has seen a thorough exploration of the stylistic possibilities of the language, particularly in the first decade or so after the Revolution. A cursory examination of Soviet literature reveals a wide variety of styles: A. N. Tolstoy, for example, writes in a style which is a direct development of that of the great nineteenth-century authors; Sholokhov's style is marked by the large number of words from the speech of the Don Cossacks; the style of Zoshchenko, and of Ilf and Petrov, is typical of the feuilletonist—racy, slangy, often ironic, sometimes facetious; Babel's very individual style, with its unexpected images, is sometimes quite expressionistic; and, Pasternak has, while maintaining a classic form, gone further than any other poet in the wealth of his imagery and the scope of his phraseological innovation. But when due allowance has been made for the metaphorical use of language and for the unfamiliarity of the institutions which Soviet authors may write about, the greatest difficulty for the foreigner in understanding Soviet literature 'lies in the extraordinarily wide vocabulary used by Soviet authors, and in the frequency with which they employ popular, vulgar, slang and dialect forms or constructions often ignored even in the most comprehensive dictionaries and grammars'.[1]

1 R. Hingley, *Soviet Prose*, p. v.

PART I

SOUND AND SYMBOL

I

Phonetics

'A speech-sound is a sound of definite organic formation and definite acoustic quality'.[1] Speech-sounds may be classified into phonemes. A phoneme is an abstraction from speech-sounds, established by virtue of the following considerations. It may be found that several speech-sounds are organically alike in many respects but differ in one or more other respects and that these differences depend on the phonetic context (including the location of stress as well as the nature of the surrounding sounds). Thus, in Russian, there are two speech-sounds of the 'e'-type: one is front and half open, the other is front and half close. The latter occurs only before soft consonants, while the former occurs elsewhere: ['eʨɪ]—['ɛtət], [ɲɛt], [ɲɛ]. The difference between these two sounds depends on the phonetic context: the two speech-sounds [e] and [ɛ] are in some sense the 'same thing', and the 'same thing' which they are is the phoneme e, conventionally written /e/. The speech-sounds [e] and [ɛ] are said to be members or allophones of the phoneme /e/. The [t]'s in [kʌˈtla], [ʌtnʌˈʃu] and [tuk] are different in that they have different releases—they are 'finished off' in different ways—but the differences between them depend on the phonetic context and they cannot occur in the *same* phonetic context. They are all members of the phoneme /t/. Russian [t] and [ṭ], however, can both occur in the same phonetic context—[tuk], [ṭuk]. The difference between them is not an 'accident'

1 Daniel Jones, *An Outline of English Phonetics*, 8th edition, p. 49.

of the phonetic context but is independent of the context: they are members of two different phonemes, /t/ and /t̩/.

The speech-sounds of Russian are presented below as already classified into phonemes, each with its constituent allophones. The system of substitution of phonemes is also described briefly.

Vowels

/i/ Allophones: [i] and [ɨ] in stressed position, [ɪ] and [ɪ̵] in unstressed position. The allophones [ɨ] and [ɪ̵] occur only after hard consonants, the allophones [i] and [ɪ] occur elsewhere—['piʃut] пы́шут—['piʃut]пи́шут,[pɪx'tet]пыхте́ть —[pɪ'ʃu] пишу́, [il] ил, [ɪ'van] Ива́н. If we write these 'phonematically', i.e. distinguishing phonemes but not allophones, they will be:

/'piʃut/, /'p̣iʃut/, /pix't̩et̩/, /p̣i'ʃu/, /il/, /i'van/

Our knowledge of the circumstances in which each allophone occurs is enough for us to determine which allophone of /i/ is represented by the letter i in each of these words.

/e/ Allophones: [e] before soft consonants, [ɛ] elsewhere— [jest̩], есть, ['eti] э́ти—[jɛst] ест, ['ɛtə] э́то/э́та. Phonematically:

/jest̩/, /'eti/, /jest/, /'eta/

([ə] being an allophone of /a/—see below)

In a common style of pronunciation the phoneme /e/ occurs only in stressed position. In unstressed position it is replaced by the phoneme /i/ (see below).

/a/ Allophones: [a], [æ] and [ɑ] in stressed position, [ʌ] and [ə] in unstressed position. [æ] occurs between two soft consonants, as in [s̩æt̩] сядь, [p̣æt̩] пять. [ɑ] (a retracted [a]) occurs before [l], as in [znal] знал, and [a] occurs elsewhere, as in [sat] сад, [p̨at] пят. Of the two unstressed allophones, [ʌ], which is rather like the 'u' in English *cup*, occurs immediately before the stressed syllable as in [dʌˈla] далá or in absolute initial position, as in [ʌb̨ɪˈs̨intsɨ] абисси́нцы, or in a succession of vowels before the stress, as in [nʌuˈgat] наугáд, while [ə] occurs in the unstressed positions where [ʌ] does not occur, as in [ˈivə] и́ва, [sədʌˈvot] садовóд, [ʌbrəzʌˈvɑl] образовáл. Phonematically, the examples quoted above are:

/s̨at̨/, /p̨at̨/, /znal/, /sat/, /p̨at/, /daˈlla/, /ab̨iˈs̨intsi/, /nauˈgat/, /ˈliva/, /sadaˈvot/, /abrazaˈval/.

It should be noted that after the stress (where [ʌ] does not occur) [ə] occurs not only after hard consonants but also after soft consonants, as in [nʌˈgajə] нагáя, but before the stress neither [ʌ] nor [ə] occurs after soft consonants. Here the phoneme /a/ is replaced by the phoneme /i/ (see below).

/o/ Allophones: [o] and [ö]. The latter, which is a fronted [o], occurs only between two soft consonants, as in [ˈt̨öt̨ə] тётя, while [o] occurs elsewhere, as in [ˈt̨otkə] тётка, [on] он, [os̨] ось. Phonematically, these words:

/ˈt̨ot̨a/, /ˈt̨otka/, /on/, /os̨/.

The phoneme /o/ occurs in stressed position and also in the position of secondary stress, as in [kʌrˌtofɪlɪkʌˈpɑlkə] картὸфелекопáлка. It occurs in unstressed position only in some words of foreign origin, such as [ˈrad̨ɪo] рáдио, [doˈs̨jɛ] досьé. Otherwise the phoneme /o/ does not occur in unstressed position. Here it is replaced in pretonic positions by /i/ after soft consonants, [ʃ] and [ʒ], but by /a/ after hard consonants other than [ʃ] and [ʒ]. In post-tonic positions it is replaced by /a/ after all consonants.

/u/ Allophones: [u] and [ü]. The latter, a fronted [u],

occurs only between soft consonants, the former elsewhere. In unstressed position occur allophones which are less close than [u] and [ü] but for present purposes it is not necessary to distinguish them symbolically.

[um] ум, ['dumə] ду́ма, [u'ma] ума́,
['ļütık] лю́тик, [ţü'fak] тюфя́к.

Phonematically:

/um/, /'duma/, /u'ma/, /'ļuţik/, /ţu'fak/.

Vowel substitutions

Certain vowel substitutions were noted above. These affect the phonemes /e/, /a/ and /o/, which in unstressed position are replaced by other phonemes. This is to say that, for instance, in unstressed position no allophone of /e/ occurs and that in this position an allophone of /i/ occurs instead. Which allophone occurs depends on the rules for the occurrence of the allophones of the phoneme which is acting as 'substitute'. Thus, after soft consonants the allophone of /i/ which replaces /e/ in unstressed position is [ı], whereas after [ʃ], [ʒ] and [ts] it is [ɨ]:

['şţɛnɨ] сте́ны /'şţeni/ — [şţı'na] стена́ /şţi'na/
[ʃeşţ] шесть /ʃeşţ/ — [ʃɨ'şţi] шести́ /ʃi'şţi/.

After a soft consonant in any position before the stress allophones of /a/ do not occur: they are replaced by the [ı] allophone of /i/

[ṗæţ] пять /ṗaţ/ — [ṗı'ţi] пяти́ /ṗi'ţi/
[tʃas] час /tʃas/ — [tʃı'sɨ] часы́ /tʃi'sɨ/.

With few exceptions (see above), no allophones of /o/ occur in unstressed position: they are replaced in post-tonic positions by allophones of /a/ after any consonant, while in pretonic positions they are replaced by allophones of /a/

after hard consonants except [ʃ] and [ʒ] but by allophones
of /i/ after soft consonants and [ʃ], [ʒ][1]

[volk] волк /volk/ — [vʌlˈkof] волко́в /valˈkof/
[ˈgorət] го́род/ ˈgorat/ — [gərʌˈda] города́ /garaˈda/
[ɲos] нёс /ɲos/ — [ɲɪˈsu] несу́ /ɲiˈsu/
[ˈʒonɫ] жёны /ˈʒoni/ — [ʒɫˈna] жена́ /ʒiˈna/

In some words the replacement of /a/ by /i/ after [ʒ] and
[ʃ] is recommended by R. I. Avanesov[2] and others. Such
words include:

[ʒɫˈḻeṭ] жале́ть /ʒiˈḻeṭ/ (cf. [ʒaḻ] жаль /ʒaḻ/)

and other derivatives of the same root,

and [ləʃtˈḍam] лошадя́м / laʃiˈḍam/ —
(cf. [ˈloʃət] ло́шадь /loʃaṭ/)

and the other oblique plural cases of ло́шадь.

Though it persists most strongly in жале́ть and other
derivatives of the same root, this feature of pronunciation
is gradually disappearing.

In the type of pronunciation which is described by R. I.
Avanesov[2] and others unstressed allophones of /e/, distinct
from the unstressed allophones of /i/ do occur. In this type
of pronunciation, known as еканье, the unstressed allophones of /e/ are retracted [e]'s which are ι-like after soft
consonants and ɫ-like after [ʒ] and [ʃ]. These allophones also
replace /o/ and /a/ in the appropriate circumstances. Hence
in еканье-pronunciation there is a system of vowel substitutions in pretonic positions which might be represented by
the following diagrams, where the letters represent pho-

1 There are one or two exceptions to this, such as [ˈʃompəl] шо́м-
пол /ˈʃompal/—[ʃəmpʌˈla] шомпола́/ʃampaˈla/.
2 For instance in his *Русское литературное произношение*.

nemes, those at the head of the arrows being the substitutes
of those from which the arrows lead:

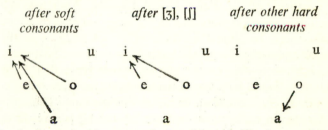

Whereas in the type of pronunciation described earlier in
this section the system of vowel substitutions is :

In both types of pronunciation [ʒ] and [ʃ] play an 'ambiguous' role in that, while being hard consonants, they have
the same substitution effect on /o/ as do soft consonants.
This is a result of the fact that they were originally soft
consonants.

At normal conversational speed the еканье type of pronunciation merges into the other type—the иканье type—
so that both [ɩ], [ɨ] and unstressed allophones of /e/ are
heard in the appropriate positions. The e-like sounds persist
most strongly in initial syllables where the spelling has э, as
in этикéтка [eţɩˈk̦ɛtkə], though here too the sound [ɩ] is
heard—[ɩţɩˈk̦ɛtkə].

In both these types of pronunciation it is not uncommon
to hear after [tʃ] and [ʃtʃ] an unstressed vowel which is very
much like, if not identical with, the [ə] allophone of /a/.[1]

1 In 'pedantic' pronunciation the vowel [ʌ] may be heard in this
position.

This is not recognized as correct by prescriptive or normative phoneticians, but the fact that it occurs is evidence of a possible shift in the Russian vowel system.

Diphthongs

The end-point of all Russian diphthongs is a vowel of the [i]-type. These vowels of the [i]-type do not form separate syllables—for then we should have a sequence of two vowels in two separate syllables, and not a diphthong—but are non-syllabic and may thus be written [i̯], following the conventions of the International Phonetic Alphabet. Although a sound represented by [i̯] may, under certain circumstances, be almost as close as, if not as close as the sound represented by [j], the latter is, in most circumstances, closer than sounds of the [i]-type. Apart from that, [j] is always followed by a vowel belonging to the same syllable. [i̯] cannot, by definition, occur in this position. Thus, the difference in distribution between [i̯] and [j] is a result of differences in the phonetic context and we shall therefore consider [i̯] and [j] to be members of one phoneme, writing that phoneme /j/. We shall consider that the sound [i̯] is a non-syllabic vowel, occurring only after another vowel, and that [j] is a consonant, occurring only before a vowel. The phoneme /j/ therefore has one member, [j], which functions as a consonant, and another member, [i̯], which functions as the end-point of diphthongs.

Any of the Russian vowel phonemes may serve as the starting point of a diphthong. Phonematically, therefore, there are five diphthongs: /ij/, /ej/, /aj/, /oj/ and /uj/. However, the allophone [i̯] of /j/ has the same effect on preceding vowels as do soft consonants and, since some of the vowel allophones do not occur in front of soft consonants, neither do they occur in diphthongs.

/ij/ Allophonically: [ii̯], [ɨi̯], [ɩi̯] and [ᵻi̯]. At normal conversational speed the two elements of [ii̯] may merge into a

single vowel [i], somewhat closer and longer than normal [i].
The elements of the diphthong [ιj] in the ending -ий are
distinct only in fairly careful or slow pronunciation. At normal conversational speed the two elements merge into a
sound which is closer than normal [ι] and may even be identical in quality with [i]. This is not so likely to happen when [ιj]
is not an ending. A similar situation holds with [ɨj], which
at normal conversational speed is reduced to [ɨ]. Thus:

[pʌrˈtij̦nɨ(j)] партийный /parˈtijni(j)/, [ˈvɨj̦du] выйду /ˈvijdu/
[ˈsin̦ɨ(j)] синий /ˈsini(j)/, [tʃɨj̦xʌˈna] чайханá /tʃijxaˈna/,
[ˈkrasnɨ(j)] красный /ˈkrasni(j)/.

The ending -ый is also pronounced [əj], this pronunciation
having once been the 'literary norm'. It is now typical of the
old Moscow pronunciation and of stage pronunciation.

/ej/ Allophonically: [ej̦] only, as in
[nʌˈl̦ej̦țɨ] налéйте /naˈlejți/, [ej̦] эй /ej/.

Those speakers who have unstressed allophones of /e/ in
their speech also use these allophones in diphthongs, where
the orthography has ей or, pretonically, ай (after a palatalized consonant) and яй. Hence, using [e̦] to indicate an
unstressed allophone of /e/

[tʃe̦j̦xʌˈna] чайханá /tʃejxaˈna/,
[je̦j̦ˈtso] яйцó /jejˈtso/.

/aj/ Allophonically: [aj̦], [æj̦], [ʌj̦] and [əj̦], as in
[ιˈgraj̦țɨ] игрáйте /iˈgrajți/,
[tʃæj̦] чай /tʃaj/,
[pʌj̦ˈdu] пойдý /pajˈdu/,
[ˈzdaməj̦] с дáмой /ˈzdamaj/.

/oj/ Allophonically: [oj̦] and [öj̦], as in
[bʌl̦ˈʃoj̦] большóй /bal̦ˈʃoj/,
[ʐɨmˈl̦öj̦] землёй /ʐimˈl̦oj/.

2+

/uj/ Allophonically: [ui̯] and [üi̯], as in

['dui̯t̮ı] ду́йте /'dujt̮i/,
[ui̯'du] уйду́ /uj'du/,
[d̮üi̯m] дюйм /d̮ujm/,
[d̮üi̯'mofkə] дюймо́вка /d̮uj'mofka/.

Consonants

We have seen above that the phoneme /t/ has at least three
allophones. Most of the other consonant phonemes also
have allophones which differ slightly among themselves.
With a few exceptions, which are discussed below, the different allophones are such that the English speaker would
automatically produce them in the right context when speaking Russian, so no further attention will be paid to them.
The majority of the consonant phonemes form pairs such
that one member of each pair consists of hard or non-
palatalized consonants, the other of soft or palatalized
consonants:

hard /p b m f v t d n s z r l/
soft /p̮ b̮ m̮ f̮ v̮ t̮ d̮ n̮ s̮ z̮ r̮ l̮/

The velar consonants [k], [g], [x] also have soft counterparts—[k̮], [g̮], [x̮]. [g̮] and [x̮] occur only before [i], [ı], [e]
and [ɛ], while [g] and [x] occur in other positions. Therefore
[g] and [x] are in complementary distribution with, respectively, [g̮] and [x̮], i.e. the occurrence of either member of
the pairs [g], [g̮] and [x], [x̮] depends entirely on the phonetic
context and where one member of a pair occurs the other
does not occur. [g] and [g̮] are therefore members of one
phoneme /g/, and [x] and [x̮] are members of one phoneme
/x/:

[nʌ'ga] нога́ /na'ga/
['nog̮ı] но́ги /'nogi/
[dʌ'xa] доха́ /dʌ'xa/
[vdʌ'x̮ɛ] в дохе́ /vda'xe/.

As for [k] and [ḵ], we find that [k] occurs in the same sort of positions as [x] but that [ḵ], while occurring in the same sort of positions as [x̣], i.e. before [i], [ɪ], [e] and [ɛ], *also* occurs in a few words before [o] and [u], thus: [tḵot] ткёт (and other forms of the same verb), [lɪˈḵor] ликёр, [ḵɪʌˈsḵor] киоскёр, [mənɪˈḵur] маникюр, [ḵuˈɣɛtkə] кювётка. [ḵ] also occurs in a few proper names before [a] and [j]: [ˈḵaxtə] Кяхта (place-name), [luˈḵjanəf] Лукьянов (personal name). The conclusion to be drawn from these facts is that [k] and [ḵ] belong to different phonemes, namely /k/ and /ḵ/ respectively, but /ḵ/ is obligatory before /i/ and /e/ (within one word) and is otherwise not common.

At the juncture of two words which are 'closely bound' the phoneme /k/ occurs before /i/ and in this case the allophone of /i/ which occurs is [i̇] or [ɨ], since [i] and [ɪ] cannot occur after hard consonants—[ˈkɪɣɪ] к иве, [kɨˈvanu] к Ивану. The other velar phonemes may also be found in similar circumstances and then their hard allophones occur, followed by [ɨ], as in [ˈsmɛxɨ ˈṣlozɨ] смех и слёзы[1]. In general a hard consonant at the end of a word remains hard when the next word begins with /e/ or /i/, the allophone of the latter then being [i̇] or [ɨ] if the two words are closely bound—[ˈsɨvɨ] с ивы (cf. [ˈivɨ] ивы), [ʌtɨˈvanə] от Ивана (cf. [ɪˈvanə] Ивана).

The phoneme /ts/ is a hard consonant with no soft counterpart, the phoneme /tʃ/ is a soft consonant and has no hard counterpart, while /j/, as we have seen, has two allophones—a palatal consonant [j] and the non-syllabic [i̯]. In one style of pronunciation the hard consonant /ʒ/ has a soft counterpart, an independent phoneme /ʑ/, which occurs only within roots and is always of double length—[ʑʑ], as in [ˈvoʑʑɪ] вожжи /ˈvoʑi/, [ujɪˈʑʑætɪ] уезжать /ujiˈʑatɪ/. Although this type of pronunciation is used by actors, radio

---

1 Phonematically–/ṣmex i ˈṣlozi/, since /ˈṣmexi.../ would be read as [ˈṣmɛx̣ɪ...].

announcers and some members of the older generation, it is
not used, by and large, by people of the younger generation,
who pronounce such words as those just quoted as [ˈvoʒʒɨ]
and [ujɨˈʒʒatʲ].

In order to assess the phonemic status of [ʃʃ] and [ʃʃ] ('soft
[ʃʃ]'), it is necessary to take into account the pronunciation of
щ and the letter sequences сч, зч, etc. Some speakers pronounce the latter as [ʃtʃ], i.e. 'soft [ʃʃ]' plus [tʃ], which, bear in
mind, is a soft consonant. (The stop element represented by
t in [tʃ] is weak.) Since the sequence *[ʃtʃ], i.e. hard [ʃʃ] followed by [tʃ], does not occur, [ʃʃ] in the speech of those who
pronounce щ, etc., as [ʃtʃ] is an allophone of /ʃ/. Other
speakers pronounce щ, etc., as [ʃʃ], a 'soft [ʃʃ]' of double
length. Since hard [ʃʃ] of double length also occurs in the
same context (cf. [ʃʃei] щей and [ʃʃei] сшей), [ʃʃ] here cannot
be a member of the phoneme /ʃ/: it is part of the independent
phoneme /ʃ/. In most positions /ʃ/ is phonetically [ʃʃʃ], but
it may be 'reduced' to [ʃʃ] before other consonants and at the
end of a word (as in [ɨˈʒæʃ(ʃ)nɨ(ɨ)] изящный, [tʌˈvarɨʃ(ʃ)]
товарищ).[1]

The sound [ɣ], which used to occur in a few words, such as
[ˈboɣə] бога, [ˈɣospədɨ] господи, is now regarded as archaic
as far as the literary norm is concerned. However, the sound
[ɣ], instead of [g], is found in some Russian dialects and it is
heard not infrequently in Moscow. Though some people in
Moscow who use this sound are natives of regions where [ɣ]
is used, others are undoubtedly not. Such people use this
sound sporadically, under the influence of speakers who
habitually use [ɣ] and of speakers of Ukrainian, in which
language the Old East Slavonic g has become [ɦ] (a 'voiced'
[h]), a sound which is not unlike [ɣ] to the untrained ear.[2]
We have here an example of the influence of the 'village'

1 For a more detailed discussion of the status of [ʃʃ] see my 'Russian
[ʃʃ] and [ʒ]', Le maître phonétique, no. 110.
2 The sound [ɣ] may also occur as an allophone of /x/ (see below).

on the 'city', a natural enough result of the vast influx of country-people to the towns during the Soviet epoch.

Consonant substitutions

If we arrange the consonants of Russian in two sets according to whether they are voiced or voiceless we find that some of them are 'paired' according to this criterion. This is to say that some of the consonants form pairs, the members of which are distinguished only by the presence or absence of voice:

voiceless: p p̡ f f̡ t t̡ s s̡ ʃ k k̡ x x̡ ts tʃ ʧ
    | | | | | | | | | | |
voiced: b b̡ v v̡ d d̡ z z̡ ʒ g g̡   m m̡ n n̡ r r̡ l l̡ j

Voiced members of the pairs do not, as a general rule, occur at the end of a word: they are replaced in this position by their voiceless counterparts:

[bʌˈba] бобá—[bop] боб,
[ˈgrud̡ɪ] грýди—[grut̡] грудь,
[glʌˈza] глазá—[glas] глаз, etc.

This phenomenon may be described briefly as 'devoicing'. Some exceptions to the phenomenon may occur under special circumstances (see below).

Devoicing happens within words too: the voiced members of the pairs do not occur before any of the voiceless consonants (paired or unpaired). Whenever, because of word-formation or form-derivation, a voiced member of a pair would have preceded a voiceless consonant (or whenever this would have happened in the past), the voiced consonant is (or has already been) replaced by a voiceless consonant. This phenomenon of internal devoicing is a type of 'assimilation'—one sound is assimilated in some respect to another. The consonant that replaces the voiced consonant is the latter's voiceless counterpart, unless one or more of the other types of assimilation is operating (see below). Thus:

[glʌˈzok] глазо́к—[glʌˈska] глазка́
[ˈnogət̬] но́готь—[ˈnokt̬ɪ] но́гти,
[nʌrˈɣeʒɨts] норве́жец—[nʌrˈɣeʃtsɨ] норве́жцы.

The converse of devoicing is voicing: the two are varieties of one and the same type of assimilation, in which consonants are assimilated to voicelessness or to voice. The voiceless members of the pairs do not occur before any of the voiced members other than [v] and [ɣ]: they are replaced by a voiced consonant. The latter is the corresponding voiced consonant, unless, as in the case of devoicing, one or more of the other types of assimilation is operating. Thus:

[suˈm̥et̬] суме́ть—[zdʌˈvat̬] сдава́ть,
[ʌtuˈtʃit̬] отучи́ть—[ʌdgʌŋæt̬] отгоня́ть.

The phenomenon may also occur when two words are 'closely bound' and the second word begins with a voiced consonant. In this event the second word is usually a particle as in [ˈroz‿bɨ] рос бы, or less commonly some other unstressed word, as in [ˈkod‿bɨl] кот был. In such circumstances voiceless consonants which are *not* members of pairs may become voiced, i.e. the normal allophone may be replaced by a rare voiced allophone, as in [duɣ‿bɨ] дух бы, [ʌˈt̬edz‿bɨ] оте́ц бы. If *devoicing* should normally have occurred at the end of the first word and the phenomenon is, so to speak, neutralized by the initial voiced consonant of the second word then we have exceptions to the final devoicing rule, as in [ˈroz‿bɨ] роз бы, [ˈgod‿bɨl] год был. It should be pointed out that instances of final voicing or neutralization of final devoicing are rare when the second word is not a particle or some other enclitic, such as да *and*.

In speaking of voicing and devoicing where two or more consonants occur together we have said that one consonant is replaced by another corresponding voiced or voiceless consonant. It could have been put another way by saying that voice or voicelessness extends over the group of two or more consonants, though it is dependent on the voice or voicelessness of the last consonant in the group. This is perhaps the simplest way of describing another type of assimilation—the palatalization of adjacent consonants. Here the feature of palatalization extends over the whole group of two or more consonants and, once again, it is the last consonant in the group which determines the presence or absence of palatalization in the rest of the group.

The palatalization of adjacent consonants occurs in 'indissoluble' forms, i.e. ones which have not been arrived at (in the history of Russian) by way of word-formation or form-derivation, such as [ṣṇɛk] снег, [tʃæṣṭ] часть, and in words which *have* been arrived at by some process of derivation, such as [ṣṭɪˈnuṭ] стянуть, (cf. [ˈstasḳɪvəṭ] стáскивать, [sʌˈgnaṭ] согнáть, etc.).

The system of palatalization of adjacent consonants is not by any means as regular as the system of voicing and devoicing. Practice varies from speaker to speaker, as an examination of the writings of various people on Russian pronunciation shows.[1] Palatalization of adjacent consonants was more extensive in the old norm of pronunciation than it is today. The 'highest common factor' of present-day practices is, roughly, that consonants formed with the same articulating organs are most likely to share a common feature of hardness or softness. This is almost always the case when the *manner* of articulation is also the same, i.e. when, for example, both consonants are stops or both are fricatives. If the manner of articulation is not quite the same or the articulating organs are not quite the same, the

1 For instance, no two of the authors Boyanus, Broch, Obnorsky, Shapiro, Jakobson, Cherry-Halle-Jakobson, Trofimov-Jones, Ushakov and Avanesov (see Bibliography) record exactly the same practice.

phenomenon is less likely to happen. Here are a few examples of palatalization of adjacent consonants where there is identity or near-identity of articulating organs and/or manner of articulation:

[ɣɣol] ввёл, [ˈɣm̻e̻s̻t̻ɪ] вместе, [ʌt̻t̻ɪˈnut̻] оттянуть,
[s̻t̻ɪˈna] стена, [ˈm̻ed̻n̻ɪk] медник, [d̻n̻i] дни,
[ˈp̻et̻l̻ɪ] петли, [ˈban̻t̻ɪk] бантик;

and, with simultaneous voicing or devoicing:

[ˈz̻d̻ɛlət̻] сделать, [ʌd̻d̻ɪˈlit̻] отделить,
[rəz̻d̻ɪˈlit̻] разделить.

In some words the palatalization of a labial consonant has 'regressed' to a preceding alveolar consonant or originally dental consonant (which has then become a palatalized alveolar consonant), as in

[z̻ɣer̻] зверь, [s̻ɣɛt] свет,
[d̻ɣɛ] две, [t̻ɣer̻] Тверь, [ˈd̻m̻it̻r̻ɪ] Дмитрий, etc.

The occurrence of this type of palatalization of adjacent consonants is, however, decreasing in frequency: some younger speakers pronounce, for example, [ˈtɣordɨ] твёрдый not [ˈt̻ɣordɨ], [l̻uˈdm̻ilə] Людмила not [l̻üˈdm̻ilə], and even [dɣɛ] may be heard, though [d̻ɣɛ] is still commoner. Moreover, palatalization of adjacent consonants is less common now when the first consonant is part of a prefix and is discernible as such—[s̻ɣir̻ˈnul] (and [s̻ɣɪr̻ˈnul]) свернул, [rəz̻ɣɪr̻ˈnul] (and [rəz̻ɣɪr̻ˈnul]) развернул, etc. The practice is even less common now when the first consonant is part of a preposition, as in [ˈs̻ɣɛrəj] с Верой. All these facts testify to the increasing restriction of the practice of palatalization of adjacent consonants. It may well be that ultimately the practice will affect only consonants formed with the same organs and in the same manner, though it would be foolhardy to make a definite prophecy.

The converse of palatalization of adjacent consonants,
i.e. hardening before a hard consonant of a consonant which
in other positions is soft, is not so common. It may be observed, with simultaneous devoicing, in such a form as
[ɪrˈlanttsɨ] ирландцы (cf. [ɪrˈlandɪts] ирландец). Such a
word as [ˈmatkə] матка (cf. [matʲ] мать) is not an example
of this phenomenon but an example of a word which has
this form for other historical reasons (note that soft [tʲ] can
also occur before [k], as in [ˈbatʲkə] батька).

Palatalization of adjacent consonants and the last type of
assimilation are, in effect, two aspects of one and the same
type of assimilation: one which concerns place and manner
of articulation. Both these sub-types can occur simultaneously with the type of assimilation which concerns the
presence or absence of voice.

This last type of assimilation affects [s] and [z]. These consonants do not occur before [ʃ], [ʒ] or [tʃ]. In these positions
they are assimilated, both with respect to voice and place
and manner of articulation, to the following consonant.
Compare, for example,

   [sxʌˈdʲitʲ] сходить, [zdʌˈvatʲ] сдавать, [stʲɪˈnutʲ] стянуть,
      [ɪsxʌˈdʲitʲ] исходить, [ˈzdʲɛlətʲ] сделать,
   [ɪzdʌˈvatʲ] издавать, [rəzdʌˈvatʲ] раздавать,   etc.

with

        [ʃʃitʲ] сшить, [ʒʒetʃ] сжечь,
     [ˈʃtʃiʂtɪtʲ] or [ˈʃʃiʂtɪtʲ] счистить,
   [rəʃʃʌˈtatʲ] расшатать, [ɪʒʒɪˈvatʲ] изживать,
   [rəʃtʃɪˈsatʲ] or [rəʃʃɪˈsatʲ] расчесать,   etc.

Before [ʃtʃ] or [ʃʃ] both [s] and [z] 'disappear'—they are
completely assimilated *by* the following consonant, as in

    [ʃtʃɪnˈkom] or [ʃʃɪnˈkom] с щенком,
    [rəʃtʃɪˈpʲitʲ] or [rəʃʃɪˈpʲitʲ] расщепить.

2*

The sounds [t] and [s] may become 'fused' into the affricate [ts]. This occurs when, for example, a root ending, orthographically, in д or т is followed by a suffix beginning with c as in сосе́дский, сове́тский. In careful speech such words are pronounced with [t] + [s], which we shall write [t-s]—[sʌˈsɛt-sķi], [sʌˈγɛt-sķɪ], but at conversational speed they are pronounced with [ts]—[sʌˈsɛtsķɪ], [sʌˈγɛtsķɪ]. The sequence [t-s] differs from [ts] in that the stop of [t] is perceptibly longer than the stop element of [ts]. In the infinitive of reflexive verbs and the third person singular and plural [t] and [s] may be fused into [ts]—

бояться   [bʌˈjat-sə], [bʌˈjatsə],
бойтся   [bʌˈjit-sə], [bʌˈjitsə],
боятся   [bʌˈjat-sə], [bʌˈjatsə].

Spelling-pronunciation

The influence of spelling on pronunciation is evident from some of the facts mentioned above. It is also felt on the last type of assimilation, for such spelling-pronunciations (regarded as 'over-correct' or 'pedantic') as the following can be heard: [ˈʂtʃiʂtɪt] счи́стить, [zʒtˈnoj] (for [ʒʒtˈnoj]) с жено́й, etc. Although, with the spread of literacy, there has been some influence of spelling on pronunciation, it has not been such as to lead to any considerable shifts in the phonetic system. Spelling-pronunciation has, however, meant that the present style of pronunciation used by the great majority of speakers is much nearer to the Leningrad norm than to the old Moscow norm. The latter is distinguished by и́канье, by the pronunciation of щ, etc., as [ʃʃʃ] and not as [ʃtʃ], by more frequent regressive palatalization and by various other features affecting individual words, sets of words and grammatical forms. Among the last one may note the pronunciation of the unstressed neuter

noun ending -e and the unstressed neuter adjective ending -oe as [ə] and [əjə], respectively: мо́ре [ˈmorə], кра́с-
ное [ˈkrasnəjə] (identical with кра́сная [ˈkrasnəjə]). Many
speakers now pronounce such words thus: [ˈmorɪ], [ˈkras-
nəjɪ]. The old Moscow type of pronunciation is still used on
the stage of some of the more important theatres but to
many members of the audience it sounds rather old-
fashioned. Some contemporary writers on the pronunciation
of Russian are somewhat reluctant to recognize the domin-
ance of the Leningrad norm over the Moscow norm.

Loan-words

In many languages the pronunciation of words of foreign
origin often 'infringes' the phonetic system which holds for
words of native origin. Such 'infringements' are found in
Russian too. Mention was made above of the pronunciation
of [o] in unstressed syllables in foreign words. One should
also note the pronunciation of hard consonants before [e]
and [ɛ].[1] In native words the only hard consonants which
can occur before these vowels are [ʃ], [ʒ] and [ts]. In many
foreign words the hard consonants [t], [d], [n], [s], [z] and [r]
also occur before [e] and [ɛ]. Hard labial consonants also
occur sometimes before these vowels. In the majority of
foreign words, however, only soft consonants occur before
[e] and [ɛ] and, as a general rule, the more widely used a
word is, the more likely is it that [e] and [ɛ] will be preceded
by soft, rather than hard consonants. Indeed many foreign
words have become thus assimilated to the phonetic system
of Russian long before this fact is recognized in print by the
writers on Russian phonetics. It is also very common to pronounce a rather open e-vowel in foreign words not only in
initial stressed position but also in initial unstressed position
(in such words as эми́р, эпите́т, эско́рт, etc.)

1 And before [ɪ], where the spelling has e.

Slurred forms

Slurred forms are, of course, common at rapid or even normal conversational speed. It is very common to find, at normal speed, the lapse of the consonant [j] between vowels, particularly when the second vowel is unstressed and especially so when both vowels are unstressed, as in [ɩˈgraɩʈɩ] for [ɩˈgrajɩʈɩ] игра́ете, [məɩˈvo] for [məjɩˈvo] моего́, etc. Such forms as [kʌˈda] for [kʌgˈda] когда́, [tʌˈda] for [tʌgˈda] тогда́, [ˈnovvə] for [ˈnovəvə] но́вого, [ˈnovmu] and even [ˈnowmu] for [ˈnovəmu] но́вому may be heard in rapid or careless speech.

Slurring is particularly common in numerals—[ˈtiʃʈʃə] or [ˈtiʃʃə] for ты́сяча is standard[1] but one also hears [ˈs̨ems̨ət][2] for [ˈs̨emdɩs̨ət] се́мьдесят, [ˈvos̨ɩms̨ət][2] for [ˈvos̨ɩmdɩs̨ət] во́семьдесят, etc. Such slurred forms, which are not peculiar to Soviet speakers of Russian, are regarded as 'bad' by school-teachers and prescriptive phoneticians and, though they may persist in 'sub-standard' and rapid speech, it seems unlikely that they will be accepted as normal for the careful, 'literary' mode of pronunciation[3].

1 [tiʃətʃə] is rather pedantic.
2 With devoicing of the last vowel.
3 Since this book went to press I have been able to read, with the author's kind permission, Dr C. L. Drage's doctoral dissertation 'The palatalization of consonants before palatalized consonants in contemporary standard Russian'. Though there are many individual variations, Dr Drage's work confirms the general impression that where there is similarity in place and manner of articulation then palatalization of adjacent consonants is more likely to occur (see p. 39) and that the phenomenon is less common in younger speakers than in older speakers (p. 40). Proximity to a stressed vowel, particularly when the stressed vowel precedes the consonant-group, increases the probability of regressive palatalization. Dr Drage does not find, however, that regressive palatization is particularly less likely when the first consonant is a prefix.

2

Stress

The phonetic system of Russian has not changed in any significant respect in the last half-century, nor indeed for a much longer time than that. The stress system, which is part of the phonetic system, has not changed either. The fundamental principles still hold—Russian stress is 'free' and 'mobile' (see below) and is closely associated with changes in vowel quality. Changes in the *location* of stress in particular words, however, are constantly occurring. There is a steady tendency to regularize the location of stress in some sets of words, yet this very tendency itself creates further 'anomalies'. This chapter contains a brief examination of the nature of Russian stress and the freedom of stress in Russian, and then a slightly more detailed examination of the mobility of Russian stress. For most of the chapter stress will be treated as a feature of individual words spoken in isolation. At the end of the chapter there will be some remarks on stress as a feature of such groups as, for example, preposition plus substantive. Otherwise stress as a feature of units greater than the single word will not be discussed.

'Stress may be described as the degree of force with which a sound or syllable is uttered.'[1] In languages such as Russian or English one syllable in a word is spoken with greater force than the other syllables. Such a syllable is called the stressed or tonic syllable and such languages are languages

1 Daniel Jones, *An Outline of English Phonetics*, 8th ed., p. 245. We are not concerned here with the mechanics of stress, i.e. the physiological processes which produce stress.

with a stress-accent. Although it is fundamentally a matter of degree of force of utterance, stress is also closely associated with intonation (not only in sentences but also in words spoken in isolation) and length (all other things being equal, a stressed vowel in Russian is slightly longer than an unstressed vowel[1]). Syllables other than the stressed syllable are usually called *unstressed syllables*, though in fact they are pronounced with varying degrees of stress weaker than that of the stressed syllable. The distribution of these varying degrees of weak stress is not the same in Russian as it is in English, where the syllable immediately preceding the stress (the 'pretonic' syllable) is one of the weakest, if not the weakest in a word, and a syllable occurring earlier still in a word may bear the second heaviest stress. This results in many long English words producing a 'two-beat' effect, as for example *òpportúnity, rèvolútion, mìsapprehénsion, pòlysyllábic*. In Russian a polysyllabic word rises, as it were, through increasing degrees of stress until it reaches the most heavily stressed syllable, after which there is an abrupt fall. In other words, the pretonic syllable in Russian is the second most heavily stressed, the pre-pretonic the third most heavily stressed, and so on, while the syllables after the stress (the post-tonic syllables) are all very weakly stressed. Russian words, therefore, both short and long, with the exception of the types mentioned below, produce a 'single-beat' effect. Stress in Russian is quite heavy, rather like that of English.

The great majority of Russian words have only one stress. There are, however, some which have two stresses—and certain types of words regularly have two stresses. Whenever there are two stresses on a word the second stress is heavier than the first, this being, in all probability, a reflex of the

1 See I. Mahnken and M. Braun, 'Zur Vokalquantität im Russischen' and 'Zum „expiratorischen Akzent" im Russischen', *Zeitschrift für Phonetik*, V and VI.

steady rise in degree of stress through the word (see above). Among double stressed words are hyphenated compounds, such as шко́ла-интерна́т[1], фа̀брика-ку́хня, and words with certain numeral prefixes, such as двух̀годи́чный, трёхзна́чный, четырёхдне́вный. The latter are examples of 'abutted compounds' (see Chapter 6) which, in general, have two stresses: сѐмяпо́чка, Сою̀зпеча́ть, etc. The oblique cases of 200, 300 and 400 also have two stresses: двумя̀ста́ми, трёхсо́т, четырёмста́м, etc. Long compound words of recent origin frequently have two stresses: карто̀фелекопа́лка, моро̀зоусто́йчивый, самолётостро́ение, зѝмневесе́нний, etc. Words of this type may be found with more than two stresses: элѐктропа̀роподогрева́тель, трёхсо̀тзна́чный, and here too the last stress is the heaviest. Multiple stress is found too in 'stump-compounds' (Chapter 6), such as о̀блдра̀мтеа́тр and particularly in those initialwords which are pronounced as initials, such as МГУ, СССР, КПСС. Stump-compounds which have become familiar, everyday words usually have only one stress nowadays: колхо́з, госба́нк, спецоде́жда, etc. Finally, the prefixes of foreign origin анти-, ультра-, супер-, транс-, контр-, про-,[2] etc., and the native prefixes после-, сверхand меж- bear a secondary stress: а̀нтинау́чный, у̀льтрафиоле́товый, су̀перобло́жка, тра̀нсатланти́ческий, ко̀нтрразве́дчик, про̀сове́тский, по̀слевое́нный, свѐрхъесте́ственный, мѐжзона́льный.

Russian stress is 'free' (разноме́стный), i.e. it can occur on any syllable and is not restricted to, say the initial syllable, as it is in Czech, or the penultimate, as it is almost entirely in Polish and, to a smaller extent, in Italian. In this respect Russian stress is akin to English, though the fre-

1 Since the 'rule' is as given above, both stresses could be indicated by the acute accent but it is convenient to use the grave accent for the first stress: it serves as a warning that there is a heavier stress coming! The letter ё, of course, always indicates stress (secondary or primary).
2 But not the native prefix про-, as in проходи́ть.

quent occurrence of final stress on polysyllabic words in Russian has no parallel in English. There are in English many types of words in which the position of the stress is more or less rigidly determined.[1] At first sight it would not appear that there are many 'rules' (for that is what the correlation of stress and word-type or grammatical form amounts to) for the location of stress in Russian. There are some obvious rules, such as the following random selection; all words ending in -ция (except фармация, but see footnote) have stress on the preceding syllable[2] (револю́ция, дифра́кция, эволю́ция) and all corresponding adjectives in -ионный are stressed on the о (революцио́нный, дифракцио́нный, эволюцио́нный); the suffixes -изм and -ист are stressed (маркси́зм, коммуни́зм, маркси́ст, коммуни́ст, реванши́ст, etc.); the suffix -олог (when it corresponds to English -ologist) is stressed on the first о, but the corresponding names of sciences in -ология are stressed on the second о (био́лог–биоло́гия, гео́лог–геоло́гия, etc., but моноло́г, where -олог does *not* correspond to -ologist); the adjective ending -ический is always stressed on the first и (коммунисти́ческий, коми́ческий, etc.); perfective verbs

---

1 For instance, words ending in -*lity* are stressed on the preceding syllable (e.g. *impenetrability, actuality*); words ending in -*tion* are stressed on the preceding syllable (e.g. *application, revolution*); words ending in -*ic(al)* are stressed on the preceding syllable (e.g. *phonetic, sporadic, technical, comical*) etc., etc. For a description and historical survey of this in English see G. P. Torsuev, *Вопросы акцентологии современного английского языка.*

2 This is in fact part of a wider rule, which runs as follows: no substantive ending in -ия has stress earlier than the antepenultimate syllable; the majority of substantives in -ия have stress *on* the antepenultimate syllable; about 7% have stress on the penultimate syllable (диспепси́я, эклампси́я, терапи́я, атони́я, фармаци́я, микроскопи́я, etc.) and most of these words are medical terms (which thus form a special sub-set of words in -ия); a few words are stressed on the final syllable (змия́, паремия́, лития́, судия́). The last, as well as the non-medical words in -ия, would have to be listed in a guide to Russian stress, whereas the rest need not be. The wider a rule is, of course, the more likely is it to have exceptions.

with the prefix вы- are always stressed on this prefix (вы́йти, вы́ставить, вы́дать, etc.); and so on. There are other rules which are 'negative' or 'partial', such as the following: only seven verbs of the -овать/-евать ~ -ую/-юю type are stressed on the conjugational endings[1]; all but a few forms of verbs with infinitive ending -чь are stressed on the conjugational endings and on the last syllable of the past tense (unless they are perfectivized by the prefix вы-)[2]; a great many adjectives formed with the suffix -н(-ый) are stressed in the long forms on the syllable immediately preceding the н, but there is a small percentage of exceptions[3] (а́збучный, безро́потный, достопа́мятный, трёхко́мнатный, etc.), including such groups as those formed with the suffixes -оч- and -тель- before -н(-ый), which are normally stressed on the syllable before the first suffix (ба́рочный, винто́вочный, заты́лоч- ный, etc.; блиста́тельный, жела́тельный, занима́тельный, изобрази́тельный, etc.). These and others are well-known rules, but many others could soon be devised.[4]

Occasionally a grammatical differentiation has been brought about by a difference in stress. Thus the adverb *little* in modern Russian is ма́ло only, whereas the short form neuter of the adjective *little* is мало́ or ма́ло. Similarly широко́, глубоко́ and далеко́ are usually adverbs, while широ́ко, глубо́ко and далёко are usually short forms

1 блева́ть — блюю́, блюёшь,	жева́ть — жую́, жуёшь,
клева́ть — клюю́, клюёшь,	кова́ть — кую́, куёшь,
плева́ть — плюю́, плюёшь,	снова́ть — сную́, снуёшь,
сова́ть — сую́, суёшь.	

2 The exceptions being мочь—могу́ but мо́жешь, etc.; лечь— ля́гу, ля́жешь, etc.; стричь—стри́гла, etc.; сечь—се́кла, etc.

3 Amounting, of course, to a large number of words since -н(-ый) is a very common suffix.

4 See J. Forsyth, *A practical guide to Russian stress*, V. Klepko, *A practical handbook on stress in Russian* and, for a historical survey as well, V. Kiparsky, *Der Wortakzent der russischen Scriftsprache*. These works also deal with the stress-patterns of grammatical forms. Much information on the location of stress according to word-type and grammatical form can be gleaned from the Academy Grammar, vol. I, *passim*, and from B. O. Unbegaun's *Russian Grammar*.

neuter of the corresponding adjectives, though they are also
found as adverbs. Such differences, indefinite as they are,
have arisen through the separation of what were formerly
stress-alternants. The utilization of these stress differences is
not yet at an end. With a few adjectives denoting size there is a
nascent differentiation, based on stress-alternants, between
the short form *simpliciter* and the short form, with final
stress, having the meaning 'excessive measure', as in Это
платье широко́ *This dress is too lose*.

A very few words have completely equivalent stress-
alternants, such as творо́г/тво́рог *curds*, ина́че/и́наче
otherwise, and о́бух/обу́х *butt-end* (of an axe). Such alternants as these arise and then are gradually eliminated from
the language. The word против, for instance, which was
used by Lermontov in his poem "Демон" (1838–1841) with
stress on the second syllable—проти́в—is given in the first
edition of Dal's dictionary[1] some two decades later with
alternative stress—про́тив. Nowadays it is stressed only
про́тив. Демон contains several more examples of words
which, in the last hundred years or so have changed their
stress, having passed through a phase of alternative stress.
Such are черти́м–че́ртим,[2] приду́т–приду́т, оцени́т–
оце́нит, кури́тся–ку́рится, хо́лмы–холмы́, сложена́–сло́-
жена, кати́тся–ка́тится, духо́в (*spirits*)–ду́хов, кладби́ще–
кла́дбище, между́–ме́жду. An examination of the words of
other poets through the nineteenth century will show similar
changes in the stress of individual words, some of them of
much later date.

MOBILITY OF STRESS

Stress in Russian is not only free, it is also mobile (подвиж-
но́й), i.e. the location of the stress may be different in dif-

1 V. I. Dal (Даль), *Толковый словарь живаго великорускаго языка* (1863–1866).
2 Lermontov's version is given first, the modern version second.

ferent grammatical forms of the same word. In conjugated verb forms the location of the stress may change from the ending in the first person singular to the root in all the other forms. In the past tense the stress may move from the root on to the ending in the feminine form. Similarly the stress may move between root and case-ending in the declension of substantives. These stress-shifts are not arbitrary, however: there is a limited number of patterns of stress-shift and, with very few exceptions, any one word can have only one pattern of stress-shift.

VERBS: CONJUGATION[1]

In Chapter 10 there is an outline of a method of classifying verbs according to the interrelationship of conjugation-type and infinitive-type (and some other factors, in the case of a few verbs). For the first conjugation there are four conjugation-types:

1. with a vowel letter (the 'stem vowel') before the endings -ю, -ешь, etc. (читáю, стреля́ю, старéю, etc.);
2. with к or г before the endings of the first person singular, but ч or ж before the other endings (пекý, печёшь . . . пекýт, берегý, бережёшь . . . берегýт, etc.);
3. with the same consonant letter before all the conjugational endings, this letter being derived by a regular set of conventions from a different letter in the infinitive (писáть—пишý, пи́шешь, плáкать—плáчу, плáчешь, etc.);
4. with the same consonant letter before all the conjugational endings, this letter not being derived as in type 3: in most verbs the same letter is found in the infinitive too (нестú—несý, несёшь, колóть—колю́, кóлешь, сосáть—сосý, сосёшь, etc.).

There is only one type for the second conjugation.

1 Present-future only. See next section for past tense.

There are two possible stress-patterns in conjugation: fixed stress and mobile stress. Mobile stress occurs *only* if the first person singular is stressed on the ending—in the other forms the stress moves back one syllable and no other pattern of stress-shift is possible. Not all verbs with stress on the ending of the first person singular have a mobile stress. Perfective verbs of any class with the prefix вы- have stress fixed on this prefix. Otherwise the following rules apply. In type 1 the stress is fixed: on the root (де́лаю, де́лаешь), on the stem-vowel (чита́ю, чита́ешь), or on the ending[1] (узна́ю, узнаёшь). In type 2 there is one verb[2] with mobile stress: могу́, мо́жешь . . . мо́гут. Otherwise the stress is fixed: on the root in ля́гу, ля́жешь . . . ля́гут but on the ending in all others: пеку́, печёшь . . . пеку́т, берегу́, бережёшь . . . берегу́т, etc. In type 3 there are some sixty verbs. Fourteen of these have fixed stress on the root, as in пла́кать—пла́чу, пла́чешь . . . пла́чут. The others with fixed stress are (given, for brevity, in the infinitive only): кли́кать, мурлы́кать, ты́кать, бры́згать, дви́гать, пря́тать, ры́скать, ма́зать, ре́зать, ка́пать, сы́пать, and two which are slightly exceptional in having the infinitive stressed differently from the fixed-stress conjugation: колеба́ть—коле́блю, коле́блешь, and колыха́ть—колы́шу, колы́шешь. All the rest have mobile stress: писа́ть—пишу́, пи́шешь, маха́ть—машу́, ма́шешь, иска́ть—ищу́, и́щешь, мета́ть—мечу́, ме́чешь, etc. In the singular the verb хоте́ть has a type 3 conjugation, with mobile stress: хочу́, хо́чешь, хо́чет, but in the plural it is an end-stressed second conjugation verb: хоти́м, хоти́те, хотя́т. In type 4 there are many

1 It being understood that in the second person plural ending -ете/-ите it is the first vowel which bears the stress.
2 Here and elsewhere in this chapter 'verb' is to be understood to mean 'basic verb from which others with the same stress pattern may be derived by means of prefixes'. Thus, as far as stress pattern is concerned, могу́, мо́жешь . . . мо́гут includes помогу́, помо́жешь . . . помо́гут, although the meanings of the two verbs are quite different.

scores of verbs of different classes but this conjugation-
type as a whole has fixed stress. The only ones with mobile
stress are:

1 The five verbs with infinitive in -оть: боро́ться—бо-
   рю́сь, бо́решься; коло́ть—колю́, ко́лешь; моло́ть—
   мелю́, ме́лешь; поло́ть,—полю́, по́лешь; and по-
   ро́ть—порю́, по́решь.

2 Those seven compounds of the verb -нять/-ять (always
   prefixed) which have -ним, -им, or -ым- in the conjugation: обня́ть—обниму́, обни́мешь; отня́ть—отниму́,
   отни́мешь; подня́ть—подниму́, подни́мешь; при-
   ня́ть—приму́, при́мешь; разня́ть—разниму́, разни́-
   мешь; снять—сниму́, сни́мешь; and изъя́ть—изыму́,
   изы́мешь. (The other compounds of -нять/-ять have
   -йм- in the conjugation and fixed stress on the ending:
   поня́ть—пойму́, поймёшь, etc.).

3 A few verbs which have an infinitive ending in -нуть:
   тону́ть—тону́, то́нешь; тяну́ть—тяну́, тя́нешь; об-
   ману́ть—обману́, обма́нешь, (с-, у-)помяну́ть—
   помяну́, помя́нешь.[1]

4 the verb стона́ть: стону́, сто́нешь.
   The remaining verbs with type 4 conjugation have fixed
   stress. Those with infinitive ending in -ти or -ть after a
   consonant have stress on the ending, except in лезть
   —ле́зу, ле́зешь and сесть—ся́ду, ся́дешь. The stress is
   also on the root in the two verbs е́хать—е́ду, е́дешь and
   жа́ждать—жа́жду, жа́ждешь. All those verbs with infinitive in -нуть which lose the -н- in the past tense have
   stress on the root: мёрзнуть—мёрзну, мёрзнешь;
   ги́бнуть—ги́бну, ги́бнешь, etc. In the productive
   class of verbs in -нуть, which retain the -н- in the past
   tense, some are stressed on the endings, others on the

---

1 The verb мину́ть shifts the stress from y in the infinitive to и in
the conjugation—ми́нешь, ми́нет—but has no first person singular.

root; and the stress is in the same place in the conjugation as in the infinitive: дро́гнуть—дро́гну, дро́гнешь; кри́кнуть—кри́кну, кри́кнешь; косну́ться—косну́сь, коснёшься; улыбну́ться—улыбну́сь, улыбнёшься, etc., etc.

In the second conjugation the fixed stress may be on the root, as in чи́стить—чи́щу, чи́стишь, or on the ending, as in запрети́ть—запрещу́, запрети́шь. Mobile stress is also found but it is much less common than fixed stress. There are some one hundred and sixty verbs of both conjugations with mobile stress, and first conjugation verbs mentioned above account for over sixty of this number. Hence there are only about ninety verbs with mobile stress in the very large class of second conjugation verbs, and a few of these have an alternative fixed-stress pattern. Moreover, the majority of second conjugation verbs with infinitive in -еть have fixed final stress as in лете́ть—лечу́, лети́шь. Four have stress on the root: ви́деть, ненави́деть, оби́деть and зави́сеть (but висе́ть), and three only have mobile stress: верте́ть—верчу́, ве́ртишь, терпе́ть—терплю́, те́рпишь and смотре́ть—смотрю́, смо́тришь. The two dozen second conjugation verbs with infinitive in -ать have fixed final stress, except слы́шать, with root stress, and держа́ть, дыша́ть, with mobile stress—держу́, де́ржишь; дышу́, ды́шишь. Гнать, which has a mobile vowel in the conjugation, should also be included here: гоню́, го́нишь.

The majority of verbs have fixed stress in the past tense, corresponding with the stress in the infinitive: де́лать–де́лал, стреля́ть–стреля́л, ходи́ть–ходи́л, etc. Fixed final stress is found in verbs with infinitive ending in -ти and -чь, the stress falling on the last syllable of the root in the past tense masculine: (при-)нёс, несла́, несло́, несли́, берёг, берегла́, берегло́, берегли́, etc.

A few verbs with monosyllabic infinitives have a mobile stress, shifting the stress on to the ending in the feminine, as in был, была́, бы́ло, бы́ли. The other verbs with this pattern are брать, взять, вить, гнать, дать, драть, жить, звать, лить, пить, плыть, рвать, спать and the archaic verb слыть. Дать has an alternative past tense neuter дало́, as well as the commoner да́ло. The verb роди́ть also has the feminine ending stressed when it is perfective: роди́л, родила́, роди́ло, роди́ли but not when it is imperfective: роди́л, роди́ла, роди́ло, роди́ли.

One or two verbs which are always prefixed or in which the prefix can no longer be separated from the root also have the feminine ending stressed: зача́ть—зача́л, зачала́, зача́ло, зача́ли, опереть—опёр, оперла́ (also опёрла), опёрло, опёрли.

Some prefixed verbs, including one or two which cannot occur without a prefix, have a stress pattern in which the stress falls on the ending in the feminine but on the *prefix* in the other forms, as in отда́ть—о́тдал, отдала́, о́тдало, о́тдали. Other verbs which have this pattern in some of their prefixed derivatives are быть (при́был, прибыла́), жить (до́жил, дожила́), клясть (про́клял, прокляла́), лить (про́лил, пролила́), пить (до́пил, допила́), and the verbs умере́ть (у́мер, умерла́), замере́ть (за́мер, замерла́), обмере́ть (о́бмер, обмерла́), перемере́ть (пе́ремер, перемерла́), запере́ть (за́пер, заперла́), отпере́ть (о́тпер, отперла́), нача́ть (на́чал, начала́) and most compounds of -нять/-ять—поня́ть (по́нял, поняла́), отня́ть (о́тнял, отняла́), etc. The verb созда́ть, though not etymologically connected with дать, has the same pattern as compounds of this verb: со́здал–создала́. Not all the compounds of these verbs have stress on the prefix in the masculine, neuter and plural: возда́л–воздала́, изда́л–издала́, надда́л–наддала́,

уня́л–уняла́, разня́л–разняла́. Some compounds of these
verbs retain the stress on the root even in the feminine:
забы́л–забы́ла, подпёр–подпёрла and a few with stressed
prefixes have alternatives with stress on the root, as in от-
ня́л, отняла́. Such alternatives are considered at present to
be colloquial but it may well be that they represent the first
stage in a slow process wherein the forms stressed on the
prefix will be eradicated.

When they are reflexive, some of the verbs listed above
have stress on the last syllable in all forms, so that in the
masculine stress falls on the reflexive particle ся, as in
заперся́, заперла́сь, заперло́сь, заперли́сь and отперся́,
отперла́сь, отперло́сь, отперли́сь and занялся́, заняла́сь,
заняло́сь, заняли́сь. Colloquial variants with stress as in
the non-reflexive form are heard, such as за́перся, запер-
ла́сь, за́перлось, за́перлись. Similarly нача́ться, with past
tense начался́, начала́сь, начало́сь, начали́сь, has colloquial variants на́чалось, etc.). A generation ago the following
verbs had stress on the reflexive particle in the past tense
masculine but now no longer do so:

> бра́лся, брала́сь, брало́сь, брали́сь,
> ви́лся, вила́сь, вило́сь, вили́сь,
> взя́лся, взяла́сь, взяло́сь, взяли́сь,
> гна́лся, гнала́сь, гнало́сь, гнали́сь,
> да́лся, дала́сь, дало́сь, дали́сь,
> дра́лся, драла́сь, драло́сь, драли́сь.

Moreover, all these verbs have alternatives, some of them
still considered colloquial, with stress on the root in the
neuter and plural forms too. The verb роди́ться (pfv.) has
past tense роди́лся/родился́, родила́сь, родило́сь, роди-
ли́сь, with alternatives роди́лась (N.B.), роди́лось, роди́-
лись.

In these reflexive verbs too a slow process of levelling or
regularization is taking place. In general they are being

brought into the pattern which has stress on the feminine ending but otherwise on the root.

PARTICIPLES

The participles of the verb have an even more straight-forward stress system. In their long forms they behave like long adjectives and thus there are no stress-shifts in their declensions. In their short forms the present passive and present active participles retain the stress where it is in the long form.

The past passive participle in -анный/-янный has stress on the root or prefix if the infinitive is stressed on root or prefix. If the infinitive is stressed on a/я, then the stress in the past passive participle moves one syllable nearer the beginning of the word, as in задáть–зáданный, расстре-ля́ть–растре́лянный. Желáть–желáнный is exceptional in not having a stress-shift and передáть–пе́реданный is exceptional in shifting the stress two syllables. The stress remains in the same place in the short forms unless the verb is one of those described in the preceding section which have mobile stress in the past tense. Thus, со́бранный—со́бран, собранá, со́брано, со́браны; зáданный—зáдан, заданá, зáдано, зáданы, etc. Дáнный has short forms дан, данá, данó, даны́.

The location of the stress in the past passive participle in -енный is deduced from the location of the stress in the conjugation of the same verb. Thus verbs with fixed stress in the conjugation have stress on the same syllable in the past passive participle: вы́явить—вы́явлю, вы́явишь, вы́явлен-ный; уговори́ть—уговорю́, уговори́шь, уговорённый; пе-ревести́—переведу́, переведёшь, переведённый, etc. In verbs with mobile stress the past passive participle is stressed on the same syllable as any of the conjugated forms other than the first person singular: скоси́ть–скошу́, ско́сишь–ско́шенный; купи́ть–куплю́, ку́пишь–ку́пленный, etc.

There are some exceptions to this rule, such as съéденный in face of съедúте, ушúбленный in face of ушибёшь, etc., укрáденный in face of украдёшь, подстрúженный in face of подстрижёшь, разгры́зенный in face of разгрызёшь, засéченный (*flogged*) in face of засечёшь, одóлженный in face of одолжúшь, etc. Some of these exceptions have arisen because the stress-pattern of the conjugation has changed but the past passive participle has retained its older stress. Such are

изменённый	in face of измé-нишь	(formerly изме-нúшь),
разделённый	in face of раздé-лишь	(formerly разде-лúшь),
осуждённый	in face of осу́-дишь	(formerly осудúшь),
освещённый	in face of освé-тишь	(formerly осве-тúшь),
оценённый	in face of оцé-нишь	(formerly оце-нúшь),

and other past passive participles from compounds of the same roots. Traces of similar changes are visible in such adjectives, formerly participles, as варёный (cf. свáренный), сложённый (cf. слóженный), учёный (cf. обу́ченный), пря́деный (cf. спрядённый), etc.

In the short form of the participle in unstressed -енный the stress remains on the same syllable as in the long form: скóшенный—скóшен, скóшена, скóшено, скóшены, but in the short form of the participle in stressed -ённый the stress falls on the final syllable: переведённый—переведён, переведенá, переведенó, переведены́; оценённый—оценён, оцененá, оцененó, оценены́, etc.

The stress pattern of the past passive participle in -тый is determined as follows. If the infinitive is in stressed -ну́ть, then the stress moves back one syllable in the participle: сомкну́ть–со́мкнутый, загну́ть–за́гнутый, etc. If the infinitive is in -оть (which is always stressed), the stress again moves back one syllable in the participle: проколо́ть–проко́лотый, перемоло́ть–перемо́лотый.

Otherwise the stress in the participle is as in the past tense masculine, including those past tenses which are stressed on the prefix: приня́ть–при́нял–при́нятый, нача́ть–на́чал–на́чатый, прокля́сть–про́клял–про́клятый (but прокля́тый—adjective), etc. Participles of the last set have a mobile stress in the short form, which thus corresponds in stress-pattern to the past tense:

при́нятый	— при́нят, принята́, при́нято, при́няты,
на́чатый	— на́чат, начата́, на́чато, на́чаты,
про́клятый	— про́клят, проклята́, про́клято, про́кляты, etc.

ADJECTIVES

There are no stress shifts in the declension of long forms. There may, however, be a difference in the location of stress between long and short forms and there may be a stress-shift within the short forms themselves. Long adjectives of more than three syllables retain the stress in the same position in the short form. Most trisyllabic long forms follow the same principle but a few[1] follow one or other of the stress-shift patterns found in the short forms of some disyllabic adjectives. Other disyllabic adjectives retain the position of the stress as it is in the long form. Adjectives which have the stress on the final syllable in all the short forms (irrespective of where it is in the long form) have in fact a *fixed* short form stress, namely 'fixed final'. It happens that the short form masculine has no ending and therefore

1 Notably those with a pleophonic root (which in Common Slavonic would be monosyllabic, e.g. дорого́й, < C. Sl. *dorg-).

the stress has to fall on the last syllable of the stem: горя́-
чий—горя́ч, горяча́, горячо́, горячи́; смешно́й—смешо́н,
смешна́, смешно́, смешны́.

Some grammarians prefer to describe this pattern as one
with a stress-shift[1] but this leads to a slightly less economical
description of the short form stress phenomena than that
implied above.

The two basic patterns of mobile stress in the short form
are (1) stem stress in all forms except the feminine, where
the stress shifts to the ending; (2) stem stress in the masculine but stress on the ending in all other forms. Examples
are: (1) чи́стый—чист, чиста́, чи́сто, чи́сты; весёлый—
ве́сел, весела́, ве́село, ве́селы; дорого́й—до́рог, дорога́,
до́рого, до́роги; (2) больно́й—бо́лен, больна́, больно́,
больны́; (до́лжный)—до́лжен, должна́, должно́, должны́.

A difference in stress pattern serves to distinguish the two
meanings of, for example, о́стрый *sharp*: остр, остра́,
о́стро, о́стры ('sharp-edged') and остр, остра́, остро́,
остры́ ('witty'); and во́льный *free*: во́лен, вольна́, во́льно,
во́льны (or вольны́) ('independent') and во́лен, вольна́,
вольно́, вольны́ ('permitted'). Such a semantic distinction is
a rare phenomenon but the alternative stress patterns be-
hind this distinction have affected other adjectives, such that
some of them now have complete alternative patterns or
partial alternative patterns. Among those with complete
alternative patterns are:

> у́мный   — умён, умна́, умно́, у́мны;
> по́лный — по́лон, полна́, по́лно, по́лны;
> ста́рый — стар, стара́, ста́ро, ста́ры.

In some adjectives only the plural has alternatives, brought
about by a mixture of conflicting influences: the influence of
the final stress of the feminine, the general tendency of the
plural and neuter to follow one and the same pattern and a

1 E.g. M. V. Trofimov, *Handbook of Russian*, II, pp. 67–68.

tendency to associate the neuter form with the adverb and thus to dissociate it from the plural. Thus one has:

вре́дный — вре́ден, вредна́, вре́дно, вре́дны́;
ну́жный — ну́жен, нужна́, ну́жно, ну́жны́;
но́вый — нов, нова́, но́во, но́вы́.

The adjective до́брый has short forms добр, добра́, до́бро and до́бры, with an alternative добры́ which seems to be limited to such expressions as бу́дьте добры́ (also бу́дьте до́бры).

The most complex result of these conflicting tendencies is found in the adjective коро́ткий, which has short forms ко́роток, коротка́, ко́ро́тко́ and ко́ро́тки́. There are, however, certain restrictions evident here, such that one has for example, ум ко́роток ('not very bright') not ум ко́роток. The neuter form коро́тко is usually restricted to the function of short form *simpliciter*, while коротко́ tends to have the function of expressing 'excessive measure', as in пла́тье коротко́ *the dress is too short*. This tendency is perhaps not quite so marked in the plural, and in the expression (*He*) *hasn't the necessary authority*, for example, where it is not clear whether 'excessive measure' is intended, one has the alternatives ру́ки ко́ротки and ру́ки коротки́.

Conflicting influences have produced an unusual stress pattern in хи́трый, for example: хитёр, хитра́, хи́тро, хи́тры. So it is recorded by Avanesov and Ozhegov,[1] where Ushakov[2] records colloquial alternatives хитро́ and хитры́, and Trofimov[3] has only хитро́, хитры́. Similarly, Mazon[4] has кра́сный—кра́сен, красна́, красно́, красны́ and глу́пый—глуп, глупа́, глу́по, глупы́, whereas more recent authorities have кра́сно, кра́сны only and глу́пы only.

1 Русское литературное произношение и ударение.
2 Толковый словарь русского языка.
3 *Handbook of Russian*—Part II, p. 68.
4 *Grammaire de la langue russe*, p. 72.

All these facts lead to the conclusion that changes in the stress patterns of some short forms are still taking place and that there is a tendency towards the stabilization of one pattern for each adjective. It is impossible to say in which direction this tendency lies and it may be that, in view of the decay of the short form as a living category,[1] stabilization will not be achieved before the category disappears entirely or reaches a point of maximum restriction.

SUBSTANTIVES

Substantives, like verbs, present at first sight a bewildering variety of stress location but here too there is limited number of basic patterns. Again, certain changes have taken place recently or are taking place now and thus giving rise to variations.

Nearly all substantives with three or more syllables and having stress neither on the first nor on the last syllable have fixed stress.[2] Other substantives may or may not have fixed stress. Feminine substantives ending in unstressed a/я have fixed stress and so do a few ending in stressed á/я́. The majority of the latter, however, have mobile stress and there are three patterns:

1 The stress remains on the ending in the singular but moves back one syllable in the plural (e.g. вдова́–вдо́вы, etc., овца́–о́вцы, etc., змея́–зме́и, etc.); a few nouns of this type stress the last syllable in the genitive plural (ове́ц, свине́й, сестёр, земе́ль, etc.).
2 Stress is final throughout singular and plural,[3] except

1 See Chapter 8.
2 See B. O. Unbegaun, *Russian Grammar*, p. 38. For lists of substantives in the various patterns see Chapter III of Unbegaun's work, but note modifications of those lists in the light of what follows.
3 In the genitive plural with zero ending stress must, of course, fall on the root.

in the nominative plural, where it moves back one syllable (e.g. губа́—гу́бы, губа́м etc., слеза́—слёзы, слеза́м etc.).

3 Stress is final throughout singular and plural except in the accusative singular and nominative plural, where it moves back one syllable (e.g. рука́, ру́ку, руки́, etc., plural—ру́ки, рук, рука́м, etc.). Some substantives such as голова́, борода́[1] form a special set within this pattern, since they move the stress back two syllables: голова́, го́лову, головы́, etc., plural—го́ловы, голо́в, голова́м, etc.

Of these three patterns, the first is the most 'viable', and is in process of attracting substantives of the other patterns. The other two, especially the third, are almost completely fossilized, though very occasionally they exert an influence on substantives of the first pattern. The following remarks illustrate recent, completed changes of pattern and changes now in process.

The substantive страна́ has moved from the category with fixed stress to pattern 1 almost within living memory. A century ago изба́ was in pattern 3 (acc. и́збу) but is now in pattern 1 (acc. избу́), though the alternative и́збу is still heard. Коса́ is given by Unbegaun as pattern 1, by Ushakov as pattern 3. Avanesov and Ozhegov give only pattern 1 for коса́=*plait* but pattern 1 *or* pattern 3 for коса́=*scythe*. Similarly the two meanings of среда́ are distinguished by different patterns: pattern 3 for среда́=*Wednesday* (acc. sing. сре́ду, plural сре́ды, сред, среда́м, etc.), pattern 1 for среда́=*milieu* (acc. sing. среду́, plural сре́ды, сред, сре́дам, etc.). Блоха́ has pattern 2 but there is a tendency for it to shift to pattern 1. Волна́ has already carried out this shift (cf. Ushakov—pattern 2, Avanesov and Ozhegov—pattern 1). Строка́ has alternative patterns—2 or 3 (i.e. acc. sing.

1 These being words with pleophonic roots which would be monosyllabic in Common Slavonic (e.g. *golv-).

стро́ку́ but plural стро́ки, строка́м), but there is a tendency for it to shift to pattern 1. Some other substantives show similar shifts of pattern.

The stress pattern of feminine substantives ending in -ь is much simpler. Throughout the singular they keep the stress on the same syllable as in the nominative singular. Любо́вь is exceptional in shifting the stress on to most of the endings (любви́, любви́, любо́вью, любви́) and so are the numerals 5 to 10, 20 and 30 (пять, пяти́, пятью́, etc.). In multiplication, however, these same numerals retain the stress on the root in the instrumental: пя́тью шесть *five times six*. The numerals 50, 60, 70 and 80 have lost the stress on the second element: пяти́десяти, пятью́десятью, etc. The stressed locative of some nouns in -ь is discussed in Chapter 7. The word грудь is exceptional in having not only end-stressed locative but also an alternative end-stressed genitive after the prepositions: до/из/о́коло/от/с/у груди́, and end-stressed dative after к and по: к груди́, по груди́. An end-stressed genitive is also found without prepositions: ширина́ груди́. In the plural, many feminine substantives in -ь shift the stress to the endings in all the cases other than the nominative-accusative: кость—ко́сти, косте́й, костя́м, ко́сти, костя́ми, костя́х.

Masculine substantives with fixed stress include some with non-final stress, embracing the majority of non-suffixed substantives and some suffixed ones, and some with final stress, in which the nominative singular has the stress on the final syllable of the root or the suffix: враг–врага́; игро́к–игрока́.

Masculine substantives with mobile stress all have final stress in the oblique cases of the plural and therefore fall into three patterns, according to the stress in the singular and the nominative plural:

1   the nominative plural is end-stressed (e.g. нос–носы́, круг–круги́, etc.);

2 the stress is retained on the stem in the nominative
   plural; most of these nouns end in -ь (e.g. гость—
   го́сти, гостéй, etc; зверь—звéри, зверéй, etc.; волк—
   во́лки, волко́в, etc.);
3 the stress shifts on to the ending in the singular oblique
   cases but remains on the stem in the nominative plural
   (e.g. конь, коня́, etc.—ко́ни, конéй, etc.).

Pattern 3 is limited to a very few nouns, pattern 2 is a little
more numerous, while pattern 1 is the most numerous and
dominant pattern. Mazon writes: 'C'est ce . . . type d'accen-
tuation opposant le singulier au pluriel qui tend visiblement
a s'imposer, ainsi que l'on constate pour tels substantifs dont
le mouvement d'accent hésite entre le génitif pluriel et le
nominatif-accusatif pluriel.'[1] He then notes that the colloquial language ('la langue commune') prefers воры́, тру-
сы́ (pattern 1) to во́ры, воро́в (pattern 2) and тру́сы, тру́-
сов (fixed) and one finds Avanesov and Ozhegov still warning against воры́ and genitive singular вора́ (patterns 1 *and*
3!) and against трусы́, трусо́в (pattern 1). У́голь has initial
or end stress in the singular—угля́, etc., but in the plural, in
the sense of *coal*, initial stress only—у́гли, у́глей, etc., while
in the sense of (*pieces of*) *charcoal* it has end stress in the
oblique cases—у́гли, углéй, etc. It is clear then that in the
masculine substantives too some levelling is going on but it
is not as extensive as in the feminine nouns.

Neuter nouns present a less complex picture. It has already been noted that nouns of three or more syllables with
medial stress have fixed stress. The stress is likewise fixed in
neuter nouns, irrespective of the number of syllables and
location of stress, when they are formed with the suffixes[2]
-ие, -ье, -ство, -ище, -ушко, -юшко, -ышко, -ишко, -ечко,
-(и)це (non-final stress) and -ьё, -ство́, -(е)цо́. Nouns ending
in -ьё mostly denote abstract ideas or collectives and, as

1 Mazon, *op cit.*, p. 43.
2 Strictly speaking, derivational suffixes plus case-suffixes (endings).
3+

such, have no plural. Some of those which have a plural have a stress-shift: копьё—plural ко́пья, ко́пий, ко́пьям, etc., ружьё—plural ру́жья, ру́жей, ру́жьям, etc. (see below). The form деревца́ serves as plural to both the singulars де́ревце and деревцо́, and to this extent may be said to 'break the rule' given above.

Otherwise neuter nouns have a stress shift between singular and plural (but not *within* the singular and plural declensions). Nouns with final stress in the singular shift the stress back one syllable in the plural while those with root stress in the singular shift the stress on to the endings in the plural. There is thus only one pattern: 'stress-shift'—with two varieties: 'backward' and 'forward'—окно́—о́кна, о́кон, о́кнам, etc., письмо́—пи́сьма, пи́сем, пи́сьмам, etc., and сло́во—слова́, слов, слова́м, etc., о́блако—облака́, облако́в (exceptional gen.), облака́м, etc. In trisyllabics of the first variety with a mobile vowel in the genitive plural the stress moves back two syllables in this case:

> волокно́ — воло́кна, воло́кон, воло́кнам, etc.,
> ремесло́ — ремёсла, ремёсел, ремёслам, etc.

In the pleophonic серебро́ and толокно́ there is no stress shift. Among the second variety, о́зеро and де́рево are exceptional in moving the stress only one syllable forward:

> озёра, озёр, озёрам, etc.,
> дере́вья, дере́вьев, дере́вьям, etc.,

while кру́жево is exceptional in the stress of its genitive plural:

> кружева́, кру́жев, кружева́м, etc.

Я́блоко and чу́чело do not have a stress shift and there are some disyllabic nouns other than those with the suffixes listed above which do not have a stress shift: with fixed end stress—

> добро́, нутро́, пшено́, тепло́

and with fixed initial stress—

блю́до, брю́хо, ве́ко, го́рло, ду́ло, жа́ло, кре́сло,
        ры́ло, со́лнце, у́тро, ши́ло.

У́тро is also exceptional in having final stress after certain prepositions: до/от/с утра́, к утру́, по утра́м, etc.

PREPOSITIONS

A number of monosyllabic prepositions draw the stress from certain substantives and numerals: на́ гору, по́д ноги, и́з дому, по́ два, на́ три, etc.[1] The commonest such combinations are those with на followed by the accusative case. За (plus accusative and, occasionally, instrumental) is rather less common, под (plus accusative) less common still; по (plus dative and accusative) and из do not enter into such combinations very often and there are only a very few combinations with без and от.

The shift does not normally occur when there is an adjective or some other word or phrase delimiting the substantive: thus—на́ гору *uphill*, but на высо́кую го́ру *up a high hill*, на́ душу брать *to take on one's conscience*, but на ду́шу населе́ния *per head of population*. Many of these expressions are virtually adverbs (as is на́ гору above), which happen to be written as two words. When the expression, though functioning as adjunct, is appreciated not as a unit but as 'preposition + substantive', then the stress shift is less likely to occur. Levelling or regularization has been at work, so that some such combinations current in the nineteenth century with stress-shift no longer have the shift and others are in the transitional stage of admitting while not requiring the shift: на́/за́ де́вять/де́сять, под ве́чер/го́лову, за́/на́/по́д со́рок, etc. The numerals are less likely to lose their stress to the preposition if followed by a substantive and со́рок

1 See Avanesov and Ozhegov, *Русское литературное произношение и ударение*, p. 704, for fuller lists.

retains its stress if it is part of a higher number: за сто
со́рок, за со́рок пять, etc.

NEGATIVE PARTICLE

The negative particle attracts the stress of the past tense
masculine, neuter and plural (*not* feminine) of быть, дать
and жить (but not their compounds): не́ был, не́ было, не́
были but не была́; не́ дал, не́ дало, не́ дали but не дала́;
не́ жил, не́ жило, не́ жили but не жила́. In nineteenth-
century Russian and somewhat later this stress-shift was
allowed in a few more verbs, such as не́ взял, не́ взяло, etc.

3
Orthography

Russian has five vowel phonemes and thirty-three or thirty-four consonant phonemes, making a total stock of thirty-eight or thirty-nine phonemes. Certain substitutions among both vowels and consonants occur, depending on the phonetic context (see Chapter 1). The language is written alphabetically but the alphabet has only thirty-two letters: nine vowel letters, и, ы, е, э, а, я, о, у, ю, twenty consonant letters, п, б, м, ф, в, т, д, н, с, з, р, л, ц, ч, ш, ж, щ, к, г, х, the letter й representing /j/, and two auxiliary letters ъ and ь, which have no sound of their own.

The value of most of the consonant letters is not known unless what follows them is also known. The examples in Chapter 1 show that the value of most of the consonant letters varies according to the nature of the consonants which follow them. Apart from that, the full value of most of the consonant letters followed by a vowel letter is known only if we know also what that vowel letter is. In other words, т, for example, signifies only dental or alveolar stop but т in та signifies voiceless dental stop and т in те signifies voiceless palatalized alveolar stop (and т in отде́лать signifies voiced palatalized alveolar stop, and so on). The vowel letters and most of the consonant letters, therefore, are used in what might be called a syllabic mode.

This is made possible by the fact that, though there are only five vowel phonemes, there are nine vowel letters. The letters ы, э, а, о and у, besides denoting certain vowel values, also signify that certain consonant letters occurring before

them represent hard consonants, while the letters и, е, я and
ю, besides denoting certain vowel values, also signify that
certain consonant letters occurring before them represent
soft consonants. The letters и, е, я and ю also denote
j + vowel when they occur after another vowel, a soft sign or
a hard sign, as in твой [tvʌˈji], моя [mʌˈja], судью [suˈdju],
съéхать [ˈsjɛxət]. Three of these letters also have this value
in initial position: я́ма [ˈjamə] éхать [ˈjɛxət], юг [juk]. И
does not have this double value in initial position, except in
the alternative pronunciation [jix], [jim], [ˈjimɪ] of их, им,
и́ми (instead of [ix], [im], [ˈimɪ]).

The vowel value of all the vowel letters except ы and и always depends entirely on the phonetic context, including the
location of stress. Thus, both у and ю in stressed position
denote the vowel value [ü] between two soft consonants but
the vowel value [u] when not between two soft consonants.
The letter э denotes [e] in stressed position before a soft consonant but [ɛ] in other stressed positions. The letter е also
has these two values in stressed position in many words but
in some words it has the value [ö] in stressed position between two soft consonants or [o] when not between two soft
consonants. The letters ы and и, however, denote different
vowel values irrespective of the surrounding consonants: ы
denotes [ɨ] or [ɪ] according to the location of the stress, while
и denotes, after all except three consonant letters, [i] or [ɪ],
according to the location of the stress. After ж, ш and ц,
however, и denotes [ɨ] or [ɪ]. This is a result of the fact that
ж, ш and ц represented *soft* consonants in Old Russian.
They have since become hard consonants and hence in pronunciation are followed by [ɪ] or [ɪ] (since [i] and [ɪ] cannot
follow hard consonants) but the old spelling жи, ши, ци is
retained. The letter ы, however, is written after ц when it is
part of a grammatical ending, as in овцы́, белоли́цый, in
the suffix -ын, as in сестри́цын, and also in a few isolated
words such as цыга́н, цыплёнок, etc. Otherwise ци is written.

Though ж, ш and ц represent hard consonants[1] one writes e, not э, after them (again for historical reasons), and here e does not have the 'softening' effect which it has on other consonants. Both e *and* o occur after ж and ш with the value [o]—e is written in certain endings and suffixes, o in others.[2] Within roots e/o after ж, ш serves to distinguish between verbal and nominal forms: изжёг, ожёг, поджёг—изжóга, ожóг, поджóг. The hardness of ж, ш and ц is recognized by the orthography in the sequences жа, ша, ца, жу, шу, цу. The sequences *жя, *шя, *ця do not occur and the sequences жю, шю, цю are restricted. Жю and шю occur in a few loan-words, such as жюри́ and параш́ют, but here ю has the same value as y. The sequence цю occurs only in foreign names, such as Цю́рих, and names of Ukrainian origin, such as Цюру́пинск, and here ю has the value [ju], the [ts] remaining hard. Similar anomalies are to be observed in the writing of vowel letters after ч and щ, which, while always denoting soft consonants, are followed on the one hand by a, not я, and by y, not ю, and on the other hand by и, not ы, and by e, not э. The value [o] after ч and щ is indicated either by e or o, according to the same rules which regulate the writing of же/жо, etc.

The letter й denotes either the second element of diphthongs or the consonant [j] between two vowels. In the latter use, however, it is found only in words of foreign origin. As a rule the following letter is then o, as in райóн, майóр, but other letters are occasionally found, as in мáйя[3]. In native words the sequence 'vowel+j+o' is written as, for example, in моё, твоё, etc. Similarly, the initial sequence 'j+vowel' is registered by means of one of the vowel letters e, ю, or я even in foreign words, unless the vowel is [o] in

1 An exception is мужчи́на [muˈʃʃinə].
2 See *Правила русской орфографии и пунктуации*, pp. 7–9, for details.
3 But this is presumably pronounced [ˈmajjə], so that й represents the semi-vowel [j̯].

that word *or some other word derived from the same root.* Thus one writes Евро́па, ю́нга, я́хта but йот, йод, йота́ция [joˈtatsɪjə], йодофо́рм [jɪdʌˈform].[1]

The soft sign and the hard sign occur only after consonant letters. The soft sign indicates that the preceding consonant is soft, if it is a member of one of the hard-soft pairs, no matter what follows: мать [mat̪], грязь [gr̪æs̪], сва́дьба [ˈsvad̪bə], вольна́ [vʌl̪ˈna], etc. When a vowel letter follows the soft sign the latter indicates not only that the preceding consonant is soft but also that the following vowel letter has the double value which it has after other vowel letters: судья́ [suˈdja], сча́стье [ˈʃʃæs̪t̪jɪ], etc. In this complex of consonant letter + soft sign + vowel letter the soft sign is said to have the function of 'separating sign' (раздели́тельный знак) as well as that of softening. The complex illustrates to what extent the syllabic mode operates, for in the дья of судья́ we know that д represents a soft consonant only because of the following ь, we know that ь has the additional function of separating sign only because of the following я, and we know that я has the value of [j] + vowel only because of the preceding soft sign. In native words only the vowel letters и, е, я, or ю can appear in this complex but in words of foreign origin the letter о occurs when the vowel to be represented is [o]—почтальо́н [pətʃtʌˈljon], шампиньо́н [ʃəmpɪˈnjon], etc. When the sonsonant letter preceding ь is ш, ж or ч, the soft sign has simply the function of separating sign, since these letters represent hard consonants (ш, ж) or a soft consonant (ч), whatever follows them: шьёт [ʃjot], мужья́ [muˈʒja], чьё [tʃjo].

The soft sign also occurs finally after ш, ж, ч and щ and here it has no phonetic function at all. It is a grammatical marker, indicating (a) after any of the four letters, that the word is a noun belonging to the feminine declension of the

---

1 According to Avanesov and Ozhegov, *Русское литературное произношение и ударение.*

кость type: вошь, ложь, речь, вещь; or (b) after ш, ж, ч, that the word is an imperative: ешь, режь, плачь; or (c) after ч, that the word is an infinitive: течь, мочь; or (d) after ш, that the word is second person singular of a verb: чит-áешь, пи́шешь; or (e) after ш, ж, ч, that the word is an adverb: наóтмашь, нáстежь, прочь.

The soft sign also has purely grammatical function in the infinitives of reflexive verbs. In боя́ться, for instance, it simply indicates that this is the infinitive and not the third person plural боя́тся, since both forms are pronounced [bʌˈjat-sə] or [bʌˈjatsə]. The reflexive particle сь/ся was formerly pronounced with hard [s] in all circumstances. The commoner practice today is to pronounce the form сь of this particle with soft [s̡]. The form ся of this particle is pronounced with hard [s] in the infinitive, the third person singular and plural, the second person singular and the past tense masculine ending in л—боя́ться [bʌˈjat-sə], бои́тся [bʌˈjit-sə], боя́тся [bʌˈjat-sə], бои́шься [bʌˈjiʃsə] боя́лся [bʌˈjalsə].[1] In these forms therefore the letter я has the value of a.

The hard sign occurs mainly between the final consonants of prefixes and initial е, я, ю of roots. It acts as a separating sign and the preceding letter then represents a hard consonant, except in the case of с and з, which may represent either, in an older style of pronunciation, a soft consonant or, in a newer style of pronunciation, a hard consonant. Thus: отъéхать [ʌˈtjɛxət̡], въéхать [ˈvjɛxət̡], съéхать [ˈsjɛxət̡]/[ˈs̡jɛxət̡].

Apart from the fact that the letters of the alphabet are used in a 'syllabic' mode, Russian orthography is also distinguished by the fact that in nearly all words the vowel and

---

1 Soft [s̡] is sometimes heard in the second person singular. Similarly, in the first person plural (бои́мся), in imperatives such as утéшься, мáжься, in the past tense masculine after consonants other than л (нёсся, обжёгся) and in such infinitives as берéчься, the с of ся represents either hard [s] or, less commonly for the time being, soft [s̡].

consonant phonemes are written as if they were in 'strong position'.[1] The strong position for vowel phonemes is the stressed position: the stressed vowels in the following examples are in strong position—[mʌˈja] /maˈja/ моя́, [stʌˈlʲi] /staˈli/ столы́, [pʲɪˈro] /pʲiˈro/ перо́. The position of secondary stress is also a strong position—[kʌrˌtofʲɪˌlʲɪkʌˈpalkə] /karˌtofʲiˌlʲikaˈpalka /ка́ртофелекопа́лка, [mʌˌrozəuˈstojtʃɪvt] /maˌrozauˈstojtʃivi/ моро́зоусто́йчивый. Unstressed positions are, of course, weak positions for vowels. In weak position the vowels are written as if they were in strong position. For many words, where the vowel is in weak position, the strong position for that vowel can be found—and hence the orthography of the vowel determined —by comparison with other forms of the same word. Thus the orthography of the vowels in some of the words quoted above is determined by, for example, [moj] /moj/ мой, [stol] /stol/ стол, [ˈpʲerjə] /ˈpʲerja/ пе́рья. What one is actually doing in such instances is determining the orthography of the vowel by reference to a form of the morpheme[2] where the vowel is stressed.

Quite frequently it happens that a particular vowel in a word never occurs in stressed position in any form of that word. A comparison may then be made with other, related words. In почтальо́н [pətʃtʌˈljon] /patʃtaˈljon/ for instance the first vowel is never stressed but in the related word по́чта [ˈpotʃtə] /ˈpotʃta/ it *is* stressed. There may, however, be no related words in which a particular vowel is stressed. This is very often the case where the vowel is part of a prefix or an ending. In such cases one compares the morpheme (prefix or ending) as it occurs in the word under consideration with other occurrences of the same morpheme in other

1 The term is a translation of the Russian си́льная пози́ция.

2 Broadly speaking, a 'morpheme' is the linguistic expression or form of an irreducible unit of meaning (and the meaning may be lexical or grammatical). Morphemes include roots, prefixes, suffixes and endings (which form a special kind of suffix).

words. Thus, the morpheme (ending) which means 'nominative singular feminine' is established orthographically as a in фа́за [ˈfazə] /ˈfaza/ by comparison with words such as жена́ [ʒɨˈna] /ʒiˈna/ where the vowel of this morpheme occurs in strong position. On the other hand the vowel [ə] in [ˈslovə] /ˈslova/ сло́во is established orthographically as o by comparison with such words as [ʌˈkno] /aˈkno/ окно́, where the vowel of the morpheme written o, meaning 'nominative singular neuter', is in strong position.

One may sometimes have to extend the field of comparison wider than in the two examples just taken. The two o's in кра́сного [ˈkrasnəvə] /ˈkrasnava/, for example, are established by comparison with the same ending not only in end-stressed adjectives, such as круто́го [kruˈtovə] /kruˈtova/, which would establish only the first o, but also in pronouns such as самого́ [səmʌˈvo] /samaˈvo/ which establishes the second o.

There may be cases where there is no comparative evidence for establishing the orthographic form of a particular vowel. For instance, in no forms of the word боло́то [bʌˈlotə] /baˈlota/ and in no related words is the first vowel ever stressed; similarly, the second vowel in ко́мната [ˈkomnətə] /ˈkomnata/ and related words is never stressed. Here, the letters o and a respectively are written for purely historical reasons: there *was* a time when боло́то and ко́мната were pronounced (approximately) [boˈloto] and [ˈkomnata]. We should expect the unstressed ending of adjectives which mean 'nominative singular masculine' to be written -ой in view of the spelling of the stressed ending in круто́й [kruˈtoj̍] /kruˈtoj/ for example. The ending -ый, however, was borrowed at an early date from Old Church Slavonic, and spelling has, so to speak, got the upper hand of pronunciation, since the ending -ый is now pronounced [ɨ(i̯)] as well as [əi̯]. It is only in a small percentage of cases that the strong position of a vowel cannot be found by comparison with other words.

This feature of Russian orthography means that it does not record vowel changes brought about simply by a shift of stress: it does not register the vowel substitutions described in Chapter 1. There are few exceptions to this statement. Among them we may note the infinitive расти́ [rʌ'şţi] *to grow* and present tense расту́ [rʌ'stu], etc., in face of the past tense poc [ros], росла́ [rʌ'sla], etc., равни́на [rʌ'vņinə] *plain* in face of ро́вный ['rovnɨ(j)] *level* and the prefix раз-/рас- in unstressed position in face of роз-/рос- in stressed position. In these and similar instances, however, the presence of a in unstressed syllables in face of o in stressed syllables is due to the example of Old Church Slavonic, where the reflex of Common Slavonic *ort- (*t* representing any consonant) is *rat-*. It is possible that the spelling of the prefix раз-/рас- may be due not only to the example of Old Church Slavonic but also to the influence of pronunciation on spelling (cf. стака́н, паро́м, etc. with Old Russian достока́нъ, поро́мъ, etc.).

The strong positions for consonant phonemes vary according to the type of consonant. Thus, some of the strong positions for voiced consonants are not strong positions for voiceless consonants, and *vice versa*. However, the position in front of the vowel phonemes /o/ and /u/ is a strong position for all the consonant phonemes. This is to say that in this position—*the* strong position for all consonants—any of the Russian consonant phonemes may occur. If a consonant has been devoiced or voiced or in some other way assimilated, in other words if it has in fact been replaced by another phoneme, the orthography continues to record the morpheme in which the consonant appears as if the consonant were still in the strong position. Thus, the orthography disregards consonant changes which have occurred for purely phonetic reasons. Some of the examples in Chapter 1 adequately illustrate this phenomenon.

There are some exceptions. Apart from a few isolated words such as нóздри ['nozdṛɪ] *nostrils* (cf. нос [nos] *nose*) and свáдьба ['svad̦bə] *wedding* (cf. сват [svat] *marriage-broker*)—where, in any case, it is doubtful whether the connection between нóздри and нос, and свáдьба and сват is any longer felt—the principal exceptions are those prefixes where, in strong position, the final consonant is /z/. These are, in strong position, (о)без-, воз-/вз-, из-, низ-, раз- (and роз-) and через-. Before voiceless consonants the spelling changes to, respectively, (о)бес-, вос-/вс-, ис-, нис-, рас- (and рос-) and черес-:

безрýкий [b̦ɪ'zruk̦ɪ]	— бескрýлый [b̦ɪ'skrᵻlt]
взойтú [vzʌj̦'ți]	— всходúть [vsxʌ'd̦iț]
издавáть [ɪzdʌ'vaț]	— испускáть [ɪspu'skaț]
низвергáть	— ниспослáть
[n̦ɪzv̦ɪr'gaț]	[n̦ɪspʌ'slaț]
разогнáть	— расписáть
[rəzʌ'gnaț]	[rəspɪ'saț]
череззéрница	— чересседéльник
[tʃʃɪṛɪ'zᶻɛrn̦ɪtsə]	[tʃʃɪṛɪsșɪ'd̦el̦n̦ɪk]

Reform of the orthography

When the first books were printed in Russia in the middle of the sixteenth century, changes in the phonetic system (notably vowel and consonant substitutions) which had taken place since the introduction of writing in the tenth century were not in general recognized in the orthography. The printed book thus established a system of spelling which in many respects did not reflect the pronunciation. Peter the Great's decree of 1708 which introduced the civil type (граждáнский шрифт) was not an orthographic reform but a typographical and alphabetical reform. The general shape of the letters was reformed on the model of West European alphabets and, with insignificant changes, the new shape has survived to this day. Some superfluous letters were abolished but in other cases pairs of alternative letters having the same phonetic function were retained (e.g. i and и, ф and ѳ, s and з), their use being determined by etymological considerations or arbitrary spelling conventions. The letter э was introduced but not the letter й, which, though it had been used as early as the fourteenth century, had not been included in the printed alphabet of the sixteenth century. Nor was a letter having the value of present-day ё introduced. This letter was invented by Karamzin at the end of the eighteenth century, until when ио or io, sometimes with a ligature (i͜o or i͡o), was occasionally used.

In his *Разговоръ . . . объ ортографіи . . .*[1] V. Trediakovsky proposed further changes in the constitution of the alphabet. He also proposed that, by and large, Russian should be spelt as pronounced, though he was not as dogmatic in this proposal as some writers on the history of the language would lead one to believe.[2] His proposals met with no success. Equally abortive were the attempts by A. A. Barsov in 1768 to have the hard sign abolished and и replaced everywhere by the alternative i, and the attempt by D. I. Yazykov to have the hard sign and ѣ abolished.[3]

During the latter part of the nineteenth century and the early twentieth century various commissions and individuals discussed the reform of Russian orthography.[4] A special commission of the Academy of Sciences, headed by Fortunatov and Shakhmatov, presented its conclusions to the Academy on April 12, 1904. These conclusions, somewhat modified (see below), were republished in 1912. The conclusions of this orthographic commission did not pass into law until 1917. On May 17 and June 22 in that year the

---

1 St Petersburg, 1748. See Bibliography for full title.
2 See his *Разговоръ . . .*, pp. 410–416.
3 See A. and T. Fesenko, *Русский язык при советах*, pp. 149–150.
4 See V. I. Chernyshev, *Упрощение русского правописания*.

Ministry of Education of the Provisional Government issued directives that schools were to adopt the new orthography. Under A. Lunacharsky, the Bolshevik Ministry of Education decreed on December 23, 1917, that all state and government organizations were to adopt the new orthography and in the following year, on October 10, the Soviet of People's Commissars prescribed the new orthography for the entire state press. Thereafter the new orthography spread until it was in general use in the Soviet Union, though outside the Soviet Union some publishers persist in using the old orthography, or at least modifications of it.

In the reformed orthography no changes were made in the basic principles of Russian orthography as described in the preceding section of this chapter. The changes made consisted of the abolition of superfluous letters and the writing of certain grammatical forms in accordance with the basic principles of the orthography where previously they had not been. Thus, the letters ѣ, ѳ and i were abolished and the use of the hard sign at the end of every word which did not end in a vowel or the soft sign was discontinued. The genitive endings -аго and -яго were henceforth to be written -ого and -его, the nominative plural endings feminine and neuter, -ыя, -ія, were to be written -ые, -ие, the feminine plurals онѣ, однѣ, однѣхъ and однѣми were replaced by они, одни, одних and одними, and ея, formerly the accusative of она and the genitive in the sense of *her's*, *its*, was replaced by её, which had formerly been the genitive only. In addition the prefixes ending in з were given alternatives ending in с, to be used before voiceless consonants (see preceding section). This last element of the reform, whereby the orthography reverted to thirteenth-century principles, does in fact violate one of the basic principles of Russian orthography and seems unnecessary.

The decree of 1917 recognized the use of the letter ё as 'desirable but not obligatory'. The paragraph concerning this letter was omitted altogether from the decree of 1918 and to this day ё cannot be considered a fully 'independent' letter of the Russian alphabet. It is merely an alternative to е, does not have independent status in dictionaries[1] and is written only to avoid ambiguity, as in всё *everything* (cf. все *everybody*), узнаём *we find out* (cf. узнáем *we shall find out*), etc. In this respect, therefore, the alphabet is 'deficient', since е has to serve as the 'softening' vowel letter corresponding to о.

The Academy commission, under Fortunatov and Shakhmatov, had proposed in 1904 that /o/ after ш, ж, ч and щ should be written о everywhere, and that ь should be omitted at the end of words after ш, ж, ч and щ. The commission also proposed to replace ъ by ь between consonant and vowel letter in such words as съёмка, субъект, etc. None of these proposals were incorporated into the decrees of 1917 and 1918. A further commission again proposed in 1930 the replacement of ъ by ь but the proposal was again rejected. The contention that й after vowels could be replaced by ь (край > краь, стой > стоь) was made by the Croat J. Križanić in the seventeenth century[2] but seems never to have been given serious consideration.

During 1954 a discussion of orthographic reform was carried on in *Русский язык в школе* and *Учительская газета*, the more radical suggestions being made by some of the contributors to the latter publication. On the basis of this discussion a set of rules for orthography and punctuation was drawn up, confirmed by the Academy of Sciences, the Ministry of Education and the Ministry of Higher Education, and published under the title Прáвила рýсской ор-

---

1 That is to say it does not affect the order of items in a dictionary as, say, а and я or у and ю do.

2 See 'Избыточные буквы в русском письме' in Roman Jakobson, *Selected Writings*, I. See also the concluding paragraphs of my 'A Critique of Russian Orthography' in *In Honour of Daniel Jones*.

фогра́фии и пунктуа́ции. The object of this publication was not to institute a reform of the orthography but to resolve certain anomalies and, in general, to carry a step further the regularization of the orthography.

Some irregularities have been left, as examples in the preceding section of this chapter show. One notes in particular the quite arbitrary decision to retain ы after ц in a few roots only and the somewhat complicated rules governing the writing of e and o after ш, ж, ч and щ. It has now been decided to write ы (representing the phoneme /i/) after prefixes ending in a consonant (безыде́йный, подыто́живать, etc.), where, before the publication of the Пра́вила, there had been a tendency to retain the и of the unprefixed form or underlying root (безиде́йный, подито́живать—pronounced, however, with hard [z] and [d]). After prefixes ending in ж and x the letter и continues to be written—межир-рига́цио́нный, сверхизы́сканный—and this accords with the principle that one writes и (with the value [i] or [ɨ]) not ы after ж and ш, and the fact that the sounds [i] and [ɨ] do not occur, within a word, after the velar consonants. The и of the underlying root is retained, however, when the prefix is of foreign origin (e.g. панислами́зм, контригра́) and this represents an anomaly in the orthography, since the final letters in such prefixes represent hard consonants. It would seem that и is retained in these cases because it is felt that in some way it reveals the foreign origin of the prefix, just as ю is, needlessly, retained in such words as параш́ю́т, жюри́ to reveal their foreign origin. The letter и is also retained in such stump-compounds ('contracted compounds'—see Chapter 6) as госизда́т, where c represents hard [s] and и represents [ɨ].

Some loan-words which in their language of origin were written with double consonants are written with double consonants in Russian, even when only one consonant is pronounced: касса́ция, эссе́нция, etc. Others are written with a single consonant: афи́ша, официа́льный, etc. There is no apparent system.

It is clear from such facts as those mentioned above that further regularization of the orthography could have been carried out at certain points. Some conservatism, or timorousness in seizing the opportunity presented by the issue of the Пра́вила, is evident. In general, however, the compilers of the new rules have acted wisely in not attempting any radical reforms, for, apart from the fact that the orthography of Russian is peculiarly suited to the language, it is a historically evolved orthography and is the vehicle, in its older, almost identical form, of an important literature and, in its present form, of a vast number of publications read by millions who are familiar with its established principles. A radical reform would lead not only to temporary but considerable difficulties in communication but also to the colossal expense of reprinting pre-reform literature or, failing this, to a situation wherein the pre-reform literature would be inaccessible to the common reader.[1]

The mobile vowel

Strictly speaking, the phenomenon of the mobile vowel is principally a feature of word-structure. It does, however, raise occasional problems of spelling and for this reason, together with the fact that it is found in substantives, adjectives, verbs, pronouns, prepositions and prefixes, it is convenient to describe the phenomenon as a whole in this chapter rather than piecemeal in chapters dealing with various parts of speech.

Briefly, the historical reason for the phenomenon of the mobile vowel is as follows. In Old Russian (and in the older stages of the Slavonic languages) there were two so-called

1 At the time of my writing this a new orthographic commission has just been formed and many articles devoted to questions of orthographic reform are appearing (particularly in *Русский яык в школе*).

'ultra-short' vowels, designated by the letters ъ and ь. Very early (*ca.* twelfth century) in the history of Russian the vowels ъ and ь in certain positions ceased to be pronounced (though the letters ъ and ь, by and large, continued to be written). A little later the remaining ъ and ь vowels became identical with, respectively, o and e.[1] Where ъ or ь became a 'normal' vowel modern Russian has a mobile vowel, alternating with zero where ъ or ь lapsed, as for example in сънъ > сън > сон—съна > сна,   ог   шьль > шьл > шел—шьла > шла. Although a knowledge of the location of ъ and ь in Old Russian is usually of great help in determining whether the mobile vowel in modern Russian is o or e, it does not always help, since analogy has in some instances produced mobile vowels where Old Russian had neither ъ nor ь. In a few instances я and и function as mobile vowels.

Several dozen masculine substantives have a mobile vowel in the nominative singular only.[2] Some of these substantives are monosyllabic in the nominative singular: сон–сна *sleep*, рот–рта *mouth*, день–дня *day*, лёд–льда *ice*, etc., some are disyllabic: уголь–угля *coal*, угол–угла *corner*, *angle*, замо́к–замка́ *lock*, дёготь–дёгтя *pitch*, хребе́т–хребта́ *crest*, *ridge*, ковёр–ковра́ *carpet*, ве́тер–ве́тра *wind*, за́яц–за́йца *hare* (where the mobile vowel я is replaced by й); and some are trisyllabic: потоло́к–потолка́ *ceiling*, за́мысел–за́мысла *project*, соловей–соловья *nightingale*. Such substantives simply have to be listed and learnt, though all the masculine substantives ending in the element

1 The factors determining the lapse of ъ and ь or their retention and ultimate conversion into o and e operated in general with great regularity and were perhaps a reflex of an ebb and flow of stress within the word.

2 Five feminine substantives have mobile o in the nom. sing. and instr. sing.—вошь *louse* (instr. во́шью, gen. вши, etc.), ложь *lie*, рожь *rye*, любо́вь *love*, це́рковь *church*. Дно *bottom* (of a vessel) has mobile o in the plural—до́нья, до́ньев, etc.

-оть lose the o after the nominative case.[1] Since there are only half-a-dozen such substantives (дёготь *pitch*, коготь *claw*, лапоть *bast-shoe*, локоть *elbow*, ломоть *slice*, ноготь *nail*), these too might as well be listed and learnt.

In the suffixal elements -ок, -ек/-ёк, which may function as suffixes themselves or as part of such suffixes as -онок, -ёнок, -ечек, -шек, etc., o and e are mobile. Exceptions include ездок *rider*—ездока, знаток *expert*—знатока, игрок *player*—игрока, челнок *canoe*—челнока. Where ок is not a suffixal element the o remains, as in восток *east*, обморок *faint*, урок *lesson*, чеснок *garlic*, etc., though there are a few exceptions to this, such as замок *lock*—замка, замок *castle*—замка, потолок *ceiling*—потолка. In the suffix -ец the e is mobile[2] unless its lapse would lead to the presence of р, л, м or н between two other consonants,[3] hence кузнец *smith*—кузнеца, храбрец *brave man*—храбреца, жнец *reaper*—жнеца. The last word would in any case retain its e under the rule that words with the suffix -ец after a vowel-less stem retain the e (cf. льстец *flatterer*—льстеца, чтец *reader*—чтеца). The letter e is retained in мертвец *dead person*—мертвеца, гордец *proud man*—гордеца and овсец *oats*—овсеца.

In the short form masculine of the adjective and the genitive plural of substantives ending in -а/-я and -о/-е there is considerable uniformity as regards the nature of the mobile vowel. First, one should note that ь and й when replaced by a mobile vowel are with very few exceptions (see below) replaced by e: горький *bitter*—горек, бойкий *smart*—боек,

1 *The Academy Grammar* (vol. I, pp. 141–142) lists several more final elements which have a mobile vowel. There are, however, too many words where these final elements do not have a mobile vowel for this list to be more than a partial aid in learning which substantives have a mobile vowel.

2 Being replaced by й after a vowel, as in боец *warrior*—бойца.

3 The letters р, л, м, н denote 'sonants', which are a special type of consonant. Where possible, the combination of consonant + sonant + consonant is avoided in Russian.

тюрьма́ *prison*—тю́рем, га́йка *nut*—га́ек, письмо́ *letter*—
пи́сем, серьга́ *ear-ring*—серёг. Про́сьба *request* is exceptional in not having this change—просьб, and so are
обо́йма *cramp-iron*—обо́йм, про́йма *opening*—пройм and
па́льма *palm*—пальм. The mobile vowel also replaces ь in
the genitive plural of neuter substantives ending in -ье
which have stressed endings in the plural: питьё *drink*—
питéй; in feminine substantives with the nominative singular in -ья; статья́ *article*—стате́й; and in four *masculine*
substantives with nominative plural in -ья: мужья́ *husbands*
—муже́й (see Chapter 7). Ружьё *rifle* is exceptional in
having genitive plural ру́жей, though the stress is not on
the ending. Otherwise, in neuter substantives ending in -ье
which do not have stress on the plural endings, as well as in
feminine substantives in -ья which are not stressed on the
endings, the mobile vowel in the genitive plural is и:
муче́нье *torment*—муче́ний, го́стья *guest*—го́стий. The
substantive яйцо́ *egg* is quite exceptional in having the
mobile и́ in the genitive plural яи́ц and so are the adjectives
досто́йный *worthy* and недосто́йный *unworthy* in having the
mobile vowel и in the short forms masculine досто́ин and
недосто́ин (cf. споко́йный *calm*—споко́ен).

After ш and ж the mobile vowel is о if stressed, е if unstressed: смешно́й *funny*—смешо́н, княжна́ *princess*—
княжо́н, тя́жкий *weighty*—тя́жек, ча́шка *cup*—ча́шек,
око́шко *window*—око́шек. Otherwise, the following rules
apply: between a hard consonant and к the mobile vowel is
о, between a soft consonant and к the mobile vowel is е:
доска́ *board*—досо́к, бе́лка *squirrel*—бе́лок, гла́дкий
smooth—гла́док, де́вочка *little girl*—де́вочек. Before ц the
mobile vowel is е: овца́ *sheep*—ове́ц, полоте́нце *towel*—
полоте́нец, кольцо́ *ring*—коле́ц. After velar consonants
the mobile vowel is о: ку́хня *kitchen*—ку́хонь, ку́кла *doll*—
ку́кол. The mobile vowel *before* velars is also о, unless one
of the above rules is operating: ро́зга *birch-rod*—ро́зог,

дóлгий *long*—дóлог; and the mobile vowel before sonants is e unless one of the above rules is operating: кислый *sour*— кисел, хитрый *cunning*—хитёр, умный *clever*—умён, веслó *oar*—вёсел, пятнó *stain*—пятен, ребрó *rib*—рёбер, земля *land*—земель.

Verb forms and pronouns showing the presence of a mobile vowel cannot all be brought under a formula and are in any case so few as to be easily learnt. They include among verbs шёл, жёг (cf. шла, жгла), беру, деру, стелю (cf. брать, драть, стлать), бей, пей, etc. (cf. бью, пью, etc.), вычесть, etc. (cf. вычту, etc.), тереть and similar verbs (cf. тру), зову, гоню (cf. звать, гнать), толочь (cf. толку), and among pronouns весь—всего etc., чей—чьё, чья, etc.

The prepositions with mobile vowel безо, во, ко, изо, надо, обо, ото, подо, передо and со occur before the various forms of весь (including весь itself) and всякий (though sometimes the form of the preposition without mobile vowel is admitted[1]), before что (во что, обо что, подо что), before those forms of the first person pronoun singular which begin with two consonants (мне, мной/ мною), usually before words beginning with clusters of consonants when the first consonant is homorganic[2] with the last consonant of the preposition, often before words beginning with consonant clusters which include a letter denoting a sonant (р, л, м, н), and in some isolated expressions such as во-пéрвых, во имя, etc. The form co also occurs before words beginning with щ or сч—со щукой, со счáстьем— and sometimes before words beginning with a consonant cluster, of which the first is ш: со/с шпионáжем.

The prefixes with mobile vowel взо-, во-, изо-, надо-, низо-, обо-, ото-, подо- разо- and со- always occur when

---

1 перед всем/всéми, etc., are preferred to передо всем/всéми, etc., which are considered very colloquial or vulgar.

2 'Homorganic' in phonetic parlance means 'formed with the speech organs (*sci.* lips, tongue) in the same position'.

the next element begins with й (войти, сойти, etc.), or with
a consonant followed by ь (изобью, волью, etc.), often
when the next element begins with a consonant cluster including a letter designating a sonant (взобраться, изо-
гнуть, отогреть, etc.) and, with the exception of низо-, before -шел (обошёл, сошёл, вошёл, etc.). Низойти, however, has past tense нисшёл, низошла, etc. The two prefixes
which consist in their basic form of one consonant, i.e. в-
and с- appear with mobile vowel before о—вооружать,
сооружать, etc., but the basically univocalic prefix о-
appears in its form об- before о—оборудование, etc. Во-
and обо- also appear before consonant clusters containing
в—водворить, обозвать, etc., while во-, изо-, разо- and
со- appear before -ткать. Со- also appears in some isolated
words where the next element begins with a single vowel—
собирать, собор, содержать, сожалеть, сочинить, со-
вершить, совещание and of course other forms of and
derivatives from these words.

PART II

FORMS AND USAGE

4
Syntax and Parts of Speech

An approach to syntax
The first part of this chapter[1] is devoted to aspects of
Russian syntax. No attempt is made at an exhaustive study
of the subject, for this would require a book to itself. The
primary object is, by way of analysis of some of the syntactical structures of modern Russian, to indicate the lines
on which a general and detailed analysis may be carried out,
such that descriptive statements for teaching and learning
purposes may be devised[2]. Some brief words of preliminary
explanation are necessary.

'The category set up to account for the stretches that carry
grammatical patterns is the "unit".'[3] The units are ranged
on a scale going from the largest at the top to the smallest
at the bottom and this scale is called 'rank'. The rank of
units for the description of Russian is:

UNITS

		sentence
	↑	clause
RANK		group(/phase)
		word
	↓	morpheme

1 I am very much indebted to Dr J. Ellis, Lecturer in English Language and General Linguistics at the University of Edinburgh, for many
discussions which I have had with him on the matter in this chapter.

2 The method of analysis used is based on that which has been
elaborated in the Department of English Language and General Linguistics at the University of Edinburgh. See M. A. K. Halliday,
'Categories of the Theory of Grammar', *Word*, vol. 17, no. 3.

3 M. A. K. Halliday, 'Categories . . .', p. 251.

Any unit above the morpheme is a structure consisting of one or more of the units next below: the sentence consists of one or more clauses, the clause of one or more groups, the group of one or more words and the word of one or more morphemes. It follows that a single word may be a group, that a single group may be a clause and that a single clause may be a sentence. Indeed a word like *Yes* or да may be one sentence which is one clause which is one group which is one word which is also one morpheme.

Not only can a unit include, in what it consists of, one or more units of one degree lower in rank than itself but also it can include a unit of rank higher than or equal in rank to itself. For instance, the sentence *Whether you agree is not important* consists of one clause and the subject of this clause is *Whether you agree*. This subject, however, is itself a clause which is occupying a place in the structure of another clause. At the first stage of analysis, the sentence *The parcel you sent me has not arrived* consists of one clause and the subject of this clause is *the parcel you sent me*. This subject is a 'nominal group' with the structure: 'modifier' (*the*), 'head' (*parcel*), 'qualifier' (*you sent me*) and this qualifier is itself a clause: it is a clause occupying a place in the structure of the subject, which is itself an element in the structure of a clause. Such transference of units is known as 'rank-shift' and units so transferred are said to be 'rank-shifted'.

In the statement of Russian clause structure four elements are needed: subject, predicator, complement and adjunct. These are symbolized as S, P, C and A respectively. Clause structures will be stated as various combinations of some or all of the elements S, P, C and A or as *one only* of these elements, e.g. SP, SPC, SPCA, PC, P, etc. A group that will be referred to constantly is the 'nominal group'. The possible elements of structure of the nominal group are 'head' (H), 'modifier' (M) and 'qualifier' (Q), as in *the* (M) *green* (M) *seld* (H) *of Earth* (Q).

The element S is present in all of the first sets of clause structures which we shall examine. In the following clause all four elements S, P, C, A are present

Двóе	сдéлают	шаг	в стóрону	*Two (will) take a*
		(Klen.)		*pace to the side*
S	P	C	A	

and the adjunct consists of preposition+nominal group, the latter consisting simply of a head. In the next examples the element A is not present.

Семéйная жизнь	крáсит	человéка	*Family life improves*
	(Arb.)		*a man*
S	P	C	

Here the subject is a nominal group consisting of modifier and head: its structure is MH.

Жéнщины не	прощáют	нам	*There's one thing*
S	P^n	C^2	*that women cannot*
одногó		(Arb.)	*forgive us*
C^1			

This sentence has two complements, C^1 the 'direct object', C^2 the 'indirect object'. The predicator is negated (P^n). Whether the genitive or the accusative is used with a negated verb the clause structure, *ceteris paribus*, remains the same. Thus the structure both of Он не купи́л маши́ны and of Он не купи́л маши́ну is SP^nC. At a further degree of 'delicacy' of analysis the complements are, of course, different. If necessary, the difference can be indicated by superscript letters, thus—C^g and C^a. The case-differentiation of the complement gives a differentiation in clause-meaning, which is discussed in Chapter 9.

Натáша	сиди́т	прямáя,	*Natasha is sitting*
S	P	C	*straight, tense*
подтя́нутая			(Klen.)
C			

Each of the two complements, this time of equivalent status,
is a nominal group consisting of a modifier only—the long
form of the adjective.

The following two examples have the elements S and P
but not C:

Моско́вский ухо́дит	*The Moscow (train)*
S P	*leaves at eleven*
в оди́ннадцать (Arb.)	
A	

Here the subject is a nominal group consisting of a modifier
alone, the adjunct consists of preposition + nominal group
and the latter consists of a numeral modifier without a head.

Плеска́лась тёплая и тёмная,	*The warm dark*
P S...............	*water splashed in*
в фиоле́товых разво́дах, вода́.	*violet arabesques*
(Klen.)	
...........................S	

The subject consists of the entire nominal group, from теп-
лая to вода (in the English translation, however, *in violet
arabesques* is the adjunct to the predicator *splashed*). The
structure of this nominal group M&MQH[1], the 'qualifier'
consisting of preposition + nominal group with structure
MH.

In the following examples there are no predicators. When
we say that an element is absent we do not mean that it is
'understood'. In structures with no adjunct or no complement the concept of an absent element is easily accepted. In
structures with no predicator it is a temptation to suppose
that the predicator is 'understood' but it is only when a predicator in a preceding structure is, so to speak, 'carried over'
that one may say the predicator is 'understood'. Even then

1 & indicates a conjunction.

the structure has no predicator—not even a 'zero predicator', if by that term is meant an element which is represented
by nothing—nor is the structure an 'incomplete' one.

(двóе сдéлают шаг в стóрону);		(*Two will take a*
двóе — шаг вперёд	(Klen.)	*pace to the side); two*
S C A		*—a pace forward*

Он сын мой.	(Arb.)	*He's my son*
S C		

The complement here is a nominal group consisting of head
and modifier (possessive pronoun). The clause structure is
similar in the next example, where the modifier is an adjective:

Охóтников — человéк внезáпный		*Okhotnikov is an im-*
	(Arb.)	*petuous person*
S C		
Ты чстýреста двáдцать дéвять		*You (have made) four*
S C........................		*hundred and*
замéсов	(Kat.)	*twenty-nine mixes*
......C		

The complement is the nominal group четýреста двáдцать
дéвять замéсов, structure MH, the element M being a
numeral. The head of the nominal group, замéсов, is in the
genitive case, one of the peculiarities of Russian syntax being that when a numeral group is the subject ('nominative')
or complement of the direct object ('nominative-accusative')
the case of the head is determined by the numeral-modifier,
if this is not ... одúн. Although it is necessary to have a
predicator in the English translation no predicator is 'understood' (in the sense defined above) in the Russian structure: nowhere in the preceding 2,500 words of the chapter
from which the example is taken is there a verb which could
be said to be 'carried over' to this sentence. It is the object of

this kind of analysis to analyse what is there, not what 'should' be there.

In the next example

Настоя́щим быть тру́дно (Arb.)   *To be a real (journa-list) is difficult*

the subject is настоя́щим быть, the complement тру́дно. S here is a rank-shifted clause with structure CP and P is an infinitive.

The structure of the next two examples consists of the elements S and A.

Ты из го́рода? (Arb.)   *Have you come from*
S   A   *town?*

Сего́дня необы́чный спекта́кль   *There's an unusual*
A   S   (Klen.)   *show on today*

Finally, in these first sets of examples, we come to clauses consisting of one element only—S. The structure of this clause

Моги́лы уло́женные и забы́тые   *Neatly laid out*
        (Klen.)   *graves and for-gotten ones*

is simply S, this being a nominal group with structure HM&M.

чёрная звёздная ночь   *a black, starry night*
        S
степна́я нака́танная доро́га   *the smooth steppe*
        S   (Klen.)   *road*

—two clauses with identical structure S, each S being a nominal group with structure MMH.

Се́рый асфа́льт моско́вских   *The grey asphalt of*
    тротуа́ров; обса́женный   *the Moscow*

молодьіми ли́пами и распи́санным де́тским мелко́м; ско́льзкий зимо́й, пы́льный ле́том и мо́крый по́сле дождя́ ... (Klen.)

pavements, planted with young limes and covered with children's chalk-scrawls, slippery in winter, dusty in summer and damp after rain...

This is one clause consisting of the element S only, S being a nominal group with structure MHQ; M&M; MM &M. The second two elements M are themselves groups consisting of participle plus nominal group, the last three elements M are also groups, consisting of adjective plus adverb or adverbial phrase.

In the next sets of examples the element P is present but not the element S. In some of the examples personal forms of the verb stand at P. Although the personal forms have the grammatical category (see below) of person there is no element S *in the clause-structure* in these examples.

The first examples have the elements P and C only.

Обвини́тельное заключе́ние
        C
зака́нчиваю   (Arb.)
        P

I am finishing off my indictment

C is a nominal group with structure MH. Similarly in the next example, though here the two component elements of the complement are separated by the predicator:

Золота́я была́ же́нщина   (Klen.)
    C...   P   ...C

She was a jewel of a woman

The structure of the following clause

... отступа́ть не́ было вре́мя
                    (Klen.)

...it was not the time for retreat

4+

is P^n (нé было) C (врéмя отступáть). C is a nominal group with structure HQ, and Q is a *rank-shifted clause* with structure P, the exponent of which is an infinitive.

In the next examples only the elements P and A occur.

Выхожý на Комсомóльскую P A плóщадь (Klen.)	*I come out on to Komsomol Square*

(. . . из Москвы́ брáтец егó явил- ся) Выступáет всю́ду (Arb.) P A	(*His brother's turned up from Moscow . . .*) *He's making speeches every-where*

Пéрвый раз на урóк
  A   A
опáздываю   (Arb.)
  P
	This is the first time I've been late for a lesson

Structures consisting only of the element P are common in dialogue: (Он был там?)   — Был; (Вы слы́шали?) — Слы́шал; Знáю; Понимáете?   — Понимáю, etc.

When the imperative is at P then S is present only in contrastive commands—Вы пиши́те, а вы читáйте *You write, and you read*—or in 'attenuated' commands—Вы напиши́те мне откры́тку (structure SPCC) *Do send me a postcard*.

Clauses consisting simply of a complement are not uncommon, especially in dialogue: (Жéнщины не прощáют нам одногó.) — Чегó? (Arb.) (*There's one thing that women cannot forgive us.*)   — *What?* (Вспоминáю, дружóк.) — Когó? (*I remember, old man*) — *Who?* (Когó вы ви́дели?) — Сóню. (*Who did you see?*) — *Sonya*; (Чем вы интересýетесь?) — Дрáмой (*What are you interested in?*) — *The drama*; Смешнóй *He's a funny one*; Ýмница *He's a clever one*; Негодя́й *He's a good-for-nothing*; Ти́хо *It's quiet*; Шу́мно *It's noisy*; Жаль *It's a pity*,[1] etc.

Clauses are found in which only the element A occurs: Поскоре́е! *Hurry up!* Домо́й! *Home!* Наконе́ц до́ма! *Home at last!* Пря́мо, пото́м нале́во, зате́м напра́во *Straight on, then left, then right.* This last is a sentence of three clauses in each of which only the element A occurs (A, AA, AA).

The clauses examined above do not, of course, exhaust all possible varieties of clause structure but represent some common—and some less common—types of structure. The sentence consists of one or more clauses and the clauses may be free ('main clauses') or bound ('subordinate clauses'). The combinations of the two classes of clauses leads to a great variety of sentence structures. Thus, an exhaustive description of the sentence is a work of considerable proportions and one which should form the subject of a separate book.

For the remainder of this section we shall examine in somewhat more detail the structure of the various elements of the clause.

The nominal group may occur at S or C or A, as some of the examples above show. As we have seen, the elements which may occur in the structure of the nominal group are M (modifier), H (head) and Q (qualifier). The minimum structure of the nominal group is H or M. In such a sentence as Моско́вский ухо́дит в оди́ннадцать *The Moscow (train) leaves at eleven* both моско́вский and оди́ннадцать are nominal groups consisting simply of a modifier, in one case an adjective, in the other case a numeral. Pronouns and participles too may constitute nominal groups consisting of modifier only. Certain pronouns, such as я, ты, вы, он, кто, что, etc., function only as heads in a nominal group. It was

1 In the last three examples a 'predicative adverb' stands at C. Predicative adverbs are discussed below.

noted above that a peculiarity of Russian grammar is that in the nominal group consisting of numeral-modifier and head it is the numeral-modifier which, in certain circumstances, determines the case of the head.

We should also note here the nominal group consisting of two heads linked by the preposition c, as in мы с тобóй *you and I*, дóктор с женóй *the doctor and his wife*, and the phrase consisting of preposition plus nominal group and acting, not as qualifier in a nominal group or as adjunct in clause-structure, but as subject or complement, as in В кóм-нате . . . смоглú поместúться óколо пятúдесяти человéк (N. Ostr.) *About fifty people could get into the room*, where óколо пятúдесяти человéк is the subject.

It is not only the nominal group which may be the subject of a clause. In such a clause as Прекратúть разговóр бы́ло бы сáмое лýчшее *The best thing would be to stop talking*, for example, the subject is прекратúть разговóр, and this we would describe as a rank-shifted clause (a clause standing where a group 'normally' stands), the structure of this clause being P (прекратúть) C (разговóр). Similarly, the structure of Мóжно войтú and Нельзя́ войтú is CS, where S is a rank-shifted clause consisting of P alone. The negative pronouns and adverbs such as нéкого, нéчего, нéгде, нéкуда, etc., also figure in rank-shifted clauses standing at S. Thus, the structure of Нéчего бы́ло дéлать *There was nothing to be done* and Нéкуда бы́ло идтú *There was nowhere to go* is, in both instances, S... P ...S (where the dots indicate that the predicator is enclosed by the two parts of the subject) and in both instances S is a rank-shifted clause. In the first instance the structure of the rank-shifted clause is C (нéчего) P (дéлать), in the second instance A (нéкуда) P (идтú). It follows that the structure of Нéчего дéлать *There is nothing to be done* and Нéкуда идтú *There is nowhere to go* is simply S and that at S is a rank-shifted clause.

Finally, any unit from morpheme to sentence, may, as a

quoted item, stand at S: Осно́вой э́того глаго́ла явля́ется
«чита-» *The stem of this verb is* 'чита-', Его́ «Иди́ сюда́!»
звуча́ло о́чень гру́бо *His 'Come here!' sounded very rude.*

As well as the nominal group, certain adverbs may also
occur as complement. There is then no predicator in the
clause or the predicator is a form of быть or of such verbs
as станови́ться, де́латься, *to become*, as in Шу́мно *It's
noisy*, Бы́ло ти́хо *It was quiet*, Ста́ло хо́лодно *It became
cold*. Some might prefer to consider that these adverbs are
in the position of adjunct, rather than complement. Their
status is discussed in more detail below, under 'Category of
State'.

As in the instance of the subject, any item or set of items
may, as quoted forms, stand at C: Я сказа́л «тя» *I said* 'тя',
Я не сказа́л «иди́те сюда́» *I didn't say 'Come here'*, «Два
ра́за ко́фе?» спра́шивает официа́нт (Klen.) *'Two coffees?'
asks the waiter*. In the last two examples, of course, C is a
rank-shifted clause (which is also a sentence).

Various other items besides the finite forms of the verb
may occur as predicators. Examples of the infinitive as predicator have been quoted above. Participles may also
appear as non-finite predicators. For instance, in such
clauses as Челове́к, чита́ющий докла́д — мой брат
The man reading the lecture is my brother and Челове́к,
то́лько что прочита́вший докла́д — мой брат *The man
who has just read the lecture is my brother* the active participles чита́ющий and прочита́вший are non-finite predicators in bound clauses which are themselves qualifiers in a
nominal group. The structure of these two clauses, each of
which constitutes a sentence, is therefore SC. A more
detailed analysis is: S—челове́к, чита́ющий докла́д and
челове́к, то́лько что прочита́вший докла́д; C—мой брат
in both cases; at S—a nominal group, structure HQ, at
C—a nominal group, structure MH; at Q—a rank-shifted
clause, structure P (чита́ющий) C (докла́д) in the first

example, A (только что) PC in the second example. The gerunds also appear as non-finite predicators in bound clauses, as in Читая доклад, он всё запинался *As he was reading his lecture he kept faltering* and Прочитав доклад, он вышел из аудитории *Having read his lecture he left the lecture-hall.* Here the bound clauses are not rank-shifted— they are subordinate clauses. Sometimes, however, a gerund may better be considered as being an adjunct, not a predicator, as in Он говорит запинаясь *He speaks with a stammer.* Some former gerunds have in fact become adverbs and no longer stand at P: Он стоит молча *He stands in silence,* Он читает лёжа *He reads lying down.*

Non-verbal predicators include не and нет, as in Он не там *He is not there,* Нет карандашей *There are no pencils,* and the deverbal interjections, such as щёлк *click,* хлоп *bang,* бух *plop,* as in . . . немец ползёт . . . я — щёлк, он и свалился набок (A. N. Tol.) *A German came crawling towards me—I clicked (the trigger) and he rolled on to his side,* С утра, как проснётся — хлоп стакан водки (Kav.) *As soon as he woke up in the morning—down went a glass of vodka,* [Свинья] . . . бух в омут (Prish.) *[The pig] . . . went plop into the water.*

Parts of speech and grammatical categories

Parts of speech may be defined as classes of words, each class occupying a certain place or places in the structure of a group which occupies a certain place or places in a clause which occupies a certain place or places in a sentence. Thus, the parts of speech are distinguished from one another by the places they occupy in structure or, to put it another way, by the functions they fulfil. In this context it is necessary to bear in mind that 'place' includes the associations which words may enter into with other words in the same group. It is this meaning of the word 'place' which makes it possible, for instance, to distinguish in Russian the part of speech 'substantives' from pronouns such as я, ты, вы, etc., to distinguish these pronouns from such pronouns as этот, тот, весь, etc., and to distinguish these from adjectives.

Some of the parts of speech include in their morphology exponents ('markers') of various grammatical meanings. These grammatical meanings are known, in traditional parlance, as 'grammatical categories'. The grammatical categories of Russian are: case (with its constituent members of nominative, genitive, dative, etc.), number (singular, plural), gender (masculine, feminine, neuter), comparison (positive, comparative, superlative), person (first person, second person, third person), tense (present, past, future), aspect I (imperfective, perfective), aspect II (determinate, indeterminate), voice (active, passive, etc.), and mood (indicative, imperative, conditional). Most of the parts of speech which have grammatical categories have more than one grammatical category, indeed several grammatical categories are frequently combined in one and the same morphological marker. Thus the ending -ом in a substantive is the exponent of case (instrumental), number (singular) and gender (not feminine), while the ending -ут in a verb is the exponent of tense (not past), person (third), number (plural), mood (indicative) and voice (active, if it is not followed by -ся).

The nominal parts of speech, i.e. the noun (*nomen*) in its widest sense, include substantives, adjectives, pronouns and numerals. The participle is both nominal and verbal. All have in common the grammatical category of case. Substantives, adjectives and most pronouns also have in common the category of number. The first and second person pronouns distinguish number not by morphological means (i.e. not by changing the ending) but radically. In other words, я is a word which means *I*, мы is a word which means *we*, and so on, though these words still form a grammatical system in which singular is distinguished from

plural.[1] The pronouns which do not distinguish number are
себя́, кто, что and derivatives of the last two (кто́-нибудь,
кто́-то, etc.). Among the numerals, 'one' and 'hundred'
have the category of number: оди́н, одна́, одно́ *one*—
одни́ *some* ('ones'), сто *one hundred*—пять сот *five hundred*.
Ты́сяча *thousand* has plural forms too but it has the syntactical characteristics of a numeral only when it is part of a
higher numeral or is not preceded by a modifier. Otherwise
it has the syntactical characteristics of a substantive: с
одно́й ты́сячей рубле́й, с двумя́ ты́сячами рубле́й (cf. с
ты́сячью рубля́ми, с двумя́ ты́сячами пятью́ рубля́ми).[2]

The category of gender is found in substantives, adjectives and pronouns II (э́тот, тот, весь etc.):

э́тот ма́ленький стол *this big table,*
ва́ша краси́вая сестра́ *your beautiful sister,*
на́ше большо́е по́ле *our big field.*

In the plural, however, gender distinctions are not found in
adjectives and pronouns, while in substantives the gender
distinctions are found only in certain cases and even there
they are poorly marked. Thus, although the nominative-
accusative plural ending -а/-я is typical of neuter substantives, there are some masculine substantives which also have
this ending. Conversely, there are some neuter substantives
which have the nominative-accusative plural ending -и,
which is typical of masculine and feminine substantives.
The zero-ending of the genitive plural is typical of certain
classes of neuter and feminine substantives but is also found
in some masculine substantives.[3] In the singular, gender

1 Logically, of course, 'we' is not the plural of 'I' in the sense that
'tables' is the plural of 'table', since 'tables' means a number of the
individual items 'table', whereas 'we' means 'I and at least one other
person'.
2 Со́тня–со́тни *hundred*(*s*), миллио́н–миллио́ны *million*(*s*), etc.,
are substantives.
3 See Chapter 7, *Substantives.*

distinction between masculine and neuter is marked only in the nominative-accusative case. Of the pronouns I (я, ты, кто, etc.) only the third person pronoun distinguishes gender: он, она, оно.

Most of the numerals do not distinguish gender. Those which do include один, одна, одно *one*, and higher numerals ending in the element 'one'—двадцать один, ... одна, ... одно *twenty-one*. In these numerals the distinction between feminine and not-feminine (i.e. masculine *or* neuter) is marked throughout the declension, masculine and neuter being distinguished from each other only in the nominative-accusative. 'Two' and higher numerals ending in 'two' distinguish gender only in the nominative-accusative два/две. The distinction is, moreover, dyadic, not triadic, since две signifies 'feminine' while два signifies 'not-feminine'. The numeral pronoun 'both' is unique in the language in that it distinguishes gender throughout the declension: feminine— обе, обеих, обеим, etc., not-feminine—оба, обоих, обоим, etc. In colloquial Russian 'both' behaves like 'two': it distinguishes gender only in the nominative-accusative оба/обе.

The category of person is found among nominal parts of speech only in the personal pronouns: я, мы; ты, вы; он, она, оно, они. Whereas in the verb, person is distinguished by endings, in the pronoun it is distinguished radically, just as number is in the first and second person pronouns.

The category of aspect appears to affect the substantive in such pairs of words as произношение *pronunciation* ('manner of pronouncing' or 'system of pronunciation') and произнесение *pronunciation* ('act of pronouncing, uttering').[1] However, the number of such pairs is very small, there is no *system* of aspectual differentiation in the substantive and it is probably better to say that such pairs consist of separate, though related lexical items than to say that

1 See Chapter 10, *Verbs*, for more examples.

4*

the substantive has the grammatical category of aspect. One nominal part of speech, the adjectives (including adjectivalized participles), has the grammatical category of comparison.

The verbal parts of speech include the finite forms of the verb, the infinitive, the gerund and the participle, which is also a nominal part of speech. They have in common the categories of aspect and voice. Tense is found in the indicative finite forms but not in the conditional or imperative. In the indicative finite forms the tense system is triadic (past, present, future), whereas in the participles there is a dyadic system in which tense is opposed to absence of tense, since the only participle which has tense is the past imperfective active participle. In so far as a rare past imperfective gerund occurs, the gerund too opposes tense to absence of tense (see Chapter 10). The category of mood is found in all the verbal parts of speech except the infinitive, the gerunds and participles. The finite verb forms (past, present, future, imperative and conditional) as well as the participles have the category of number. In the present and future, and in the imperative, but not in the past and conditional, the category of person is found, whereas the past and conditional have the category of gender. Here, as elsewhere in the language, with the few exceptions noted above, gender is distinguished only in the singular. The participle also has the category of gender and, in addition, the category of case. Thus, the only grammatical categories common to all verbal parts of speech are aspect and voice, just as the only category common to all nominal parts of speech is case.[1] In this respect the participles occupy an intermediary position, since they have not only the verbal categories of aspect and voice but also the nominal category of case.

1 Indeclinable substantives and the one or two 'formless' verbs such as aa (see chap. 5) lack exponents of the categories.

The adverb is a separate part of speech, with a range of places in structure illustrated by Он рабо́тает бы́стро, Он идёт туда́, Э́то о́чень интере́сная кни́га, Чте́ние вслух помога́ет, В ко́мнате светло́.

The only grammatical category which is found in adverbs, and then not in all of them, is comparison, which they have in common with many adjectives.

Words which do not fall into any of the above categories are called by some grammarians 'particles of speech'. They do not have grammatical categories. These particles of speech include prepositions (с, до, на, согла́сно, благо- даря́, etc.), conjunctions (и, но, что, что́бы, пре́жде чем, etc.), interjections (ага́, а́хти, го́споди, чёрт, бух, хлоп, etc.) and particles of various kinds (deictic—вот, вон; in- tensive—же, и, да́же; modal—так, да, не, нет, бы, ли, ра́зве, неуже́ли, etc.). Some of these, as we have seen, can function as predicators (не, нет, бух, хлоп, etc.).

Category of state

Many Russian grammarians postulate the existence in Russian of another part of speech with the cumbersome name of слова́ из катего́рии состоя́ния *words from the category of state*, or more briefly катего́рия состоя́ния *category of state*. What gives rise to the notion of category of state is the occurrence of short adjectives and some adverbs in, let us call it, predicative function, as in Я печа́- лен *I am sad*, Он был гото́в *He was ready*, Темно́ *It's dark*, Бы́ло хо́лодно *It was cold*, Мо́жно *One may*, Нельзя́ *One may not*, Нельзя́ бы́ло *It was not allowed/possible*, etc., etc.

Several factors have led Russian grammarians, even as early as Lomonosov in the eighteenth century, to the con- clusion that there is something 'odd' about predicative adjectives and adverbs which distinguishes them from other parts of speech. These factors are: (1) the absence of a verb in the present tense; (2) the presence in the past tense (and the future tense) of the verb 'to be' not in the logical sense of 'exists' or 'is a member of the class x' but in the function of asserting a logical relation or ascribing a property to a term; (3) the fact that the short form of the adjective has no other than predicative function; (4) the fact that in such complete clauses as Темно́, Светло́, no subject—either grammatical or logical—can be elicited; (5) the fact that adverbs are expected *a priori* to refer to verbs or adjectives or substantives, etc., and yet in Нельзя́, Жаль, there is nothing to which these words, if they are adverbs, could refer.

In the first half of the nineteenth century some grammarians (I. F. Kalaidovich, A. Kh. Vostokov, for example) classified the short adjectives as verbs. This idea or variations of it have persisted to this day. It was L. V. Shcherba, in his 'О частях речи в русском языке',[1] who coined the term катего́рия состоя́ния. Shcherba proposed to include in the category of state not only short adjectives and predicative adverbs but also impersonal verbs (e.g. запреща́ется *it is forbidden*), the verb 'to be' plus substantives in the instrumental (as in Я был солда́том *I was a soldier*) and such phrases as быть без чувств *to be insensible*, быть в сюртуке́ *to be wearing a frock-coat*, etc. This has led some grammarians (cf. Kalaidovich and Vostokov above) to say that, for example, хо́лодно has tense forms: present tense—хо́лодно, past tense—бы́ло хо́лодно, future tense—бу́дет хо́лодно, which means that бы́ло, бу́дет here are not verb forms themselves but parts of the analytic verb forms бы́ло хо́лодно, бу́дет хо́лодно, as бу́ду, бу́дешь, etc., are parts of the analytic future imperfective бу́ду чита́ть, etc.

Nowadays, most grammarians who postulate the category of state would admit to that class of words only short adjectives and predicative adverbs, or only the latter. Some

---

1 in *Русская речь*, New Series, II, 1928; reprinted in *Избранные работы по русскому языку*, 1957.

grammarians do not postulate a category of state at all. As Ye. M. Galkina-Fedoruk, etc. write, 'one should note that the question of the category of state is not entirely settled'.[1]

What seems to have given rise to the concept of the category of state is the desire to see in almost every type of clause a predicate and to allot to some word in the clause the role of nucleus of that predicate. Thus, if one says that in such a clause as Я печа́лен there is a subject and predicate then obviously печа́лен is the predicate, and if one says that in such an 'impersonal' clause as Темно́ there is a predicate but no subject (and that there is nothing which could be 'understood' to be the subject) then obviously темно́ is the predicate. Moreover, since these clauses refer to the present, then the present tense must somehow be contained within печа́лен and темно́. When, therefore, the clause refers to the past—Я был печа́лен, Бы́ло темно́— the predicates печа́лен and темно́ have been put into the past tense and hence the 'past tense' of печа́лен is был печа́лен, and the 'past tense' of темно́ is бы́ло темно́. This sort of reasoning seems to derive from the idea of the *logical proposition*, in which the predicate tells us what is the relation that holds.

The method of analysis used in this chapter is based on what is *given* in the clause. The concept of predicate is discarded, as being a logical concept, not a grammatical item. The element *predicator* is an element of clause structure and, as we have seen, a predicator, like a subject, is not an obligatory element in Russian clause structure (though, of course, almost any clause may be re-expressed *as a logical proposition* having logical subject and predicate). Because of its meaning, Shcherba and others have classified быть not as a verb but as a copula, which is not in their opinion a verb

1 Ye. M. Galkina-Fedoruk, etc., *Совреме́нный ру́сский язы́к*, p. 379.

(since it does not express an action, nor even a state presented as an action). Быть, however, has all the morphological characteristics of other verbs, though it has no present tense, and also acts as the element predicator in clause structure. Быть, we conclude, is therefore a verb, having various logical meanings, such as ascribing a property to a term, assertion of a logical relation, the expression of identity, the expression of existence and the indication of membership of a class.

For these reasons the concept of a special part of speech called the category of state seems unnecessary. In я печа́лен the element S of clause structure is occupied by я, the element C is occupied by печа́лен and there is no element P. In бы́ло темно́ the element P is occupied by бы́ло, the element C by темно́ and there is no element S. Similarly in нельзя́ бы́ло: C—нельзя́ P—бы́ло. Hence some adverbs can stand at A, as in гори́т светло́ *it's burning brightly*, or at C, as in здесь светло́ *it's bright here*. The fact that words such as нельзя́, мо́жно, жаль, etc. cannot occur as adjunct but only as complement need not deter us from classifying them as adverbs.[1] They have a restricted place in structure, it is true, but other adverbs too are restricted in various ways. Such restrictions would lead, at a further degree of delicacy of analysis, to the setting up of various classes of adverbs. Some might consider that in, for example, здесь светло́ and нельзя́ бы́ло, the words светло́ and нельзя́ are exponents of the adjunct and not the complement. In either case it seems unnecessary to postulate a part of speech called 'the category of state'.

1 Cf. W. K. Matthews: 'As for the bulk of the syntagmas, nominal and adverbial, allocated to the 'category of state', we can fit them without undue strain into a broadly defined adverbial category as Peškovskij (*op. cit.*) has done.' ('Russian Grammatical Design', p. 31.)

5
Sources of Words I

Grammar deals with linguistic structures. In the preceding chapter the objects of analysis were structures longer than words. Such structures are analysed and described by that branch of grammar which is traditionally called 'syntax'. The structure of words is treated by that branch of grammar which is traditionally called 'morphology'. In a language such as Russian the structure of words from many of the parts of speech depends on the place which the words occupy in structures of higher rank, i.e. the endings of verbs, substantives, adjectives, etc., change according to their syntactical role. The division of morphology which treats this phenomenon is traditionally called 'accidence' or 'form-derivation' (словоизменéние or формобразовáние). Words also have structure, however, irrespective of their place in structures of higher rank, i.e. when stripped of the elements which indicate their place in higher structures they can be seen to consist of one or more units of the lowest rank (morphemes). The study of word-structure in this sense is also a division of morphology, known as 'word-formation' or 'word-derivation' (словообразовáние). Words may also be formed without recourse to morphological processes. This and the following chapter are devoted to an examination of word-formation in Russian, with particular attention to morphological processes.

At any one epoch a language has an inherited stock of words and the potential to change that stock by the removal of some items and the addition of others. In the language of a large, sophisticated community both phenomena are going on all the time, accretion being the dominant one of the two. The inherited lexis has been created by very much the same processes which at the given epoch lend it the potential to extend itself, though some processes, like the words they create, may become restricted in their application and ultimately be discarded, while others take their place. Processes which have been discarded are non-productive,[1] even though they may still be—and indeed often are clearly discernible. Processes which are still operating are productive. The degree of productivity is not the same in all processes: some are more highly productive than others and some elements in a productive process may be much more widely used than others. For instance, the prefix *un-* in English is much more frequent than the prefix *super-*, simply because of the difference in meaning: far more different types of words can be negated by adding *un-* than can be given a superlative degree by adding *super-*. So, although it has usually been taken implicitly that the larger the number of items produced by a particular process or element then the higher the degree of productivity of that process or element, it is clear that the range of applicability of a process or element should also be taken into account. When therefore the degree of productivity is qualified below by such terms as 'high', 'low', 'weak', it should be understood that these are approximations and, moreover, that they are determined on the whole by the number of items formed by the process being described. Attention will sometimes be focussed on peripheral ('weakly productive') processes or elements which are recent, partly because they *are* peripheral or recent

1 But, as B. O. Unbegaun says, 'even a dead suffix [suffixation being one of the processes of word-formation in Russian], so long as it may be detected as such, may on occasion be employed to form a new word'. (*Russian Grammar*, p. 34.)

and partly because they may become more productive in the future: they may be part of the 'growing edge' of the lexis.

Two processes of word-creation are probably common to all languages. The first is creation using simply the phonetic resources of the language without, if the structure of the language will permit it, using any of the formal or grammatical processes of the language. Onomatopoeia is an obvious case of word-creation by this process. The recent word *blip* (a trace on a radar-screen) may have been formed by onomatopoeia but *bop* (a kind of jazz) seems to be simply a 'clip' or 'stump' of *be-bop* or *re-bop*, itself part of a nonsensical refrain 'Hey, bobba-re-bop'. A common case in the modern world of words invented 'from nothing' is provided by trade-names—*Kodak*, *Omo*, etc.

The second common process is borrowing from another language. In Russian this may be combined with the processes described in C2 below (usually C2b and C2c, less commonly C2a and not at all with C2d). In the past Russian has taken words from many languages: Old (Church) Slavonic, Indo-Iranian languages, Turko-Tatar languages, Greek, Latin, Polish, German, English, French.[1] During the last half-century words have been borrowed largely from English and French and to a lesser extent from German. Many of the recent loans are technical and sporting terms: хронометра́ж *time-and-motion study*, кало́рия *calorie*, конте́йнер *capsule* (of an artificial satellite), циклотро́н *cyclotron*, моторо́ллер *motor-scooter*, магнитофо́н (with adaptation of German *Magnet* to Russian магни́т) *tape-recorder*, телеви́зор (originally an English trade-name) *television set*,

---

1 See P. Ya. Chernykh *Очерк русской исторической лексикологии —древнерусский период*; L. P. Yakubinsky *История древнерусского языка*, pp. 331–350; P. Ya. Chernykh *Историческая грамматика русского языка*, pp. 304–330; Ye. M. Galkina-Fedoruk, *Современный русский язык—лексика*, pp. 90–112; W. K. Matthews, *Russian Historical Grammar*, pp. 252–264; W. J. Entwistle and W. A. Morison, *Russian and the Slavonic Languages*, pp. 257–263.

нейло́н *nylon*, спортсме́н *athlete*, чемпио́н *champion*, старт *start*, фи́ниш *finish*, футбо́л *football*, гол *goal*, бу́тсы (with addition of a Russian plural ending) *football-boots*, кросс *cross-country*, матч *match*, нока́ут *knock-out*, смеш *smash* (tennis), ке́ды[1] (originally an American trade-name) *rubber-and-canvas shoes, plimsolls*, etc. Feminine substantives have been created from some of these by the addition of native suffixes (see below): спортсме́нка, чемпио́нка, etc.

In recent decades there has been a tendency to replace some of the English sporting terms by native words: врата́рь (голки́пер)[2] *goalkeeper*, защи́тник (бек) *back*, полузащи́тник (ха́вбек) *halfback*, уда́р сни́зу (апперко́т) *uppercut*, захва́т (клинч) *clinch*, ноль (ляв) *love*, три́дцать (се́рти) *thirty*, меня́ться сторона́ми (ченж о́вер плиз) *change over, please*, etc.[3]

In the case of some technical words it is difficult or impossible to say from which language they have come, since they are formed from Greek (and Latin) roots and are found in various European languages. Furthermore, Russian has also created words by attaching prefixes and suffixes (or compounding elements) of Greek and Latin origin to native roots (see below) and by creating words of entirely Greek and/or Latin parts (with the possible addition of native suffixes), where words of similar origin do not exist in other European languages or are formed in a slightly different way. Though these are in fact examples of compound words (see below) a few examples are given here: диафи́льм *film-strip*, телесту́дия *television-studio*, кинеско́п *television tube*, телепрогра́мма *television-programme*, телекино́ *tele-cinema*, микроци́д (name of a

1 'И ску́льптор в ке́дах баскетбо́льных' (Ye. Yevtushenko) *And a sculptor in basketball boots.*

2 The earlier, borrowed word is given in brackets.

3 For more details see Morton Benson 'English Loan Words in Russian Sport Terminology', *American Speech*, December 1958.

germicidal agent), космона́вт *spaceman, cosmonaut*[1], etc.

The other processes of word-creation in Russian are as follows:

A. *Resemanticization and polysemanticization*, i.e. endowing a word with a completely different meaning or with additional meanings without transferring the word to another part of speech. The latter is the commoner and is found throughout the history of Russian and other languages. Recent examples include площа́дка *platform*, now also (tennis) *court, launching pad*, etc.; дво́йка *two, pair*, now also *two-piece suit, doubles match*; ста́нция *station*, now also (interplanetary) *station* or *satellite*; отрывно́й *tear-off* (отрывно́й календа́рь) now also *escape* (отрывна́я ско́рость); пробе́г *run*, now also 'continuous service' (as in парово́з находи́лся в пробе́ге дво́е су́ток *the engine was on continuous duty for forty-eight hours*) and 'life' (as in пробе́г ши́ны *the life of a tyre*), достиже́ние *achievement*, now also in the sense of 'thing achieved'; оснаще́ние *equipping*, now also in the sense of *equipment*.

B. *Recategorization* or *transference*, i.e. transferring a form, without further changes, to another part of speech. This is one source of many adverbs and some prepositions and the only source of new pronominal words. Thus the instrumental has given rise to many adverbs, some of them now semantically divorced from the original substantive: круго́м *around*, верхо́м *on horseback*, гусько́м *in single file*. Prepositions have arisen from case-forms of substantives and from other parts of speech: путём *by way of*, посре́дством *by means of*, благодаря́ *thanks to*, включа́я *including*. Among substantives and adjectives which sometimes have purely pronominal or almost purely pronominal meaning

1 The English is formed on the analogy of the Russian, not *vice-versa*.

are: вещь, де́ло, шту́ка, челове́к, лицо́, да́нный, изве́ст-ный, etc., while the word о́ба/о́бе is essentially of pro-nominal meaning.

C. *Formal processes*, including root or stem modification, affixation and deaffixation.[1]

1. ROOT OR STEM MODIFICATION

(A) REDUPLICATION

This process was productive in primitive Indo-European, where it consisted of an anticipation of the first part of a root (rarely the whole root), often with some phonetic modifica-tion of the root. In primitive Indo-European, however, reduplication was usually a process of form-derivation rather than word-creation. Examples are Greek léloipa *I have left* (cf. léipō *I leave*, élipon *I left*), Sanskrit dadhāmi *he puts* (cf. adhāt *he put*), gharghara *gurgling* (cf. gharati *it gurgles*). There are a few traces in Russian: глаго́л *verb* (of Old Slavonic origin, implying a Common Slavonic *golgol) and such words, originating in the language of children, as дя́дя *uncle*, тя́тя *daddy*, ма́ма *mummy*, па́па *papa, daddy* (possibly borrowed from French[2]), пипи́ *to make water*, аа́/кака́ (*to go to*) *stool*, тю́-тю́ *ready*, (exclamation used in hide-and-seek), сюсю́кать *to lisp*, си́ся *nipple*. Apart from the occa-sional word created by children it is no longer productive. Of a somewhat different order is the repetition of a root in such fixed expressions as давны́м давно́ *long long ago*, бего́м бежа́ть *to run hard* and the composition, by means of repetition, of adverbs and adjectives having an intensive force ти́хо-ти́хо (*very*) *quietly*, до́лго-до́лго *for a long (long)*

1 Compounding is another formal process. It is treated separately in the next chapter.
2 Though the stress of the Russian word suggests either that it is of native origin or entered Russian through German *Papa*.

time, большо́й-большо́й *very big*. The latter process is slightly productive.[1]

(B) PHONETIC MODIFICATION

Changes in vowel or consonant brought about purely by the phonetic context have been described in Chapter 1 and cannot *of themselves* be used to produce new words. Apart from these changes there are others, not dependent on the phonetic context, which were established in the past, either in the pre-Russian period or during the history of the Russian language. They include such features as the alternating vowels in the roots нес-/нос-, вед-/вод-, etc., соб-ой/ себ-е, etc., бр-ать/бер-у/со-бир-ать, etc., дыш-ать/дух, and so on. In some instances a difference in meaning is apparent, as in the e/o alternation of нес- ('determinate root') and нос- ('indeterminate root'), in others the difference in meaning is almost purely formal, as in бр- ('non-prefixed infinitive group and pfv. infinitive group'), бер- ('non-prefixed present group and future pfv.'), -бир- ('prefixed impfv. group'), -бор- ('nominal'). In any event these alternations cannot of themselves be used to form new words. The alternation of -ов-/-ев- with -у-/-ю- in verbs with the infinitive ending in -овать/-евать is also inherited. It is a living alternation in that any new verb formed with the suffix -ов-/-ев- in the infinitive must have the alternation but it does not of itself produce differences in meaning. The situation is similar with the inherited consonantal alternations, such as б/бл, д/ж, к/ч, etc. Though these may occur in new and recent words and in that respect are living alternations[2] they are always associated with certain suffixes—

1 It is sometimes found in verbs too: Горя́т-горя́т зелёные/огни́ (Larisa Rimarchuk) *The green lights burn so brightly.*

2 It is worth noting that the alternation of velars with fricatives or affricates is no longer living in new adjectives derived from places or names of peoples. One has the older forms пра́жский (< Пра́га,

they are in fact a function of these suffixes. The same holds good with the vowel alternation o/a in such verbs as сбро́-сить, сбра́сывать *to throw off*: the alternation (and stress-shift—see below) is a function of the suffix -ыв-/-ив-. In the case of the vowel-zero alternation one simply has variant forms of the same root and again the occurrence of each form is determined by the following element (or absence of following element): день/дн-я, дн-ев-н-ой; сон, сон-лив-ый/сн-а, сн-о-видение; мох/мх-а, etc. The alternation of (stressed) e with ё is limited to a certain number of morphemes and is also determined by the nature of the following element (or absence of a following element):`жён-ы, жён/жен-ский, etc.

The great majority of those substantives derived from adjectives by removing a suffix and softening the final consonant are not new words (топь *swamp*, гладь *smooth expanse*, новь *virgin soil*, etc.) but a few are still occasionally formed. One finds them, for example, in the poetry of Mayakovsky—рьянь *zeal* (<рья́ный)—and Yesenin—хлюпь *squelch*, *sogginess* (<хлю́пкий). In these words the softness of the final consonant is a function of deaffixation (see below)—such substantives cannot be formed from roots which do not already have adjectives based on them. Hence it is possible to say that new words cannot be created in Russian simply by means of vowel or consonant changes.

(C) STRESS DIFFERENTIATION

Some new words have in the past been created simply by means of a shift of stress or stress-differentiation. Thus: си́дя *in a sitting position*—сидя́ *sitting* (gerund), сто́я *in a standing position*—стоя́ *standing* (gerund), су́дя (по) *to*

Prague), ри́жский (<Ри́га *Riga*) but the newer forms бу́гский (<Буг *Bug*), эдинбу́ргский (<Эдинбу́рг *Edinburgh*), нью-йо́ркский (<Нью-Йо́рк *New York*), каза́хский (<каза́х *Kazakh*), узбе́кский (<узбе́к *Uzbek*), etc.

judge (*by*)—судя́ *judging* (gerund), пя́тью *five times*—
пятью́ *five* (instr.), ше́стью *six times*—шестью́ *six* (instr.),
etc. In some instances composition is involved too—по-
мо́ему *in my opinion*, cf. по моему́ мне́нию *in my opinion*;
вплотну́ю *close* (*up to*), cf. в плóтную . . . *into the dense* . . .;
зачасту́ю *frequently*, cf. за ча́стую . . . *for/beyond frequent*
. . . . It is just possible that new words might be formed in
this way and the process may therefore be said to be potentially productive. The shift of stress involved in the formation of such verbs as ны́рнуть *to plunge* (< ныря́ть), кив-
ну́ть *to nod* (< кива́ть) and in such verbs as перепи́сывать
to transcribe (< переписа́ть), образо́вывать *to form* (< об-
разова́ть), are functions of the suffixes -ну- and -ыв-/-ив-
and cannot of themselves produce new words. Moreover,
such words as ки́внуть, образо́вывать, etc. are examples of
form-derivation, i.e. the derivation of items with possibly
new grammatical meaning but not with new lexical meaning.
Stress-differentiation is in general highly operative in form-
derivation (including inflection) in Russian but is not a
productive source of new words (with the possible exception
noted above).

2. AFFIXATION AND DEAFFIXATION

The addition of affixes to a root is the commonest process
whereby new words are created in Russian. There are three
varieties of this process: prefixation, which very occasionally
involves the phonetic modification of the following root;
suffixation, in which certain suffixes require certain modifications of the preceding root; and a combination of the two—
prefixation-suffixation.

At the beginning of this chapter we noted that word-
creating processes are not all equally productive at any one
epoch in the history of a language. It has also become
apparent that word-creating processes do not operate with

equal productivity in all parts of speech. This is particularly true of those processes which we shall be considering for the remainder of this chapter. Thus, prefixation is a weakly productive process in the substantive and adjective but is highly productive in the verb, while its productivity in the adverb is very low, if it can be said to occur at all. On the other hand, suffixation is a highly productive process in the creation of substantives and adjectives, where it is in fact the fundamental process, but less productive in the creation of new verbs (though it is more productive in *form-derivation*— the derivation of aspects). The number of suffixes used to create adjectives is much less than the number used to form substantives but they have a great range of productivity. Similarly, the only three productive suffixes used to form new adverbs are very active. The combination of prefixation with suffixation is most productive in the adjective, though less than suffixation alone, while in the substantive it has low productivity, and even lower productivity in the verb, where, however, it operates more productively in form-derivation. As for the adverb, this process really does not occur at all, for the apparently prefixed-suffixed forms are in fact derived either by the compounding of a preposition and another word (e.g. вплотную) or from prefixed adjectives by means of a suffix (e.g. поголо́вно < поголо́вный).[1] In examining these processes in more detail we shall pay little or no attention to unproductive prefixes and suffixes[2] but shall concentrate on those which are productive today. Endings, stem-vowels, etc. are special kinds of suffixes. To derive, by formal process, a word belonging to one part of

1 In general one must take care to distinguish 'secondary' derivation, by means of prefixation of an already suffixed stem or by means of
suffixation of an already prefixed stem, from 'primary' derivation by
simultaneous prefixation and suffixation. This is borne in mind in what
follows.

2 Note, however, B. O. Unbegaun's remark quoted above (page
112, footnote 1).

speech from a word belonging to another part of speech it is necessary in Russian to add and/or remove one of these special kinds of suffixes. For example, to make the verb старе́ть *to grow old* from the adjective ста́рый the suffix (ending) -ый has been removed and the suffixes -е- (stem-vowel) and -ть (infinitive ending) have been added. *Prefixation alone* can create words only from other words belonging to the same part of speech.

(A) PREFIXATION

Substantives: The prefixes[1] which can now form substantives are: анти-, as in а̀нтимате́рия *antimatter*, а̀нтипрото́н *antiproton*, а̀нтифаши́ст *antifascist*, а̀нтидарви-ни́зм *antidarwinism*, etc.; не-, as in неурожа́й *poor harvest*, непого́да *bad weather*, невнима́ние *inattention*, невы́-ход *absence* (from work), etc.; co- as in сосуществова́ние *co-existence*, соа́втор *co-author*, сореда́ктор *co-editor*, сорежиссёр *co-director*, etc.; and, somewhat less productively, пред- as in предысто́рия *prehistory*, про-, as in проре́ктор *vice-principal*, при-, as in при́звук *glide* (in phonetics). One or two other foreign prefixes, besides анти-, are mildly productive, e.g. а̀рхиске́птик *arch-sceptic*, у̀льтраимпериали́зм *ultra-imperialism*, псѐвдонау́ка *pseudo-science*, квѐзимаркси́ст *quasi-marxist*.

1 Not all initial morphemes are to be considered to be prefixes. For our purpose we shall consider a prefix to be an initial morpheme which modifies the meaning of the following morpheme(s) without adding any other nominal or verbal notion. Thus, prefixes may 'intensify', as do архи- *arch-*, ультра- *ultra-*, сверх- *ultra-*; negate, as do не-, *a-, in-*, etc., без- *-less*; add a prepositional notion, as do co- *co-*, при- *ad-*; add an adverbial notion, as in пере- *again, re-, trans-, от- away*, *a(b)-*, and so on. For this reason such initial morphemes as авиа- *aviation, aircraft*, аэро- *aircraft, aero-*, сам(о)- *self-*, все- *all, omni-* etc. are not considered to be prefixes but the initial morphemes of non-prefixal compounds. On the other hand we shall consider квази- *quasi- 'as if'* to be a prefix, and also псевдо- *pseudo-*, *not* (*in spite of appearances*).

The element экс- appears at the beginning of a few dozen words but has been borrowed along with the following element in most cases; it is a productive prefix only with names of offices or positions held, as экс-министр *ex-minister*, экс-чемпион *ex-champion*, экс-рекордсмен *ex-recordholder*. Вице- *vice-* appears to have been borrowed together with its following element in all instances, while the only possible isolatable instance of экстра- is in экстра-почта *express delivery* (used at least as early as 1846, by Belinsky). These prefixes then are not productive, though they have the potentiality of becoming productive.

Adjectives: Very few prefixes, either of native or of foreign origin, can be used to form adjectives *without simultaneous suffixation.* The prefixes which are used most commonly in this way are не- and без-, as in некультурный *vulgar*, ненаучный *unscientific*, безответственный *irresponsible*, безопытный[1] *inexperienced*, небезынтересный[1] *not without interest*, and the foreign prefix анти-, as in антинаучный *antiscientific*. The prefixes пре-, наи- and раз- *most, very* could perhaps be considered as form-deriving prefixes, since they convey the idea of superlative degree, as in презабавный *most amusing*, наивысший *highest*, разлюбезный *most kind*. Пре- and наи- are productive, раз- is rare in the literary language. Some would include in the same category of form-deriving prefixes сверх-, архи- and ультра-, as in сверхдальнобойный *super-long-range*, архиважный *most important*, ультраправый *ultra-right*. Псевдо- and квази- occur in, e.g., псевдонаучный *pseudo-scientific*, квазимарксистский *quasi-marxist*, and have the potentiality of further productivity. The prefix a- has usually been taken over together with some following element— аморальный *amoral*—but there are occasional indications that it may be isolatable and thus potentially productive—

1 Though this could be construed as a coalesence (see next chapter).

алоги́чный *non-logical*. A few other prefixes are occasionally used in forming adjectives without simultaneous suffixation.

Verbs: In all but a few instances, the addition of a prefix to a verb results in perfectivization, so, unless the prefix is an 'empty' one, prefixation in the verb is at one and the same time a process of word-creation and form-derivation. The formation of verbs by prefixation is very highly developed and we shall therefore do no more than list the productive and unproductive prefixes. Productive are: в-/во-, вз-/вс-, взъ-/взо-, вы-, до-, за-, из-/ис-/изо-, на-, над-/надо-, об-/обо-, от-/ото-, пере-, по-, под-/подо-, при-, про-, раз-/рас-/разо-, с-/со- and у-. Unproductive are Old Slavonic variants of some of these: воз-, о-, пре-, and the old Slavonic prefixes низ-/нис-/низо- and пред-/предо-[1]. The prefix не- can be added to verbs already having the prefix до-, as in недосказа́ть *not to finish* (what one is saying), недоде́лать *not to finish* (what one is doing). It is clear that in some instances the two prefixes have been added *simultaneously*, with the meaning 'not enough', to a single verb, as in недооцени́ть *to underestimate*. A few foreign prefixes enjoy a limited productivity: демобилизова́ть *to demobilize*, дезорганизова́ть *to disorganize*, дисквалифици́ровать *to disqualify*, реорганизова́ть *to reorganize*.[2]

Adverbs: Such adverbs as по-дру́жески *in a friendly fashion*, по-ста́рому *in the old fashioned way* are examples not of prefixation but of composition (preposition plus adverb or adjective), though it could be argued that the type represented by по-дру́жески is an example of prefixation. The type represented by по-ру́сски *in Russian* is an example of simultaneous prefixation and suffixation (по-русск-и).

1 Пред- is productive, however, in non-verbal derivatives. See above.

2 And even sometimes with native verbs—реиспари́ть *to reevaporate*. Переиспари́ть would be more usual.

По- is also added to comparative adverbs with the meaning 'a little, rather' and sometimes 'as . . . as possible', as in повы́ше *a little higher, as high as possible*, пода́льше *a little further, as far as possible*. These are certainly prefixed forms but may be considered examples of form-derivation ('attenuated comparative') rather than of word-creation.

(B) SUFFIXATION

Substantives: Well over a hundred substantive-forming suffixes can be isolated but not more than a few dozen are productive at present. Substantives denoting persons can be formed with the suffixes -ец, its extension -овец/-евец; -ик, its extensions -ник -щик/-чик, -льщик, -овщик; -ист and -ант; and the feminine suffixes -ка[1], its extension -овка/-евка; -ица, its extensions -ница, -щица/-чица, -льщица; and -ша.

Here are some examples of fairly recent words formed with these suffixes: комсомо́лец *comsomol*, ву́зовец (university or technical college) *student*, метростро́евец *construction worker* (on underground railway), зао́чник *correspondence course student*, до́менщик *blast-furnace worker*, лётчик *pilot*, боле́льщик '*fan*', фрезеро́вщик *milling machine operator*, футболи́ст *footballer*, танки́ст *tankman*, курса́нт *student* (on a course); комсомо́лка *comsomol*, ву́зовка *student*, метростро́евка *construction worker* (on underground railway), зао́чница *correspondence course student*, домрабо́тница *domestic help*, забасто́вщица *striker*, краси́льщица *dyer*, конду́кторша *conductress*, маникю́рша *manicurist*.

The suffix -ец has given rise to several other extensions: -анец/-янец 'of such and such nationality', -инец 'inhabitant of . . .', -ианец/-ьянец 'adherent of . . .'. They have a potential productivity: тихоокеа́нец *Pacific Islander*, баки́-

1 Throughout this chapter the case-number-gender suffixes (endings, *désinences*) а/я, о/е are not separated from preceding suffixes.

нец *inhabitant of Baku*, фабиа́нец *Fabian*. The suffix -ик also has an extension -овик/-евик, which has had some productivity: фронтови́к *front-line soldier*, большеви́к *bolshevik*, меньшеви́к *menshevik*.

The suffix -анин/-янин, 'inhabitant of . . .', has potential productivity and so have its extensions -чанин and -овчанин, as in сумча́нин *inhabitant of Sumy* (Су́мы), горьков-ча́нин *inhabitant of Gorky* (Го́рький). The suffix -ич, 'inhabitant of . . .', has a low productivity while the suffix -ич, 'son of . . .', and also -ович/-евич, have potential productivity, since they can, as the occasion demands, be used to form new patronymics. The same applies to their feminine equivalents -ична, -овна/-евна. The suffix -ёнок/-онок and its extension -чонок, 'little, young . . .', continue to have potential productivity too— буйволёнок *young buffalo*, татарчо́нок *Tatar child*.

As a means of deriving words denoting persons the suffix -тель and its extension -итель are said to be very productive in the Academy Grammar, whereas, according to Galkina-Fedoruk, etc.[1] the suffix -тель is of very low productivity in this respect (but not as a means of deriving words denoting objects—see below). It must be admitted that of the many words in -тель denoting persons most are old creations and therefore the productivity of -тель in this respect is indeed low. A very low degree of productivity, if any at all, is found in the suffixes -ун, -арь and the epicene suffixes -ла, -яга, though the last has recently been used to produce стиля́га *teddy-boy*. Little productivity is evinced either by -ыш or -ёныш, and the two feminine suffixes -иха and -уха are very weakly productive.

The elements of foreign origin -тор and -ент have usually been borrowed together with the elements which precede them. The same holds good for -ёр (< Fr. -*eur*), though there are a few words where this element has been used as a

1 *Современный русский язык.*

suffix to form new words, as for example шумёр *sound-effects man* and, more recently, киоскёр *kiosk attendant*. The element -ионер, as in революционёр *revolutionary* and a few other words, shows no signs of productivity. The element -мен (< -*man*) appears in some eight words borrowed from English, such as спортсмён *athlete*, лайнсмен *linesman*, яхтсмён *yachtsman*, клубмён *clubman*, бизнесмён *businessman*, etc. In several of the corresponding English words there is an *s* before -*man*, hence -смен in Russian. It is presumably because this element appears in a few borrowed sporting terms that it has been used as a 'suffix' to create рекордсмён *recordholder*.[1] Like киоскёр, the word рекордсмён has been created by adding an element of foreign origin to a foreign root, thus producing a word which looks as though it has been borrowed as a whole. The foreign element -ал has so far not been exploited as a productive suffix but the number of words ending in this element is large enough to make its future exploitation just feasible.

We should also consider here certain other foreign and native elements which Galkina-Fedoruk, etc.,[2] consider to be 'analogous to suffixes'. They have in mind the foreign elements -лог, -граф, -ман, -фил, -фоб and the native elements -вед, -вод, and -носец. The difficulty in analysis arises from the fact that, like suffixes, none of these elements appears (with the same meaning) as an independent item but, unlike suffixes, they are connected to the preceding element by the connecting vowel o/e in the same way that the elements of compound words are connected. A further difficulty is presented by the fact that, as far as -лог, -граф, -ман, -фил and -фоб are concerned, some of the preceding

1 Several of these words in -(с)мен can take feminine and other suffixes: спортсмёнка, спортсмёнский, спортсмёнство, рекордсмён-ка, . . . ский, . . . ство, etc.
2 *Op. cit.*, p. 250.

elements that are found with these elements do not appear as independent items either. Words containing these elements will be regarded in this book as compounds and will be treated in the next chapter.

Certain suffixes are productive in forming hypocoristics of Christian names. They express various degrees of endearment.[1] A peculiarity of most hypocoristic Christian names is that the underlying normal form ('stem') is reduced to one syllable (sometimes including a consonant or consonants from the next syllable), this syllable usually being the first syllable of the underlying form, more rarely the second. The suffixes include, -я (rarely -a), as in Вася (< Василий *Basil*), Митя (< Дмитрий *Dimitry*, NB apocope of initial д), Катя (< Екатерина *Catherine*), Стёпа (< Степан *Steven*); -ша and -уша/-юша, as in Гриша (< Григорий *Gregory*), Наташа (< Наталия *Natalie*, NB two syllables of original), Андрюша (< Андрей *Andrew*); -ня, as in Таня (< Татьяна *Tatiana*), Соня (< Софья *Sophia*). Nearly all such suffixal forms are, however, already established and therefore the possibility of creating new ones is restricted. Secondary hypocoristics are derived from primary hypocoristics and sometimes from the full Christian name by means of the productive suffixes -енька, -очка/-ечка and (with pejorative force) -ка. The suffix -ушка (primary) is added to the full stem of the Christian name, as in Иванушка (< Иван *John*), Аннушка (< Анна *Anne*). Various combinations of suffixes may be heard in the family circle.

New family names are today created only by means of the suffixes -ов/-ев (e.g. Абдулжалилов, Цыдендамбаев) and sometimes -ин, with the addition of the feminine suffix -a when necessary (e.g. Ахмадуллина).

The only productive suffixes used in the formation of names of animals are those used to derive the names of

1 See B. O. Unbegaun, *op. cit.*, pp. 88–89.

female animals. They are -ица and -иха, as in тигри́ца *tigress*, слони́ха *cow-elephant*.

The two most productive suffixes for the creation of abstract substantives are -ость/-есть and -ние. By means of -ость/-есть abstract substantives are formed from very many adjectives and some passive participles, e.g. углова́тость *angularity*, обтека́емость *streamlining*, тягу́честь *ductility*, населённость *density of population*. The letter н which frequently occurs before -ость comes from the stem of participles in -нный or adjectives in -ный and does not combine with -ость to form a productive suffix.[1] On the analogy of such words as обтека́емость (< обтека́емый), обита́емость *habitability* (< обита́емый) have been created such words as заболева́емость *incidence of illness*, воспламеня́емость *inflammability*, where a new and slightly productive extension of -ость, namely -емость, is attached to the verb stem. Similarly such words as сравни́мость *comparability* (< сравни́мый) have given rise, by analogy, to ходи́мость *durability*, гори́мость *incidence of fire-outbreaks*, where there is no underlying participle in -(и)мый. Here therefore we have a very slightly productive suffix -мость attached to a verb stem ending in и. The analogy of such words as населённость (< населённый) has led to the rise of a very slightly productive suffix -нность, attached to the verb stem, as in слётанность, derived from слета́ться (pfv.) *to be welded into a team by flying together*, and сработанность, derived from срабо́таться *to be welded into a team by working together*. It is clear that this is a very peripheral suffix. The productive suffix -ние is always preceded by a stem vowel е or а/я and gives rise to the large number of abstract nouns ending in -ение, -ание/-яние.

Three more very productive suffixes are -ство/-ество, -ка and -изм. The suffix -ство/-ество produces substantives

1 The suffix -ность, as in бу́дущность *future* (< бу́дущий) is no longer productive.

from other concrete substantives and from adjectives in -ский (including -анский/-янский and -ческий) but is no longer productive with regard to other adjectives and to verbs: áвторство *authorship*, студéнчество *student-body*, каутскиáнство *Kautskyism*, etc. It is this suffix which is used to produce abstract substantives from substantives ending in -вод and -фил (see above), with palatalization of the preceding л—шелковóдство *silk-worm breeding* (< шелковóд), русофúльство *russophilism* (< русофúл). The extensions of this suffix -тельство and -овство are now hardly, if at all, productive, while other extensions are no longer productive. The suffix -ка is now mainly productive in deriving substantives from verbs in -ировать—планирóвка *planning* (< планúровать), дифференцирóвка *differentiation* (< дифференцúровать), бомбардирóвка *bombardment* (< бомбардировáть)—its extension -ежка now being hardly productive—бомбёжка *bombing* (< бомбúть). The suffix -изм is usually correlated with the suffix -ист (see above), as in материалúзм *materialism* (cf. материалúст), империалúзм *imperialism* (cf. империалúст), though not always—ленинúзм *Leninism* (cf. лéнинец), большевúзм *bolshevism* (cf. большевúк[1]).

Another productive suffix of foreign origin, -ация, is correlated with verbs in -ировать, as in агитáция *propaganda, agitation* (cf. агитúровать), коллективизáция *collectivization* (cf. коллективизúровать). After л this suffix takes the form -яция, as in ассимиляция *assimilation* (cf. ассимилúровать), дистилляция *distillation* (cf. дистиллúровать), while its extension -фикация is associated with verbs in -фицировать, as in электрификáция *electrification* (cf. электрифицúровать). The somewhat less productive suffix -ия is also ultimately of foreign origin. It is used to derive abstract substantives from concrete substantives ending in

1 However, the term большевúст was current at one time (cf. the adjective большевúстский).

5+

-тип, -метр and the bound morphemes -лог, -граф, -ман, -фоб (see above) and -скоп, as in линотипия *linotype printing*, спектрометрия *spectrometry*, эндокринология *endocrinology*, петрография *petrography*, балетомания *balletomania*, англофобия *anglophobia*, микроскопия *microscopy*. Other technical terms are formed with this suffix. in particular new medical terms (when it is stressed -ия, as in шизофрения *schizophrenia*—see p. 48). Much less productive, indeed now only in the sense of 'quantity', is the foreign suffix -аж, as in тоннаж *tonnage*, листаж *number of pages*.

The native suffix -щина, as in иностранщина *things foreign*, стахановщина *Stakhanovism*, has some productivity, while the following suffixes of abstract substantives either have a very low productivity or have, so to speak, exhausted their productivity, being limited to derivations from restricted word-classes: -ота, -ие/-ье, -тие/-тье, -еж, -ица, -ня, -ура.

Suffixes which are productive in the creation of substantives denoting objects include -тель, -льник, -лка, -щик/ -чик, -тор and -ка, as in гаситель *extinguisher*, холодильник *refrigerator*, зажигалка *cigarette-lighter*, бомбардировщик *bomber*, коммутатор *commutator, switch-board*, зенитка *anti-aicraft gun*. Slang makes use of the suffix -ка in such words as Ленинка *The Lenin Library* (библиотека имени Ленина), Литературка *The Literary Gazette* (Литературная газета), микоянка *automatic soft-drink dispenser*. The suffix -ит, of foreign origin, is restricted to medical and technical terminology, as in полиомиелит *poliomyelitis*, фосфорит *phosphorite*, and the native suffix -ина/-атина/-ятина *meat of . . .* is, by its very meaning, extremely restricted, though it continues to have potential productivity—верблюжина *camel-flesh*, собачина *dog-flesh*, кошатина *cat-flesh*. Weakly or very weakly productive are the suffixes -ик, its extension -ник, -ок, -овка/-ёвка and -ло, as in ноздреватик *porous stone*, приёмник *receiver*,

слёпок *mould*, путёвка *holiday-grant*, поддувáло *air-vent*.
The suffixes -льня and -лка are mildly productive in the
formation of substantives denoting *place where . . .*, as in
раздевáльня and, colloquially, раздевáлка *cloakroom*.

The large variety of diminutive and hypocoristic suffixes
of all genders also fall into productive, weakly productive
and unproductive groups. The more highly productive ones
include -ик, -чик, -ка, -очка/-ечка, -онька/-енька, -це/-цо,
-ице/-ицо, the weakly productive ones -ец, -ок/-ек (and its
extensions -очек, -ечко, -ушек, -ышек), -ушка/-юшка,
-инка, -ишка, -онка/-енка, -(и)ца, -ашка, -урка, -ешка,
-(и)ко, -ушко/-юшко, and -ышко/-ишко, some of these
hardly being productive at all. The three productive augmentative suffixes are -ище, -ища and, with lower productivity, -ина.

The only singulative suffixes are -ина and its extension
-инка, as in виногрáдина *grape*, солóминка *straw*. The
collective suffix -ура is potentially productive in deriving
collective substantives from substantives denoting persons,
as in профессýра *professorial body*, аспирантýра *post-
graduate students* (also *post-graduate study*). The suffix -ат
is also occasionally found in this sense, as in инспекторáт
inspectorate. Otherwise, the element -ат, also -тура and one
or two others, are found in words of foreign origin and have
not been isolated for productive purposes.

New place-names are created by means of the suffixes -ск
and, to a smaller extent, -о as in Лéнинск, Кúровск,
Свердлóвск, Лéнино, etc. In the non-Russian regions
other, native suffixes or compounding elements may be
used, as in Ленинакáн, Кировабáд, Сталинúсси.

Adjectives: In the derivation of adjectives the most productive suffixes are -ный and -ский/-еский/-цкий.[1] Only
slightly less productive is -овый/-евый. B. O. Unbegaun

---

1 Throughout this section adjectival suffixes are given together with
the nom. sing. masc. suffix (ending) -ый/-ий.

writes[1]: 'It may be said that there are no nouns from which an adjective may not be formed with the aid of one of the three commonest suffixes: -н-, -ск- or -ов-.' If one takes into account the extensions of these suffixes, then the statement is largely true, though one should add the proviso that it does not apply to those substantives from which adjectives have already been derived by no longer productive suffixes. However, in some of these cases the forms with dead suffixes have been replaced by forms with productive suffixes, e.g. отцо́в *father's*, now replaced by отцо́вский. In view of the fact that with the three suffixes -ный, -ский, etc. and -овый such a great number of adjectives has been created and is constantly being added to we shall not discuss the basic forms further but shall look at their extensions from the point of view of productivity.

The most productive extensions of -ный are -льный, -альный, -ивный, -онный and -ичный. The first of these is used with stems of both native and foreign origin, as in купа́льный *bathing*, копирова́льный *copying*, the others only with stems of foreign origin[2] (-онный being correlated with substantives in -ия). Thus: театра́льный *theatrical*, акти́вный *active*, экскурсио́нный *excursion*, цини́чный *cynical*. Less productive is -озный, also associated only with stems of foreign origin and usually having medical or technical significance, as in карио́зный *carious*, целлюло́зный *cellulose*. A further extension is used after a few stems ending in -a, as in экзематозный *eczema*, коматозный *comatose*.

Further extensions of -альный are -иальный, which has given a few derivatives, such as принципиа́льный *in principle*, экваториа́льный *equatorial*; -ональный, which has given about a dozen derivatives, such as национа́льный *national*, функциона́льный *functional*; and -уальный,

---

1 *Op. cit.* p. 109.
2 -ичный with number stems, as in едини́чный *single*, is no longer productive.

which has given текстуа́льный *textual*, интеллектуа́льный *intellectual* and процессуа́льный *judicial*, but is not other-wise separable from preceding elements.

The most productive extension of -ский is -и́ческий, as in коммунисти́ческий *communist*, диалекти́ческий *dialectical*. Adjectives of this type are correlated with substantives in -изм and/or -ист. Less productive is -ческий, as in языко-ве́дческий *linguistic*, животново́дческий *animal husbandry*.

Adjectives denoting nationality or philosophical school, and ending in -анский/-янский, such as америка́нский *American*, гегелья́нский *Hegelian*, фабиа́нский *Fabian*, are in effect derived by means of -ский from substantives in -анец/-янец. The suffix -и́йский denoting country of origin, is still potentially productive, since new nations are con-stantly being formed. The element -ейский as in арме́й-ский *army*, is less likely to become productive. There is no evidence of any extensions of -овый/-евый.

Other productive suffixes include [j], which occurs in adjectives derived from names of animals, the [j] being ab-sent, however, in the nominative singular masculine—лиси́й, ли́сья, etc. *fox's*—and -ин, which can now be used to derive adjectives only from Christian names and sub-stantives of kinship, as in Са́шин *Sasha's*, сёстрин *sister's*. Others are -ли́вый, -чи́вый, -и́стый, -ова́тый/-ева́тый, -ча́тый, -а́стый, as in говорли́вый *talkative*, усто́йчивый *resistant*, по́ристый *porous*, круглова́тый *roundish*, весну́ш-чатый *freckled*, зуба́стый *big-toothed*. Less productive are -ови́тый/-еви́тый, -а́тый, -кий, as in плодови́тый *fruitful*, борода́тый *bearded*, но́ский *durable*. The last is used to form adjectives only from verbal or nominal-verbal roots and is not to be confused with the non-productive -кий attached long ago to original adjectival roots (as in у́зкий, ре́дкий, etc.). The suffix -лый is now hardly, if at all, pro-ductive, while the suffix -имый/-аемый, although productive, is nearly always associated in simultaneous prefixation-suffixation with the prefix не-.

Finally, we should note the productive diminutive suffix -енький/-онький, as in кру́гленький *round*, ти́хонький *quiet*, and the much less frequent augmentatives -ющий/-ущий and -енный as in большу́щий *huge*, толсте́нный *great fat*. The language of folk-songs, folk-poems, etc. makes use of the extended diminutive suffixes -ёхонький/-охонький and -ёшенький/-ошенький, as in легóхонький, легóшенький *light, little*.

Verbs: The creation of verbs by suffixation alone is, with one set of exceptions, not strongly developed. A. Mazon writes[1]: 'C'est dans le domaine du verbe, si l'on fait abstraction des emprunts étrangers, que la faculté de développement de la langue se montre la plus restreinte.' Deverbal suffixation, i.e. the creation of verbs from other verbs by means of suffixes, is restricted to form-derivation—the creation of aspectual forms by means of the productive suffixes -ывать/-ивать[2] (impfv.) and -нуть (pfv.). Denominative suffixation, the creation of verbs from substantives and adjectives (and from some pronouns and interjections), is non-aspectual in that it produces new verbs with the 'basic' imperfective aspect, from which perfectives may then be created by deverbal suffixation or prefixation.

Though there are many hundreds of verbs ending in -ать/-ять, the suffix -ать/-ять alone is not as active in verb-creation as -овать and its extensions. The point is that -ать/-ять is nearly always added to native stems and the possibilities of its combination with these stems have already been very thoroughly exploited. The same applies to its extension -кать, used to derive verbs from interjections and pronouns

1 *Lexique de la guerre et de la révolution en Russie*, p. 35.
2 Throughout this section verbal suffixes are given together with the infinitive suffix -ть.

ending in a vowel—аукать, тыкать, etc.—and to -ничать, used to form verbs of occupation and behaviour—столярничать, умничать. The potentiality is there but the means to realize that potentiality are largely exhausted. The suffixes -ить and -еть are in a similar state. They are potentially productive in deriving verbs from adjectives (e.g. белый *white*, белить *to whiten*, белеть *to turn white*) but again the potentiality has been thoroughly exploited and seemingly new creations of this type often turn out to have been used in the nineteenth century.[1]

The suffixes -ить and -еть can also be used to derive verbs from nouns. Here too new creations are often 'peripheral'— they are slang, facetious, or highly colloquial. Thus while хулиганить *to behave like a hooligan* is accepted by the literary language, бомбить *to bomb* and телефонить *to telephone* are regarded as colloquial in comparison with the literary бомбардировать and телефонировать, while the recent туить *to fly by Tu 104* is clearly ephemeral slang.

The suffix -овать can be attached to stems of native or foreign origin. In the first case its potential productivity has already been considerably exploited but in the second case it is still productive—стартовать *to start*, коксовать *to coke*, etc. The extensions of this suffix, -изовать, -ировать and -изировать, are very productive with foreign stems. The first of these is less productive than the other two, however, and there are some doublets in -изовать and -изировать, the latter often being regarded as preferable: индустриализовать/индустриализировать *to industrialize*, национализовать/национализировать *to nationalize*, вулканизовать/вулканизировать *to vulcanize*, экранизовать/экранизировать *to (adapt for the) screen*, etc. Only the suffixes -изовать and -изировать can form paired verbs without distinction of meaning. The few pairs distinguished

1 It may be, of course, that on the periphery of such word-classes verbs are *recreated* by individual authors.

by -ировать/-изировать are distinct in meaning too: теле-
фони́ровать *to telephone*—телефонизи́ровать *to provide
with telephones*; экрани́ровать *to screen, to protect*—экра-
низи́ровать *to (adapt for the) screen*. These suffixes are
sometimes found with native stems, as in украинизи́ровать
to Ukrainianize, военизи́ровать *to put on a wartime basis*,
большевизи́ровать *to bolshevize*, советизи́ровать *to
sovietize*, and their further productivity in this direction
cannot be excluded.

Adverbs: The productive adverb-forming suffixes are
-о/-е and -и, the latter being restricted to derivations from
adjectives in -ский or -цкий. Some adverbs in -о are stressed
differently from the neuter short form of the corresponding
adjective, e.g. светло́ *brightly* and све́тло *bright*. Most such
examples of stress differentiation are established ones but
there is some vacillation (see Chapter 2) and it is possible
that further such stress differentiations may arise. However,
new adverbs formed by means of the suffix о are unlikely to
be differentiated by stress from the neuter short form of the
corresponding adjective.

(c) PREFIXATION-SUFFIXATION

In considering the derivation of words by simultaneous prefixation and suffixation one must be careful not to confuse
this process with either the prefixation of already suffixed
stems as in а̀нти-гегелья́нец *anti-Hegelian*, безотве́тствен-
ный *irresponsible*, or the suffixation of already prefixed
stems, as in антифаши́стка *anti-fascist*, переку́рка *break for
a smoke*.

Substantives: In the sphere of the substantive prefixation-
suffixation is weakly productive. Such a word as оку́рок
cigarette-end is derived by this means. If, however, 'coalescences' (see Chapter 6) are regarded as examples of derivation

by prefixation-suffixation, then this process is somewhat more productive. (It will be seen in Chapter 6 that many suffixed substantives and adjectives with, for example, the initial element без- are regarded as a special type of compound which is derived by coalescing a phrase consisting of a preposition and a substantive.)

Adjectives: Here too the process is weakly productive, unless the coalescences described in Chapter 6 are regarded as examples of derivation by prefixation-suffixation.

An undoubted instance of prefixation-suffixation (i.e. *not* coalescence) is provided by the slightly productive process of prefixation with не- and suffixation with -мый/-емый, as in неистощи́мый *inexhaustible*, непромока́емый *waterproof, showerproof*.

Verbs: Although prefixed verbs with the suffix -ывать/ -ивать[1] are imperfectives, i.e. examples of aspect formation, they have the meaning (additional to that of the verb root) given them by the prefix, and are to that extent also examples, apparently, of word-creation. They can almost always be correlated with prefixed perfectives (some of these having the suffix -нуть) and it is probably best to consider most of them simply as examples of aspect formation. The process whereby they are arrived at can be shown by the following series: пры́гать *to jump*, imperfective—пры́гнуть, perfective, with the -нуть suffix meaning instantaneous action—подпры́гнуть *to jump up* (once), perfective, and an example of word creation by prefixation—подпры́гивать *to jump up and down*, imperfective, an example of aspect formation by substitution of -ывать for -нуть. However, there are verbs of this type which cannot be correlated with

1 See footnote 2, p. 134.

5*

perfectives. The verb припля́сывать *to execute a few dance-steps* is derived by simultaneous prefixation and suffixation from пляса́ть *to dance*. Such verbs are very few in number. For these reasons we can say that the derivation of new verbs from other verbs by simultaneous prefixation and suffixation is very weakly developed, is indeed 'peripheral'.

The case of verbs derived from nouns or adjectives by this process is very different. Here there is productivity. The productive suffixes are -ить and, to a smaller extent, -еть. The productive prefixes are those used in the creation of verbs by prefixation alone (see above), except до-, над-, низ- and пред-. Most productive are об- and у-, as in обу́глить *to carbonize*, упласта́ть *to pave*. These verbs are perfective and such new ones as are created form imperfectives by means of -ывать/-ивать, as in обу́гливать, упла́стывать.

The prefix о- has been used to derive verbs in -ить and, to a lesser extent, in -еть from phrases with the preposition без, as in обезле́сить *to deforest*, обезле́сеть *to become deforested*. Strictly speaking, therefore, such verbs are not examples of derivation by the addition of a prefix and a suffix to a root but of derivation by means of coalescence, with simultaneous prefixation-suffixation. They are therefore prefixed-suffixed compounds. However, such verbs as those quoted have given rise to a productive prefix обез-/обес- which can be added to nominal roots to produce, with suffixation, verbs such as обезлю́дить *to depopulate*, обезлю́деть *to become depopulated*, обесто́чить *to deprive of electricity supply*, etc.

Very similar to the prefixation-suffixation method of creating verbs from nominal roots is the creation of new verbs from verbs by simultaneous prefixation and addition of the reflexive particle -ся, which here has no reflexive meaning and behaves in fact very much like a suffix. This type of verb has varied in productivity during the last cen-

tury or so[1] but it is still productive today. Several prefixes
are used to form these verbs, but the most productive are
до-, за- and на-, as in дозвони́ться *to ring till one receives
an answer*, зачита́ться *to become absorbed in a book*, начи-
та́ться *to have one's fill of reading*, насиде́ться *to sit until
one is tired of sitting*.[2] These verbs are perfective and form
their imperfectives with the suffix -ыва/-ива, as in зачи́ты-
ваться, etc.

Adverbs: The only productive process of prefixation-
suffixation in the adverb is that with the prefix по- and the
suffix -и, by means of which adverbs are derived from
adjectives of nationality and origin and relative adjectives
in -ий, as in по-ру́сски *in Russian, à la russe*, по-моско́вски
in the Moscow fashion, по-во́лчьи *wolfishly*.

(D) DEAFFIXATION

The only part of speech in which words can be created by
deaffixation (*sci.* desuffixation) is the substantive. In the
past, many substantives have been created from prefixed
verbs by removing the stem-vowel of the verb (and, of
course, the infinitive suffix -ть), as in проры́в *break-through*
(<прорыва́ть), о́тдых *rest* (<отдыха́ть), вы́ход *exit*
(<выходи́ть), призы́в *call, conscription* (<призыва́ть).
As a general rule, such nouns are formed from imperfective
non-reflexive verbs but there are exceptions to this, such as
осмо́тр *inspection* (<осмотре́ть, pfv.), о́быск *search*

1 See F. P. Filin, 'О двух значениях глаголов, образованных
посредством префикса *на-* и суффикса *-ся*', *Вопросы грамматики*,
pp. 446–453.
2 Cf. Я ведь вся́кого напро́бовался! (Arb.) *I've had a go at
everything, you know!*; За три дня в Москве́ я наглота́лся
ды́ма. (Klen.) *I've swallowed my fill of smoke during these three
days in Moscow*; Я намакаро́нился! *I've had too much macaroni*,
quoted by K. Chukovsky in *От двух до пяти*.

(<обыска́ть, pfv.), надо́й *milk-yield* (<надои́ть, pfv.), о́тзыв *testimonial* (<отзыва́ться, impfv. reflexive).

With the loss of the suffixal stem-vowel, the stress has of course to shift back to the root. In some cases, however, the stress shifts back to the prefix, as in вы́ход, о́тзыв. Phonetic modification takes place in those instances where the last consonant of the verbal stem is soft: desuffixation is accompanied by hardening of this consonant, as in вы́ход, осмо́тр. Those substantives derived by this process which have a soft ending are not instances of retention of the softness of the final consonant but instances of the creation of feminine substantives of the кость-type, instead of masculine substantives. Examples are про́резь *hole* (<прореза́ть), про́рубь *hole* (<проруба́ть[1]), за́пись *record* (<записа́ть). This type is rarer than the hard-ending masculine type.

This process of substantive creation remains potentially productive but it has already been very thoroughly exploited and it usually turns out that apparently new words formed in this way have already been used earlier. In such words as налёт (*air-*)*raid*, пробе́г *life* (of a tyre), etc. we have examples not of new creations by way of desuffixation but examples of extension and change of meaning, often associated with change of meaning in the connected verb.

The creation of substantives from adjectives by desuffixation was touched on above, under *Phonetic Modification.* Though substantives have been created by this process in the past (зе́лень *greenery*, новь *virgin-soil*, голь *nakedness*) and though, as was pointed out above, Yesenin and Mayakovsky created words by this process, it can be said that apart from its very occasional use for 'poetic' or 'folksy' effect this is no longer a productive process.

1 Or < проруби́ть, pfv.

6
Sources of Words II

Where a substantive or adjective is derived by prefixing to an already existing substantive or adjective an element which is neither nominal nor verbal in origin, such a derived word is considered to be an example of derivation by prefixation. This has been dealt with in the preceding chapter. There are, however, words of complex structure which have been derived by coalescing a phrase (preposition + substantive), with simultaneous suffixation in the case of substantives, with or without simultaneous suffixation in the case of adjectives. Examples of this are:

безрабо́тица	*unemployment*, from
	{без + рабо́т(ы)} + ица,
беспроце́нтный	*without interest*, from
	{без + проце́нт(ов)} + ный

Such derived words may be considered by some to be derived by simultaneous prefixation and suffixation of a root (see Chapter 5). They may, however, be regarded as a different type of derived word, to which the name 'coalescence' is attached here.

Coalescences would include, among substantives:

безрабо́тица *unemployment*, беспризо́рник *homeless waif*, подмоско́вье *environs of Moscow*, etc.,

and among adjectives:

безволо́сый *hairless*, бескры́лый *wingless*, безбро́вый *browless*, беспроце́нтный *without interest*, безотка́т-

141

ный *recoilless*, внѐбюджѐтный *extra-budgetary*, вну-
трѝпартѝйный *intra-party*, закулѝсный *behind-the-
scenes*, мѐждугорóдный *interurban*, пòслевоéнный
post-war, внеплáновый *outside the plan*, свѐрхзвуковóй
supersonic, свѐрхплáновый *above the plan*, предвы́-
борный *pre-election* (with underlying preposition
перед transposed into its prefixal correlate пред-).
The type illustrated by противовѝрусный *anti-virus*,
противоснарáдный *anti-missile* is outstanding in
having a connecting-vowel.

Coalescences are productive, particularly in the adjectives,
where, however, the type without suffixation may be already
exhausted. The foreign prefixes про-, and транс-, which
were prepositions in their language of origin, are also
slightly productive in this sphere, as in прòгермáнский *pro-
German*, трàнсафрикáнский *trans-African*. Here the derivation is from an underlying phrase of the nature of 'for
Germany/the Germans' (rather than 'for German') and
'across Africa' (rather than 'across African') and such
adjectives are therefore not examples of adjectives derived
by prefixation from suffixal adjectives. It is arguable that at
least some of the adjectives with the initial element анти-
should also be regarded as coalescences.
The rest of this chapter is devoted to compounds and by
a compound is meant here a primary derivative arrived at
by blending into one word two or more elements of which at
least two elements are of nominal or verbal origin. Some
words are formed by simultaneous compounding and suffixation and these too are treated as compounds. Words
such as ю́го-зáпадный *south-western* are secondary derivatives arrived at by suffixing a compound (a primary derivative) and are not regarded here as compounds. We deal first
with 'whole compounds', i.e. compounds in which the nominal or verbal elements are not abbreviated.

WHOLE COMPOUNDS[1]

The derivation of substantives and adjectives by compounding has been and continues to be highly productive. Both compound substantives and compound adjectives may be classified into several types according to the elements which enter into their composition, the number of elements and the way these elements are combined and the behaviour of the elements within the compound. Some types are more productive than others.

1. *Compound substantives*

Not more than four elements may enter into the composition of first stage compound substantives. Those compounds with more than four elements are second stage compounds, in which at least one element is already compound. Some types of compounds have the connecting vowel o/e, others do not, and of those which have the connecting vowel some are formed by simultaneous suffixation while others are not.

(A) WITHOUT CONNECTING VOWEL O/E

(i) *'Hyphenated':* There are three types of compound substantive which do not have the connecting vowel. One of these is distinguished from all other compound substantives by several features. This is the type in which the two compounding elements are substantives which retain their grammatical identity, i.e. both parts decline. The two elements are linked, orthographically, by a hyphen, though not all hyphenated substantives decline both elements (see below). Compounds of this type are appositional in function, i.e. one element is in apposition to the other, 'basic' element. In other types of compound substantives the appositional function is rare. Almost always the appositional element

1 Hereafter, 'whole compounds' will be referred to simply as 'compounds'.

follows the basic element, as in шко́ла-интерна́т *boarding-school*, член-корреспонде́нт *corresponding member*, заво́д-автома́т *automated factory*, кни́жка-па́мятка *memo-book*, ваго́н-рестора́н *dining-car*, врач-инте́рн *intern*, though very occasionally the appositional element may come first, as in пила́-ры́ба *sawfish*, жернова́-печа́ти *seals like mill-stones* (Klen.), геро́й-цели́нник *heroic virgin-lands worker*. This type is quite productive and is common in nonce-words such as жернова́-печа́ти above, and дошко́льники-малыши́ *tots of pre-school age*, брю́ки-одино́чки *trousers* (not as part of a suit), etc. In all other types of compound substantives only the last element declines.

(ii) '*Abutted*': In the second type of compound without connecting vowel the two elements are also substantival. In these 'abutted' compounds the first element delimits the second, as in врѐмяпрепровожде́ние *pastime*, врѐмяисчисле́ние *chronology, calendar*, сѐмядо́ля *cotyledon*, сѐмяпо́чка *seed-bud*. More recent additions to this type have first elements ending in a consonant. In some of them the first element may have arisen from the abbreviation of an adjective (see 'Stump-compounds' below) but such words now present the appearance of abutted compounds and give rise to others of similar structure. Compounds of this kind are, of course, very common in English, but they have hitherto been unusual in Russian. Their number is still not large but the type is productive and may easily provide the language with many more words. Examples include бо̀ртпроводни́к *steward*, бо̀ртжурна́л *log-book*, бо̀ртинжене́р *flight-engineer*, пионѐрла́герь *pioneers' camp*, пионѐрвожа́тый *pioneer-leader*, пионѐротря́д *pioneer-detachment*, трѳ́ддисципли́на *labour-discipline*, трѳ́дколо́ния *work-colony*, трѳ́дшко́ла *labour school*, спо̀рткружо́к *sports circle*, спо̀рткл ́уб *sports club*, спо̀ртсоревнова́ние *sports* (*competition*), спо̀ртинвента́рь *sports equipment*, Сою́зпеча́ть *Union Press*, утильтáпочки *'utility sandals'* [1] (lit. 'light shoes made of (leather) scraps'). Some of the abutted compounds are written with a hyphen, though structurally they do not differ from those without a hyphen: дѝзель-мотóр *diesel-engine*, дѝзель-пóезд *diesel train*, крѐкинг-процéсс *cracking process*, крѐкинг-завóд *cracking factory*.

Closely associated with these abutted compounds are such words as стòп-крáн *emergency brake*, стòп-сигнáл *braking light*, in which the interjection стоп (< English *stop*) acts as delimiter, and часы̀-пѝк *rush-hour(s)*, where пик (< English *peak*) delimits часы̀ and stands in second place. The type of compound represented by киловàтт-чáс *kilowatt-hour* is slightly different since it is hardly a case of the first element delimiting the second but of two substantives joined to form another substantive which is different in meaning from either.[2]

The abutted compound is productive in the creation of place-names with the second element -грaд (the compounding form of гóрод in place-names), as in Ленингрáд, Калинингра́д, Сталингрáд. Occasionally, however, the connecting vowel is found in place-names ending in -грaд, which are then compounds with three elements: Кировогрáд (formerly Зинóвьеск and, before that, Елизаветгрáд), Волгогрáд (formerly Сталингрáд). Abutted compounds are also formed with the initial element авиа-, which is not free-standing and has the meaning 'by means of or pertaining to aircraft', as in авиапóчта *airmail*, авиаремóнт *aircraft repair*, авиамáтка *aircraft carrier*.

(iii) *With numeral element:* Compound substantives without a connecting vowel, having a numeral as first element

1 Ilf and Petrov, *Директивный бантик.*
2 An hour being a unit of time, a kilowatt being a unit of power, but a kilowatt-hour being a unit of energy consumed (at a rate of one kilowatt for one hour).

and substantive[1] as second element, can be formed. Any numeral other than один, тысяча, миллион, биллион can enter into the formation of such compounds. There is simultaneous suffixation, the usual suffixes being -ие and -ник, so that the structures have three elements. In all except those with the numerals сто and девяносто the numeral appears in its genitive, as in десятилетие *decade*, пятиугольник *pentahedron*, сорокалетие *fortieth anniversary*, восьмисотлетие *octocentenary*.[2] Of the alternative numeral first elements тре- and трех- the former is no longer productive while the numeral element двух- seems to be in process of ousting дву- as a productive element (see below).

The numerals сто and девяносто, as in столетие *centenary*, девяностолетие *ninetieth anniversary*, are at best very weakly productive in the *primary* derivation of substantives, such a word as стометровка *hundred-metre sprint*, for example, being in all probability a secondary derivative, by way of suffixation, from стометровый. Compounds with these elements are discussed again below under adjectives.

Compounds with first element 'half' should also be mentioned here. In modern Russian *half* is половина, the form пол (Old Russian полъ) now occurring as a free-standing item in a limited number of expressions in the colloquial language. In compounds, however, *half* is пол- or полу- (from the Old Russian genitive полу), and both are productive. With полу- the second element remains in its nominative

---

1 In three quarters of the compounds with сто- there is secondary stress on this element. Nowhere else does secondary stress fall on the connecting vowel, so сто- in compounds is regarded not as ст- plus connecting vowel о but as the nominative-accusative сто. It is preferable to regard девяносто- in the same way.

2 <восемьсот + лет + ие. Professor A. Yefimov, of Moscow University, has pointed out to me that, during the octocentenary period in Moscow, the man in the street spoke of восемьсотлетие, using an abutted compound of a colloquial type, in which the numeral element appears in its nominative-accusative form.

form, as in полушёлк *half-silk*, полуфинáл *semi-final*, полуфабрикáты *semi-finished goods*, whereas with пол- the second element appears in its genitive form, as in пол-лúтра *half a litre*, полминýты *half a minute*, полчасá *half an hour*. In the oblique cases of these words, however, the first element is полу-, thus: получáса, получáсу, etc. The type with полу- as first element and simultaneous suffixation, as in полугóдие *half a year*, полукрýжие *semi-circle*, полустúшие *hemistich*, is non-productive or, at most, has a very weak potential of productivity.

(b) WITH CONNECTING VOWEL o/e

All other types of compound substantives have the connecting-vowel o/e as second element. They may be classified according to the nature of the third element. We shall take first those which consist of three elements.

(i) *Substantival third element:* The type with a substantive as third element has a substantive, adjective or pronoun[1] as first element, as in рельсоуклáдчик *plate-layer*, металло-лóм *scrap-metal*, частокóл *palisade*, легковéс *light-weight*, тяжеловéс *heavy-weight*, самокрúтика *self-criticism*, само-анáлиз *self-analysis*. Here the first element delimits the third. Those with substantival first element also include compounds in which one element does not delimit another. Instead, the sum of the two notions A and B gives rise, as it were, to a third, C, which is neither A nor B (cf. кило-вàтт-чáс above). Such compounds, which are not numerous, include овцебы́к *musk-ox*, светотéнь *chiaroscuro*, железо-

---

1 Throughout this chapter, when we say that a substantive, adjective, numeral or pronoun enters into the formation of a compound we mean the root or stem of the word. In the case of substantives and pronouns the root or stem will often be identical with the nom. sing. of the word as a free-standing item. Bear in mind that o/e is an element in the structure of the compound.

бетóн *reinforced concrete*, лесостéпь *wooded steppe*,[1] лесо-
тýндра *wooded tundra*,[2] юго-зáпад *south-west*, сèверо-
востóк *north-east*. This type is very weakly productive,
though it has given rise to such fairly recent words as
человèко-чáс *man-hour*, человèко-дéнь *man-day*. It is possible to argue that in some of these words the first element
does, in some sense, delimit the third. Железобетóн, for
instance, is still бетóн, which is 'армúрованный желéзом'.

(ia) *Bound morpheme as third element:* In these compounds
the third element is of foreign origin and, though it has substantival significance, it cannot occur on its own—it is a
bound morpheme. Many of these substantives *could* be said
to be derived by deaffixation from abstract substantives,
e.g. физиóлог < физиолóгия, but it makes for a more
economical description to consider that a word such as
физиолóгия is derived by suffixation from the compound
физиóлог. This not only puts физиóлог, etc. in the same
class as фòтотéхника, etc., but is also in accord with the
very restricted role that is played by deaffixation in the
creation of words (see *Deaffixation* in the preceding chapter).

Examples are: методóлог *methodologist*, эпидемиóлог
epidemiologist, физиóлог *physiologist*, кристаллóграф
crystallographer, этнóграф *ethnographer*, балетомáн *balle-
tomane*, галломáн *gallomane*, русофúл *russophile*, библио-
фúл *bibliophile*, русофóб *russophobe*, спектроскóп *spectro-
scope*, фазомéтр *phase-meter*. One or two words formed
with some of these elements lack the connecting vowel, e.g.
каллигрáф *calligrapher*, ваттмéтр *watt-meter*, while ми-
нералóг *mineralogist*, by virtue of haplology, has 'lost' an
entire syllable.

---

1 Strictly speaking, the transitional zone between the steppe on the
one hand and the forest on the other hand.
2 Cf. preceding note.

(ib) *Bound morpheme as first element:* There are several elements, again of foreign origin, which stand as the *first* part of compound substantives and like -лог, etc., are bound morphemes. They are associated with substantival third elements which can function as free-standing items. It matters little whether these bound morphemes are said to be substantival or adjectival in significance. Examples are:

аэросъёмка   *aerial photograph*,   аэрофи́льтр   *air-filter*, микрооргани́зм *micro-organism*, микрокни́га *micro-book*, макрорайо́н   *macro-region*,   фо̀тоте́хника   *phototechnics*, фо̀тосни́мок *photograph*,   фо̀тобума́га *photographic paper*, агрого́род *agricultural centre*, агрокружо́к *agricultural club*.

Some of these initial elements may have arisen by way of abbreviation of substantives or adjectives, but they have now become, as it were, independent of the original substantives or adjectives, capable of forming compounds in the same way as substantives, adjectives, etc. Other elements which are used in this way are кино- and мото- as in кѝнотеа́тр[1] *cinema*, кѝносту́дия *cine-studio*, мо̀тоспо́рт *motor-racing*, мо̀тошлём *crash-helmet*.

(ii) *Deverbal third element:* The type with a deverbal third element has as first element a substantive, which delimits the deverbal element, i.e. in the underlying phrase the substantive would be the complement of a verb. Examples are: пылесо́с *vacuum-cleaner*, ледоко́л *ice-breaker*, языкове́д *linguist*, табаково́д *tobacco-grower*. Less productive is a type with an adverb or pronoun as first element, as in вез-дехо́д '*jeep*', самоса́д *home-grown tobacco*, where the first element is not the complement of a verb in the underlay.

(iii) *Four-element substantives:* First stage compounds

1 Note that the free-standing item кино́ *cinema* has stress on the second syllable, whereas кино- has (secondary) stress on the first syllable.

with four elements have the connecting vowel as the second element and a suffix as the fourth element. If the third element is derived from a substantive, then the first element is adjectival, as in красноармéец *red armyman*, новолýнье *new moon*, гололéдица[1] *ice-covered ground, black ice* or adverbial, as in многотирáжка *periodical with wide circulation*[2], or numeral, as in одногóдок *year old animal*, тысячелéтие *millennium*. The only numeral elements which participate in this kind of compound are одн-, тысяч-, миллион-, биллион-.

If the third element is deverbal, then the first element is derived from a substantive or, less commonly, from a pronoun or adverb, as in орденонóсец *one honoured by an order*, огнетушѝтель *fire-extinguisher*, самоýчка *self-taught person*.

2. *Compound adjectives*

In describing the structure of compound adjectives the endings -ый, -ая, etc., will be discounted. The number of elements spoken of below therefore includes all elements except the ending, and the structures are those of the adjectival stems to which the endings are attached. Two types of compound adjectives have two-element structures. All others have at least three elements and in all except two types the second element is the connecting vowel. Some compound adjectives with the connecting vowel also have a suffix, so that four elements are present. Underlying some compound adjectives is a co-ordinate group ('A and B') while underlying many others are various non-co-ordinate phrases or groups. In the latter instance the element which delimits always comes first.

---

1 Also гололёд, a three-element compound—adjective + o + substantive.

2 Recent slang has микролитрáжка '*mini-car*', with the initial element микр-, of foreign origin.

(A) 'NON-CO-ORDINATE' ADJECTIVES

(i) *Two-element structures:* One type of compound adjective having two elements is illustrated by such words as изжелта-красный *yellowish-red*, иссиня-зелёный *bluish-green*. Here the second element is a colour adjective and the first a special kind of adverb, itself derived from a colour adjective and occurring only in this kind of compound adjective.

(ii) *Structures with three or more elements:* Compound adjectives with three or more elements may be classified according to the nature of the third, or, in two types, the second element.

(a) Those with a substantival third element may be sub-divided according to the nature of the first element and the presence or absence of a suffix. Some have an adjectival first element and no suffix, such as чернобро́вый *black-browed*, узкоплёчий *narrow-shouldered*, others have a suffix as well—железнодоро́жный *railway*, коро́тково́лновый *short-wave*, высо́кочасто́тный *high-frequency*. The latter type is slightly more productive.

The majority of compound adjectives with the initial element сто- have secondary stress on this element. Here the о is not a connecting vowel and the numeral element is in its nominative-accusative form. Simultaneous suffixation is the rule in contemporary derivatives with сто- and their structure therefore has three elements: сто́метро́вый *hundred-metre*, сто́клёточный *'hundred-square'* (variety of chess), сто́эта́жный *hundred-storey*. Девяно́сто *ninety* is potentially productive of this kind of compound adjective and is also best considered to be in its nominative-accusative form when it does occur in compounds.

The numeral elements одн-, тысяч-, миллион-, биллион- are associated with the connecting vowel and simultaneous suffixation in the productive derivation of four-element compound adjectives, as in однообъекти́вный *single-objective* (microscope, etc.), тысячекилогра́ммовый *thousand-kilogram*.

A type with pronominal first element is weakly productive—всесою́зный *All-Union*, всекита́йский *All-China*, ежесу́точный *every twenty-four hours*. The last example shows the pronominal element еж-, which has no free-standing form. Words such as шарообра́зный *spherical*, парово̀зоремо́нтый *engine-repair*, кукуру̀зоубо́рочный *maize-harvesting*, illustrate a type with substantival first element and suffix. This type is fairly productive.

A type without connecting vowel is illustrated by those with numeral elements: трёхле́тний *three-year*, пятиуго́льный *pentagonal*, трёхсо̀тзна́чный *having three hundred digits*. The alternative compounding form of три, namely тре-, is no longer productive and while the alternative compounding forms of два, namely двух- and дву-, seem to have been almost equally productive in the past, the former is now dominant. Many of the adjectives which in Dal's dictionary[1] have the numeral element дву- now have the element двух- and of the modern words having alternatives дву-/двух- the latter are commoner.

The geographical adjectives illustrated by за̀паднокав-ка́зский *West Caucasian*, ю̀жнокоре́йский *South Korean*, etc., could be analysed in various ways but in most cases it seems that the underlying phrase is, for example, за́падный Кавка́з, ю́жная Коре́я, etc. Their structure therefore could be said to be adjective+connecting vowel+substantive+suffix—a four-element structure. Such adjectives as сѐверо-коре́йский *North Korean*, сѐверокавка́зский *North Caucasian* raise a difficulty, however, and it becomes necessary to say that the adjective се́верный drops its suffix н in forming compounds. Adjectives such as ю̀го-за́падный

---

1 *Словарь жива́го великору́скаго языка́*, 1st edition, 1863–1866.

south-west, сѐверо-восто́чный, *north-east* are not compound adjectives as understood here but adjectives derived by suffixation from compound substantives (< ю̀го-за́пад, сѐверо-восто́к).

(b) Another set of non-co-ordinate compound adjectives consists of those in which the third element is an adjective. Some have as first element a substantive which in the under-lying group would be part of a phrase qualifying the adjective, as in рабо̀тоспосо́бный *efficient*, жаропро́чный *heat-resistant*, моро̀зоусто́йчивый *frost-resistant*, others have an adjectival initial element, such as сѝне-зелёный *bluish-green*, ржа̀вокори́чневый *rusty brown*, древнегре́ческий *ancient Greek*, новогре́ческий *modern Greek*, электро̀нно-счётная маши́на *electronic computor* ('electronic-calculating machine'), and some have an adverb as first element, such as высо̀кокалори́йный *high-calorie content*, скороспе́лый *early ripening*.

Such forms as ослепи́тельно-бы́стрый *dazzlingly swift*, аристократи́чески-краси́вый *aristocratically beautiful*, which are common in the writings of I. A. Bunin and others, are idiosyncratic compounds at the most. Little or nothing has been added by inserting a hyphen between adverb and adjective.

The type with a pronominal first element, such as самодо-во́льный *self-satisfied*, appears to be no longer productive.

(c) Compound adjectives with a participle as third element, in contrast to those with adjectival third element, *are* productive with a pronominal first element, as in самоопро-ки́дывающийся *self-tipping*, самозагружа́ющийся *self-loading*, самосма́зывающийся *self-lubricating*.

The participial type with an adjective as first element, as in главнокома́ндующий *Commander-in-Chief* (substanti-vized), мертворождённый *still-born*, appears to be no longer productive, whereas that with adverbial first element is productive—дикорасту́щий *growing wild*, новонаселён-ный *newly settled*, новойзданный *newly published*. Such words as вы́шеизло́женный *set out above*, нижеука́зан-ный *indicated below*, consisting of adverb + participle, with no connecting vowel, are written conventionally as one word but, like certain adjectives mentioned above, gain nothing from being so written and could in fact be written as two words. The participial type with substantival first element, such as мета̀лоре́жущий *metal-cutting*, бо̀леутоля́ющий *sedative*, is fairly productive.[1]

(d) Compound adjectives with a deverbal (but not parti-cipial) third element have a substantival first element and a suffix, as in плодоро́дный *fruitful*, сноповяза́льный *sheaf-binding*, цветодели́тельный *colour-refraction*, ста̀лепла-ви́льный *steel-smelting*, снотво́рный *soporific*. Some of these might be considered to be of the type substantive + o/e + adjective, since вяза́льный and плави́льный, for example, are free-standing adjectives derived from verbs by suffixa-tion. The type consisting of adjective + deverbal (e.g. животво́рный *life-giving*) is non-productive.

(B) 'CO-ORDINATE' ADJECTIVES

Two main types of co-ordinate adjective may be distin-guished—one with adjectives as the principal[2] elements and one with substantives as the principal elements.

In the first type two adjectival elements are joined by a

1 The word мѐдьсодержа́щий *copper containing/bearing* is an abutted compound adjective consisting of substantive + participle. It could be written as two words but, if more adjectives of this structure appear, then a new type of compound adjective will have been estab-lished.

2 'Principal 'here means 'having lexical meaning', as distinct from the purely formal elements—the connecting vowel and suffix.

connecting vowel, as in ру́сско-францу́зский *Russo-French*, зи́мне-весе́нний *winter-spring*, глухонемо́й *deaf and dumb*, беспроце́нтно-вы́игрышный (биле́т) *lottery (ticket) without interest*, вы́пукло-во́гнутый *concavo-convex*, чёрно-бе́лый *black and white*. This type may be extended to five or more elements, as in ру́сско-неме́цко-францу́зский (слова́рь) *Russian-German-French (dictionary)*, а́нгло-ру́сско-неме́цко-францу́зский (слова́рь) *English-Russian-German-French (dictionary)*.

A four-element type is derived from two substantives with connecting vowel and simultaneous suffixation, as in това́ро-пассажи́рский (по́езд) *passenger-goods (train)*, мя́со-моло́чные (проду́кты) *meat and dairy (products)*, грудобрю́шная прегра́да *diaphragm* ('thorax-abdomen partition'). A five-element type has the structure: substantival element + suffix + connecting vowel + substantival element + suffix, as in профе́ссорско-преподава́тельский *professors' and teachers'*, экскурсио́нно-тури́стский *tourists' excursion*. The last example, however, could be shown to have a non-co-ordinate five-element structure with the delimiting element in fourth place instead of first place (< экску́рсия для тури́стов). Moreover, this five-element structure might in general be considered to be simply a three-element structure derived from adjective + connecting vowel + adjective, like ру́сско-францу́зский, etc.

Finally, one should note that such adjectives as ди́зель-мото́рный *diesel-engine*, социа́л-демократи́ческий *social democratic*, like ю́го-за́падный *south-west*, се́веро-восто́чный *north-east* (see above), are not compound adjectives in our sense of the term but are, structurally, simple adjectives derived by suffixation from compound substantives.

3. *Compound adverbs*

The compounding of preposition with substantive to produce an adverb has been very fruitful in the past and still has potential productivity, the prepositions most likely to take part in this process now being в, на and, to a smaller extent, с. The compounding of по with the dative case of adjectives is still potentially productive too.

4. *Compound verbs*

Compound verbs are occasionally created by means of the pronominal element сам-, as in самоуспокóиться *to become complacent*, самоустранúться *to give up one's duties of one's own accord*, самозакáливаться *to self-temper*, самоокупáться *to be financially self-supporting* (of an enterprise).

STUMP-COMPOUNDS

'Clips' or 'stump-words', such as the colloquial зам for заместúтель *deputy*, are not common in Russian. On the other hand a fruitful source of substantives in modern Russian has been the incorporation of stumps into compound words. Words produced in this way are known in Russian as сложносокращённые словá ('compound-contracted words') or аббревиатýры. The term 'stump-compounds' is used in this book.

There were some stump-compounds in the language before 1917, such as the names of firms or products Продамéта, Продýуголь, Монотóп, хатóп, ростóп,[1] the names of political parties and their members ка-дэ́[2] > кадéк, кадéт, зс-э́р[3] > зсéр (giving derivatives эсéрка, эсéрский, эсéровский) and military terms—главковéрх, главкофрóнт, штабáрм, наштадúв,[4] etc. The number of stump-compounds began

1 In full these are, respectively, Óбщество для продáжи издéлий рýсских металлургúческих завóдов, Óбщество для продáжи ýгля, Монопóлия тóплива, хáрьковское тóпливо, ростóвское тóпливо.

2 Конституциóнный демокрáт.

3 Социалúст-революционéр.

4 In full these are, respectively, верхóвный главнокомáндующий, главнокомáндующий фрóнтом, штаб áрмии, начáльник штáба дивúзии. See A. Mazon, *Lexique de la guerre*, etc., pp. 1 to 5 *et seq.*

to increase after the Revolution, with the creation of new institutions, offices, departments and so on, and there have been thousands of such words created in the forty-odd years since 1917.[1] The tendency to create such words was particularly strong in the 1920's and went in fact to extremes. Most of the stump-compounds created in that period have since disappeared but the process is still very active: within a few days of the launching of the first sputnik in October 1957, the abbreviation ИСЗ (иску́сственный сателли́т земли́ *artificial earth satellite*) appeared in the press and a week after the launching of the Venus probe in February 1961, *Pravda* used the abbreviation АМС (автомати́ческая межпланéтная стáнция *automatic interplanetary station*). These two examples illustrate the fact that some stump-compounds or abbreviations arise first in some specialized institute or place of work and later become common coin. Many, if not most, of the stump-compounds 'arise spontaneously—often the popular language creates them first and they then be-become naturalized'.[2]

Several types of stump-compounds may be distinguished: (a) those consisting entirely of parts of words (usually, though not always, single syllables), (b) those consisting of part of a word and a complete word, (c) those consisting of initials (with two sub-types—see below), and (d) a mixed type, consisting of initials and part of a word or parts of words.

Since stump-words are, by definition, derived from free-standing whole words it follows that they cannot contain the bound, deverbal elements which are common in ordinary compounds. They are derived therefore from combinations of adjective and substantive or substantive and substantive.

(a) The predominant underlay of this type is adjective +

1 Edgar Scheitz, in *Russische Abkürzungen und Kurzwörter*, lists over 20,000.
2 E. Scheitz, *Russische Abkürzungen . . .*, p. ix.

substantive. Usually the first syllable together with the next consonant of each underlying element is taken, as in колхо́з (< коллекти́вное хозя́йство) *collective farm*, техре́д (< техни́ческий реда́ктор) *technical editor*, юнна́т (< ю́ный натурали́ст) *young naturalist*, райко́м (< райо́нный комите́т) *regional committee*, физру́к (< физи́ческий руководи́тель) *physical training instructor*. Sometimes two consonants following the initial syllable are included, as in партко́м (< парти́йный комите́т) *party committee*, парто́рг (< парти́йный организа́тор) *party organizer*. Very occasionally the connecting vowel o/e may be inserted, as in технору́к (< техни́ческий руководи́тель) *technical instructor* (cf. техре́д above).

When an underlying element begins with a prefix it is usual to take the prefix and the following syllable into the compound, as in госизда́т (< госуда́рственное изда́тельство) *State Publishing House*, исполко́м (< исполни́тельный комите́т) *executive committee*[1]. Similarly, if the first syllable alone might lead to misunderstanding or to an unintentionally humorous form, then two syllables are taken, as in политру́к (< полити́ческий руководи́тель) *political instructor*, where it is desirable to avoid *полрук 'half-instructor' or even 'sex-instructor'. A compound adjective entering into the formation of a stump-compound may itself be reduced to the initial syllables of its underlying elements, as in леспромхо́з *timber enterprise*, derived from лесопромы́шленное хозя́йство. The incorporation of three syllables is rare—универма́г (< универса́льный магази́н) *department-store*.[2]

A less widespread variety of type (a) is that with the

---

1 But cf. ликбе́з and детги́з below.

2 For a more detailed discussion of the various factors affecting the length of the elements incoporated in stump-compounds see A. Baecklund, *Die univerbierenden Verkürzungen der heutigen russischen Sprache.*

underlay substantive + substantive, the second substantive
acting as qualifier to the first. Examples of this are прораб
(< производи́тель рабо́т) *construction superintendent*, лик-
бе́з (< ликвида́ция безгра́мотности) *campaign against
illiteracy*, завхо́з (< заве́дующий хозя́йством) *manager*,
замза́м (< замести́тель замести́теля) *sub-deputy*, команд-
а́рм (< кома́ндующий а́рмией) *army commander*. In the
last, which replaced the pre-revolutionary кома́рм, two
syllables of кома́ндующий have been incorporated presumably to avoid confusion with ком- < коммунисти́ческий.
In управдо́м the second element may be a false whole, since
the underlying group is управля́ющий до́мом *house-
manager*, управля́ющий being a substantivized participle.

A rare type is that with underlay substantive + substantive, in which the *first* element represents the qualifier, as in
кожими́т (< имита́ция ко́жи) *imitation leather*. Two other
rare types are that with underlay adjective + substantive +
qualifier, as in комсомо́л (< коммунисти́ческий сою́з
молодёжи) *comsomol organization*, and that with underlay
of two co-ordinate substantives, as in агитпро́п (< аги-
та́ция и пропага́нда) *agitation and propaganda*.

(b) The most widespread underlay in this type is also
adjective + substantive. Indeed, apart from the case of the
very long stump-words which are names of organizations,
and hence proper names, this seems to be the only productive underlay for type (b). Examples are стенгазе́та (< стéн-
ная газе́та) *wall newspaper*, прозоде́жда (< произво́д-
ственная оде́жда)[1] *overalls*, литкружо́к (< литерату́рный
кружо́к) *literary circle*, зарпла́та (< за́работная пла́та)
wages, запча́сть (< запасна́я часть) *spare part*, физкуль-
ту́ра (< физи́ческая культу́ра) *physical training*, ветфе́льд-
шер (< ветерина́рный фе́льдшер) *veterinary assistant*,
нарсу́д (< наро́дный суд) *people's court*, облсу́д (< облacт-

1 N.B. the lapse of и in the stump-compound.

ной суд) *district court*, культтова́ры (<культу́рные
това́ры) *educational and cultural requisites*, сельмаши́ны
(<сельскохозя́йственные маши́ны) *agricultural machines*,
парторганиза́ция (<парти́йная организа́ция) *party organization.*

In this type too one notes such features as the occasional
insertion of a connecting vowel, as in трудоде́нь (<тру-
дово́й день) *working-day*, кубоме́тр (<куби́ческий метр)
cubic metre, or the incorporation of prefix *and* following syllable, as in разведро́та (<разве́дывательная ро́та) *reconnaissance company*, разведдонесе́ние *reconnaissance
report*. The incorporation of more than one syllable is also
seen in such words as перфока́рта (<перфори́рованная
ка́рта) *punched-card*, мотомехча́сть (<мо́томеханизи́ро-
ванная часть) *motorized division* and possibly тѐлесту́дия
(<телевизио́нная сту́дия)[1] *television studio*. The reduction
to initial syllables of the underlying elements of a *compound*
adjective is illustrated by сельхозарте́ль (<сельскохозя́й-
ственный арте́ль) *agricultural co-operative*, Ремстройтре́ст
(<ремо̀нтностро́ительный трест) *repair and building
combine*, and the incorporation of elements from more than
one adjective is illustrated by о̀блдра̀мтеа́тр (<областно́й
драмати́ческий теа́тр)[2] *district dramatic theatre*.

This type is somewhat more productive than the type:
stump-adjective + stump-substantive (see above), since it has
the advantages that the ending and hence the declension of
its original substantive are retained and the normal process
of derivation by means of suffixes can operate, as in проф-
сою́з-ный   *trade-union*,   стенгазе́т-ный   *wall-newspaper*,
кубоме́тр-овый *of a cubic metre*, физкульту́р-ный *physical*

---

1 But more likely derived by substituting теле- for the кино- of
кѝносту́дия. Теле- has begun to be used as a 'prefix' or initial bound
morpheme, while кино- and мото- have already given rise to several
dozen compounds in this way (see above).
2 Conceivably, <областно́й дра̀мтеа́тр.

training. This is not to say that other words cannot be derived from type (a)—witness колхо́з-ный *collective-farm*, комсомо́л-ьский *comsomol*, комсомо́л-ец *young communist*, кожими́т-ный or кожими́т-овый *of imitation leather*, and so on.

Such substantives as физкультмину́та *physical training minute*, физкультпа́уза *physical training break* are the result of several stages in the process of word-formation. The foreign adjective 'physical' and substantive 'culture' are borrowed and given Russian endings: физи́ческая, культу́ра. From the two together a type (b) stump-compound is created: физкульту́ра. From this, by suffixation of a substantival stem, an adjective is derived: физкульту́рный. Finally физкультмину́та is derived by stump-compounding from физкульту́рная мину́та.

(c) Of the two types of initial-words one simply consists of (i.e. is pronounced as) the names of the constituent letters, as in СССР *U.S.S.R.*, КПСС *Communist Party of the Soviet Union*, МГУ[1] *Moscow State University*, впп (взлётнопоса́дочная полоса́) *aircraft landing-strip*, while in the other the initial letters produce a grapheme which is treated as an 'ordinary' word, i.e. is pronounced as spelt. Thus: ТАСС [tas], МХАТ [mxat], вуз [vus][2]. Initial-words of the first type do not decline, most of those of the second type do decline (as masculine substantives) and can give rise to derivatives—ву́зовский, ву́зовец, ву́зовка, etc. A hybrid type, as far as pronunciation is concerned, is represented by

1 In full: (О́рдена В. И. Ле́нина) Моско́вский Госуда́рственный Университе́т (и́мени М. В. Ломоно́сова). Colloquially, students treat МГУ as the second type of initial word—Он у́чится во мгу [vam'gu] *he's studying at Moscow University*.

2 In full these are, respectively, Телегра́фное аге́нтство Сове́тского Сою́за *Telegraph Agency of the Soviet Union*, Моско́вский худо́жественный академи́ческий теа́тр *Moscow Art (Academic) Theatre*, вы́сшее уче́бное заведе́ние *higher educational establishment*.

a few words, such as ЦДСА (Центра́льный дом Сове́т-
ской А́рмии) *Central House of the Soviet Army*, pronounced [tsɛdɛ^Isa]. It is the type ending in a vowel which, in
most instances, neither declines nor gives rise to derivatives.
ОНО́ (отде́л наро́дного образова́ния) *department of
popular education*, for example, does not decline or give
derivatives but the mixed type о́блоно́ (< областно́й *provincial* + ОНО́) gives the derived adjective облоно́вский.

(d) The mixed type of stump-compound, consisting of
syllables and initials, is less common in everyday speech than
either of the two purely initial types but is still productive.
Examples are: губчека́, райфо́, облоно́, РОСТА́, ИМЛИ́.[1]
A very curious type is Детги́з consisting of the initial syllable of де́тское, the initial *letter* of госуда́рственное and
the initial syllable of изда́тельство (cf. госизда́т above,
with two syllables from изда́тельство)—*State Publishing
House for Children's Literature*. There are sometimes several
variants for one and the same institution. E. Scheitz records,
for example,[2] ЦНИИЧМ, ЦНИИЧЕРМЕТ, ЦНИИЧер-
мет and ЦНИИ чёрной металлу́ргии for Центра́льный
нау́чно-иссле́довательский институ́т чёрной металлу́р-
гии *Central Research Institute for Ferrous Metallurgy*.
We have seen that the nominal group which underlies
most stump-compounds is adjective + substantive and that
the nominal groups consisting of substantive + qualifier or
adjective + substantive + qualifier are much rarer. In the
usually much longer stump-compounds which are names of
organizations and institutions, as well as in initial-words,
the latter two structures are not at all uncommon. For

1 In full, respectively губе́рнская чека́ (< чрезвыча́йная коми́ссия)
Provincial Cheka, райо́нный фина́нсовый отде́л *district financial
department*, областна́я организа́ция наро́дного образова́ния *district
organization for popular education*, Росси́йское телегра́фное аге́нтство
Russian Telegraph Agency, Институ́т мирово́й литерату́ры *Institute
of World Literature*.
2 *Op. cit.*

example, the underlay of Южура́лмашзаво́д consists either of qualifier—ю́жного Ура́ла, brought forward from its usual 'syntactical' position, an adjective—маши́нный, and a substantive—заво́д, or of two adjectives plus substantive —ю́жноура́льский, etc: *South Urals Machine Factory*. Лѐна̀втоуправле́ние has an underlay consisting either of adjective—ленингра́дское, substantive—управле́ние, and qualifier—автотра́нспортом, or of a substantive with a qualifying group—управле́ние автотра́нспортом Ленин-гра́да *Leningrad Transport Administration*. Another feature which is frequent in such words and in initial-words, though it is not frequent in everyday stump-compounds, is the omission from the compound of any element represent-ing the head of the underlying group. For instance the under-lay of Госпла́н consists of two adjectives and a substantive not represented in the compound—госуда́рственная пла́новая коми́ссия *State Planning Commission*, while the underlay of Гла̀вмо̀са̀втотра́нс consists of a substantive, such as управле́ние, not represented in the compound, two adjectives—гла́вное, моско́вское, and a qualifier—авто-тра́нспортом: *Main Autotransport Administration of Mos-cow*. There is a similar underlay in the common substantive о̀блздра́в (< областна́я коми́ссия по здравоохране́нию) *district health service commission*, while in загс there is an underlay consisting of a substantive (not represented in the initial-word) and qualifying nominal group: отде́л (or бюро́) за́писи а́ктов гражда́нского состоя́ния '*department for the registration of deeds of civil status*' = *registry office*. In ширпотре́б *consumer-goods*, on the other hand, we have an example either of extension of meaning, from *wide-scale consumption* (широ́кое потребле́ние) to 'goods of wide-scale consumption', i.e. *consumer-goods*, or of ellipsis (това́ры/проду́кты ширпотре́ба > ширпотре́б).

7
Substantives

The loss of the vocative case and the dual number in the Old Russian period, together with the interaction and partial combination of paradigms, has led to the modern Russian system of three basic types of declension, with six cases. The three types of declension, however, refer only to the singular, since declensional distinction has been largely obliterated in the plural. Two of the three basic declension types appear in hard and soft varieties, i.e. the final consonant of the stem is hard in some substantives, soft in others, and this leads to regular variations in the form of the case-endings. The distribution of gender among these three declensions is largely regular. Thus, the first declension embraces masculine and neuter substantives, the second declension feminine substantives (and a handful of masculine and epicene substantives) and the third declension feminine substantives only (the masculine путь, however, being a very close 'satellite' of this declension). A vestige of the Old Russian consonantal-stem declension is found in the subsidiary neuter declension which embraces the ten substantives ending in -мя in the nominative singular. Adjectival substantives, i.e. words which were originally adjectives but now function as substantives, have of course an adjectival declension. A small number of substantives have no declension: they are invariable. While resulting in what at first sight appears to be a fairly regular and small set of declension types, the development of the language from the Old Russian period has in fact left some anomalies

—vestiges of older declensions or the results of the influence of one declension upon another. The eradication of these anomalies is still going on but it is a very slow process.

Masculine

Nearly all masculine substantives belong to the first declension. The hard variety ends in a hard consonant (but see below) in the nominative singular, the soft variety ends, phonetically, in a soft consonant or [j], orthographically in ч, щ, ь or й. Here are two typical paradigms:

Hard		*singular*	*plural*
	nom.	стол	столы́
	gen.	стола́	столо́в
	dat.	столу́	стола́м
	acc.	стол	столы́
	instr.	столо́м	стола́ми
	prep.	столе́	стола́х

Soft			
	nom.	дождь	дожди́
	gen.	дождя́	дожде́й
	dat.	дождю́	дождя́м
	acc.	дождь	дожди́
	instr.	дождём	дождя́ми
	prep.	дожде́	дождя́х

When the final consonant of the stem is ш, ж, ч, щ or ц the instrumental singular ending of the hard declension is -ем when unstressed—му́жем (but ножо́м). The genitive plural ending for nouns with ш, ж, ч or щ as stem consonant is -ей—луче́й, ноже́й—but for nouns with ц as stem consonant it is -ев when unstressed—ме́сяцев, and -ов when stressed—отцо́в. The spelling conventions, of course, do not allow ы after ш, ж, ч or щ, hence the nominative plural ending of nouns with these stem-consonants is и. These features

are reflexes of the fact that in Old Russian all these consonants were soft (as ч and щ still are) and were therefore
followed by the front vowel [i], denoted by и, and not by the
non-front vowel [ɨ], denoted by ы.[1]

Substantives ending in -й follow the same pattern as
дождь (the -й being replaced by the case-endings), except
in the genitive plural, where they have -ев when the ending
is unstressed (случаев) and -ёв when stressed (краёв). The
few substantives of this type with и before й form the prepositional singular in и: о ра́дии—*about radium.*

The substantive путь *path, way* is unique among masculine substantives in that its singular declension follows, in
all cases except the instrumental, that of feminine substantives of the type кость (see below). The stress, however, falls
on the endings: gen., dat., prep.—пути́, instr.—путём.

Other oddities of the declension of masculine substantives, which, so to speak, violate the regular system, are as
follows. The two substantives сосе́д *neighbour* and чёрт
devil have a hard-ending singular declension but a soft-ending plural declension—сосе́ди, сосе́дей, сосе́дям, etc.,
че́рти, черте́й, чертя́м, etc. In Old Russian masculine substantives of the so-called o-stem declension had the nominative plural ending и, accusative plural ending ы.[2] Under the
influence of the feminine plural declension the accusative
ending ы replaced the nominative ending и and thereafter

---

1 Ц was also a soft consonant in Old Russian. Documentary evidence shows that ш and ж were hardening from the fourteenth century
onwards, whereas ц was hardening only from the sixteenth century onwards. The first printed books (mid-sixteenth century) adopted the old
spelling ши, жи but when ц subsequently hardened this was recognized
by the orthography and цы replaced ци. Today цы is written in endings
and suffixes and a few roots. The majority of roots containing the sound
sequence [tsi] have been borrowed from foreign languages where the
native spelling has the letter *i* and this is recognized by the Russian
spelling ци (цирк, цинк, etc.).

2 The other plural endings being: genitive -ъ, dative -омъ, instrumental -ы, prepositional -ѣхъ.

the feminine plural endings in general replaced the masculine endings. For reasons which are not clear the words
сосе́д and чёрт retained the soft-ending nominative plural,
and on the analogy of this the new type (formerly feminine)
endings for the other plural cases were also adopted in their
soft variety.

The irregular instrumentals plural of лю́ди *people* and
де́ти *children*, viz. людьми́, детьми́, like those of some
feminine nouns (ло́шадь *horse*—лошадьми́, дочь *daughter*
—дочерьми́) are derived from an Old Russian declension
(the so-called i-stem declension), which has persisted largely
unchanged in feminine nouns of the type кость (see below).
The irregular zero-ending for the genitive plural found in
some masculine nouns (глаз *eye*, солда́т *soldier*, ту́рок
Turk, цыга́н *gypsy*, сапо́г *boot*, чуло́к *stocking*, партиза́н
partisan, раз *time*, вольт *volt*, челове́к *person*, во́лос *hair*—
gen. pl. воло́с, etc.) represents in fact the persistence of the
Old Russian genitive plural ending -ъ, which letter is of
course no longer written at the end of a word. The fact that
some regularization is still taking place here is shown by
such occasional vacillations as пого́н *shoulder strap*—
genitive plural пого́н/пого́нов[1], and by the alternative geni-
tives plural of грамм, килогра́мм, etc., given in Avanesov
and Ozhegov's 'Pronouncing Dictionary'[2]—гра́ммов
('more literary'), грамм ('more colloquial'). Moreover, the
number of masculine substantives with zero-ending genitive
plural has decreased slightly during the last hundred years
or more.[3]

The zero-ending genitive plural is, however, a regular
feature of substantives with the suffix -анин/-янин. In the

1 In Fadeev, *Молодая гвардия*, quoted in the Academy Grammar,
vol. I, 1st edition, p. 153.
2 *Русское литературное произношение и ударение.*
3 See L. A. Bulakhovsky, *Исторический комментарий к русскому литературному языку*, pp. 146–149, and *Русский литературный язык первой половины XIX века*, pp. 68–70.

singular they decline like normal hard-ending masculine nouns, but in the plural they lose the syllable -ин and decline thus: nom. англича́не, gen. англича́н, dat. англича́нам, etc. Notice the nominative plural ending -e, which is unique to this type of substantive, though it is regular in the nominative plural of adjectives and some pronouns. In Old Russian too these substantives showed two different types of declension, the plural being consonantal-stem declension (of which only the nominative and genitive have persisted), the singular, derived from the plural stem by means of the singulative suffix -ин, being of the common hard-ending masculine declension ('o-stem'). Substantives of the type жеребёнок *foal*, which have a singular declension of the type стол (with mobile vowel), have a different suffix in the plural and a plural declension of the neuter type, with zero-ending in the genitive plural: жеребя́та, жеребя́т, жеребя́там, etc.

Some two dozen masculine substantives[1] have a unique change of stem in the plural. In the singular most of them have a hard stem-consonant—брат, стул, etc.—but in the plural the stem-consonant, if not already soft, is replaced by the corresponding soft consonant and is followed by [j]. The plural stem therefore ends in soft consonant + [j], except in the case of муж, since there is no soft consonant corresponding to [ʒ]. Moreover, the nominative plural marker of these substantives is /a/ (phonetically [ə] or [ᶦa]). Thus: брат *brother*—nom. pl. бра́тья, gen. pl. бра́тьев, dat. pl. бра́тьям, etc.

This anomalous plural declension owes its origin to the fact that in Old Russian the word бра́тья, for example, was nominative singular of a feminine substantive—a collective substantive, denoting '(a group of) brothers'—which, because of its meaning, came to be interpreted as *grammatically plural*—an unusual nominative plural. It was then

1 And eight neuter substantives ending in -o in the nominative singular (see next section).

endowed with the soft plural endings. By analogy with бра́тья and one or two other similar substantives other masculine substantives, such as муж *husband*, then took on the same morphological characteristics. The use of бра́тья, etc., as a plural is observed as early as the fourteenth century and is more or less established by the seventeenth century, though бра́тья can still be found as a singular at that time.

Most of the substantives of this type are stressed on the stem and have genitive plural in -ев: бра́тья—бра́тьев, ли́стья *leaves*—ли́стьев, сту́лья *chairs*—сту́льев, etc. Eight of them have stress on the endings and, of these, four form the genitive plural in -ьёв, four in zero (with the insertion of a mobile vowel, hence orthographically -ей) thus:

де́верь *brother-in-law* (husband's brother)—деверья́, де-
    верьёв;
зять *son-in-law*, *brother-in-law* (sister's husband or hus-
    band's sister's husband)—зятья́, зятьёв;
шу́рин *brother-in-law* (wife's brother)—шурья́, шурьёв
    (without the suffix -ин in the plural);
кум *'kinsman'*, *gossip*[1]—кумовья́, кумовьёв (with the
    suffix -ов- from the Old Russian u-stem declension)[2];
князь *prince*—князья́, князе́й;
муж *husband*—мужья́, муже́й;
друг *friend*—друзья́, друзе́й (with change of г to з);
сын *son*—сыновья́, сынове́й (with the suffix -ов- from the
    Old Russian u-stem declension).

Except for the fact that some of these words are now old-fashioned or 'historical' (кум, князь) and some are not common, at least among townspeople (де́верь, шу́рин), the group as a whole seems to be solidly established. Some of

---

1 In its original sense.
2 Дядья́–дядьёв *uncles* also occurs, but дя́ди–дя́дей is more usual.
*6

them have 'normal' nominatives plural with different meanings, e.g. ли́стья *leaves* (of a tree)—листы́ *leaves* (of paper),
коре́нья *root-crops*—ко́рни *roots* (of a tree), сыновья́ *sons*—
сыны́ *sons* (of the fatherland, motherland), etc.

The occurrence of the nominative plural ending -а́/-я́ in
masculine substantives has been explained as being due to
the influence of the neuter nominative plural ending -а/-я,
which in many words is stressed, or to the Old Russian
nominative *dual* ending -а/-я of the commonest masculine
declension. Though the dual may have been dead as a grammatical category in the literary language at the time when
the masculine nominative plural ending -а́/-я́ arose (late sixteenth or early seventeenth century), it could nevertheless
have continued to exert an influence on the plural declension
by way of fossilized expressions and/or from dialects. The
masculine nominative plural in -а́/-я́ may be due to a combination of both these influences and it is just possible that
forms such as мужья́, which were more or less established
by the seventeenth century, played a contributory role.

Only a few masculine substantives with the nominative
plural ending -а́/-я́ are recorded by eighteenth-century
writers, such as Kantemir and Lomonosov,[1] and it is significant that the words they record with this ending are the
names of objects which occur in pairs (and hence were
originally nominatives dual). The number of these substantives increased considerably in the early nineteenth century
and, while some have since lost the possibility of taking this
ending, yet others have been added in the twentieth century. There are now several score masculine substantives
taking the nominative plural ending -а́/-я́, among them such
common ones as дом *house*—дома́, до́ктор *doctor*—док-
тора́, а́дрес *address*—адреса́, го́лос *voice*—голоса́, па́с-
порт *passport*—паспорта́, учи́тель *teacher*—учителя́,
я́корь *anchor*—якоря́, сле́сарь *locksmith*—слесаря́, etc.,

1 See Bulakhovsky, *Исторический комментарий* . . . p. 142.

etc.[1] The colloquial language has tended to make extensive use of this ending, particularly for the names of professions and especially when they are of foreign origin, but the purists and prescriptive (or 'normative') grammarians have tried to stem the tide. Some of the words quoted in the Academy Grammar[2] have alternative nominatives plural in -ы/-и or -á/-я́ and of these alternatives Avanesov and Ozhegov[3] omit some (волоса́, инспе́кторы, ште́псели), categorize some as obsolete (корре́кторы), others as permissible (прожектора́, цеха́, инструктора́), others as colloquial (редактора́) and others as impermissible (бухгалтера́). It is clear that the situation is still somewhat fluid and one would need a considerable amount of statistical information before one could try to predict which way the tide will turn. Suffice it to say that, by prescribing some forms in -ы/-и and others in -á/-я́, the grammarians still leave the way open for a continued influx of forms in -á/-я́.

Some of these alternatives have been endowed with different meanings and there is thus no longer any question of one being preferred to the other. Among them are образа́ *ikons*—о́бразы *images*, пояса́ *belts*—по́ясы *zones*, счета́ *bills*—счёты *abacus*, тона́ *hues*—то́ны *tones*, тормоза́ *brakes*—то́рмозы *obstacles*, учителя́ *teachers* (in a school) —учи́тели *teachers* (originators of particular doctrines), etc.

We have mentioned above the Old Russian u-stem declension of masculine nouns. In this declension the genitive ending was -у, the prepositional ending -ý. Though originally this declension included no more than a handful of substantives, it has provided the alternative genitive in -у (and, by extension, in -ю) and prepositional (locative) in -ý (and, by extension, in -ю) for several dozen masculine

1 For a longer list see Academy Grammar I, pp. 148–150.
2 Vol. I, p. 149.
3 *Op. cit., passim.*

substantives. These forms in -у/-ю were much more wide-spread in the sixteenth and seventeenth centuries, and, to a smaller extent, in the eighteenth century. Their number continued to diminish in the nineteenth century and has diminished still further in the twentieth century. Although earlier they could be found in substantives denoting animate beings as well as inanimate things and abstract ideas, they are now not found in substantives denoting animate beings.

The genitive in -у/-ю has several functions. First, it expresses the partitive idea and hence many of the substantives with this form denote divisible matter or groups: мно́го са́хару, лу́ку, пе́рцу, виногра́ду, су́пу, ча́ю, ще́бню, наро́ду. Such substantives have the genitive in -у/-ю only if the partitive idea is present: стака́н ча́ю *a glass of tea*, but цена́ ча́я *the price of tea*; килогра́мм са́хару *a kilogram of sugar* but беле́е са́хара *whiter than sugar*, etc. If there is a modifier the genitive in -у/-ю is most unusual, even though the partitive idea may be present: стака́н горя́чего ча́я *a glass of hot tea*, килогра́мм куско-во́го са́хара *a kilogram of lump-sugar*. Although the partitive genitive in -у/-ю is very common with some substantives, it is not obligatory: мно́го сне́гу/сне́га *much snow*, нема́ло му́сору/му́сора *not a little rubbish*. The genitive in -у/-ю is also found in a few abstract substantives and it then has no special significance but is merely a stylistic alternative, with a colloquial nuance, to the normal genitive: бле́ску/бле́ска *glitter*, просто́ру/просто́ра *space, room*.

The genitive in -у/-ю is also found in a limited number of substantives after one of the prepositions без, от, из, or с: и́з лесу, и́з дому, без спро́су, от ды́му, со стра́ху. With the preposition in a spatial sense the stress usually falls on the preposition and the substantive is not stressed at all. Here too the forms in -у/-ю are not obligatory: one finds из ле́са, из до́ма, etc.[1] Some at least of these expressions where the substantive ends in -у/-ю are felt to be invariable adverbial expressions, which, if they persist, may possibly become one-word adverbs, as have све́рху, сни́зу, о́троду, etc.

Thirdly, there are some fixed expressions, with prepositions (без, от, из, с, до), or the negative particle ни, the negative predicators нет, не́ было, не бу́дет and some other verbs (negated or not), etc., where the genitive in -у/-ю is obligatory. Among them are: бе́з году неде́лю *for a short while*, с гла́зу на́ глаз *face to face, tête-à-tête*, ни ша́гу наза́д *not one step back*, спо́ру нет *there's no denying*, спать без про́сыпу двена́дцать часо́в *to sleep the clock round*, мно́го шу́му, да ма́ло то́лку *much cry and little wool*.

Apart from the fixed expressions with the genitive in -у/-ю, the facts cited above testify to the slow decay of the genitive in -у/-ю. This form is being replaced by the normal genitive in -а/-я or is becoming embedded as a linguistic fossil in fixed adverbial expressions.

The situation with regard to the prepositional in -у́/-ю́ is not quite so fluid. This form occurs in a limited number of substantives and only after the prepositions в and на, *when they have the significance of spatial location*.[2] One says, for example, Он был в лесу́ *He was in the wood* but Он зна́ет толк в ле́се *He knows a thing or two about forestry*. With many substantives the form in -у́/-ю́ is obligatory, with others there is a choice between the form in -у́/-ю́ and the form in -е: на ветру́/ве́тре, во мху́/в мо́хе, в отпуску́/о́т-пуске, в чаю́/ча́е, with yet others the form in -у́/-ю́ appears

---

1 There is a difference in meaning, however, between и́з дому and из до́ма, the former meaning *out of one's house (home)*, the latter *out of the house/building*.

2 In such expressions as варе́нье на меду́ *preserve made of honey* the spatial meaning is attenuated or not at first sight evident.

in some expressions, the form in -e in other expressions: я́блони в цвету́ *apple-trees in blossom*/во цве́те лет *in the bloom of life*, рабо́та на дому́ *work done at home*/на до́ме *on the house*. Where there are alternatives, the form in -e occurs when an adjective is present. Again the facts cited testify at least to the beginning of a process whereby forms in -у́/-ю́ will become adverbialized or fossilized while the forms in -e will replace them elsewhere.

Our last remarks on particular aspects of the morphology of the masculine substantive concern the form of the genitive after the numerals два, три, четы́ре. In some substantives the genitive, while not normally stressed on the ending, *is* stressed on the ending after these numerals: бо́лее ша́га but два, три, четы́ре шага́; до́льше ча́са but два, etc. часа́;[1] одного́ ря́да but два, etc., ряда́. These variations are reflexes of the fact that the genitive after два, три, четы́ре was originally not the genitive singular, but the nominative dual часа́, etc., occurring after the word два and then extended to три and четы́ре.

Irregularities and anomalies in declension are slightly more numerous in the masculine substantives than in the closely associated neuter substantives[2] and considerably more so than in the feminine substantives. The reasons are, naturally enough, historical: in general it is the masculine declensions which have undergone more extensive remodelling than the feminine declensions. It has become evident, however, that a slow levelling out of anomalies and special forms in the masculine declensions is still in process.

Neuter

All neuter substantives, except those ending in -мя, belong

1 The form часа́ also occurs in, e.g. че́тверть часа́.
2 Though, as we shall see, the genitive plural of neuter substantives is more of a 'patchwork' of forms than, by and large, that of the masculine and feminine substantives.

to the first declension, the hard variety ending in the nominative singular in -o, the soft variety in -e.

Hard in -o

	singular	*plural*
nom.	сло́во	слова́
gen.	сло́ва	слов
dat.	сло́ву	слова́м
acc.	сло́во	слова́
instr.	сло́вом	слова́ми
prep.	сло́ве	слова́х

Substantives with к as the final consonant of the stem
form the nominative plural in -и unless the stress shifts from
the stem in the singular to the ending in the plural. Thus one
has, on the one hand, блю́дечко *saucer*—блю́дечки,
око́шко *window*—око́шки, я́блоко *apple*—я́блоки, ве́ко
eyelid—ве́ки,[1] ли́чико *face*—ли́чики, but on the other hand
во́йско *army*—войска́, о́блако *cloud*—облака́, о́блачко
little cloud—облачка́ (or о́блачки, with no stress-shift).
A masculine-type genitive plural in -ов is found in neuter
substantives formed with the diminutive suffix -ик-, as in
ли́чико (*little*) *face* ли́чики, ли́чиков; плечико (*little*)
shoulder—плечики, плечиков; in those formed with the
suffix -к- and having stress on the ending, as in очки́ *spec-
tacles*—очко́в, ушко́ *eye* (of a needle)—ушки́, ушко́в; and
in one or two other substantives ending in -ко, as in о́блако
—облака́, облако́в, дре́вко *shaft*—дре́вки, дре́вков. The
word су́дно *ship* also has this genitive ending and, moreover, has no н in the plural cases: суда́, судо́в, суда́м, etc.

There are several dozen neuter substantives with ц as the
final stem consonant. When stressed on the endings, they
have exactly the same endings as the сло́во-type: кольцо́
ring, ко́льца, коле́ц, ко́льцам, etc. When stressed on the

---

1 Cf. век *age, century*—nom. pl. usually века́ but ве́ки in some expressions (e.g. во ве́ки веко́в *for ever and ever*).

stem, they have -e in the nominative-accusative singular, -ем in the instrumental singular, but otherwise the same endings as the сло́во-type: се́рдце *heart*, се́рдца, се́рдцу, се́рдцем, etc. The two substantives ending in -же—ло́же *couch*, цветоло́же *receptacle* behave in the same way.[1] A few dozen substantives end in -ще and have the same endings as those ending in -це. In some of them, however, the letter щ is part of the augmentative suffix -ищ- and substantives derived from masculine substantives by means of this suffix retain the masculine gender and may have nominative plural in -a or -и: доми́ще—доми́ща/доми́щи.

The substantive плечо́ *shoulder* is the only declinable neuter ending in -чо.[2] It has endings like those of сло́во, except in the nominative plural, which is пле́чи. The nominative plural плеча́ and the genitive plural плече́й are now archaic.

The substantives не́бо *sky* and чу́до *miracle* are exceptional in having an additional syllable -ес- (a vestige of the Old Russian consonantal-stem declension) before the plural endings: небеса́, небе́с, небеса́м, etc., чудеса́, чуде́с, чудеса́м, etc. Other anomalies include the plural of у́хо *ear* and о́ко *eye* (archaic): у́ши, уше́й, уша́м, etc., о́чи, оче́й, оча́м, etc. These last two sets of forms derive from the Old Russian neuter dual declension.

The forms уше́й and оче́й show the genitive plural ending -ей found in the two substantives по́ле *field* and мо́ре *sea* and in those ending in the nominative singular in -ьё (see below). Го́ре *grief* has no plural but in the singular has the same endings as по́ле and мо́ре[3]:

1 The only substantives ending in -ше are such indeclinables as саше́ (n.) *sachet*, атташе́ (m.) *attaché*, etc.

2 Харчо́ (kind of Caucasian soup) and каприччо *capriccio* being indeclinable.

3 Ве́че '*veche*' (city council in medieval Russia) is the only substantive ending in -че. It has the same endings as по́ле, мо́ре (allowance being made for the orthographical conventions) but retains the stress on the stem in the plural: ве́ча, ве́чей (and веч), ве́чам, etc.

	singular	*plural*
nom.	мо́ре	моря́
gen.	мо́ря	море́й
dat.	мо́рю	моря́м
acc.	мо́ре	моря́
instr.	мо́рем	моря́ми
prep.	мо́ре	моря́х

Substantives in -ье have similar endings, though there are one or two points to be noted. Those stressed on the ending in the singular have nominative-accusative in -ьё, instrumental in -ьём: питьё *drink*—питьём. Those stressed on the ending in the plural have genitive in -ей: питей, in which e is the mobile vowel replacing ь, while those not stressed on the ending in the plural have genitive in -ий: мученье *torment*—мучений, in which и functions as a mobile vowel replacing ь.[1] Ружьё *rifle* is exceptional in having genitive plural ру́жей although the stress is on the stem. Подмастерье *apprentice*, in spite of its ending, is masculine in gender and hence has genitive-accusative singular подмастерья and genitive-accusative plural подмастерьев. This genitive ending -ев, exceptional for substantives ending in -ье, is found in a few more substantives (which are neuter in form *and* gender), such as верхо́вья *upper reaches*—верхо́вьев, низо́вья *lower reaches*—низо́вьев, лохмо́тья *rags*—лохмо́тьев, пла́тья *dresses*—пла́тьев, у́стья *estuaries*—у́стьев (or у́стий), поме́стья *estates*—поме́стьев (or поме́стий), etc. Остриё *point, edge* is unusual both in its nominative singular and its genitive plural остриёв.

The two substantives житие́ *life, hagiography* and бытие́ *being, existence* show signs of their Church Slavonic origin

2 In both types, therefore, the genitive plural ending is zero (e.g. nom. sing. ɲi'tj+o, gen. pl. ɲitj+zero, with inserted mobile vowel—ɲi'tej).

in their nominative singular, instrumental singular житиём (not *житиём), prepositional singular житий (not *житиé), and genitive plural житий. These endings—without stress—are shared by substantives ending in -ание/-яние/-ение, of which there are scores in modern Russian and which have also been derived from or formed on the direct or indirect analogy of Church Slavonic words: здáние *building*—здáния, здáнию, здáние, здáнием, здáнии, plural—здáния, здáний, здáниям, etc.

The eight neuter substantives mentioned in the preceding section as having nominative singular in -о, but plural in -ья, etc., are дéрево *tree*—дерéвья, дно *bottom*—дóнья, звенó *link*—звéнья, колéно *node*—колéнья, крылó *wing*—крылья, перó *feather, pen*—пéрья, полéно *log*—полéнья and шúло *awl*—шúлья. All are stressed on the stem in the plural and all have genitive plural in -ев: дерéвьев, etc. In Old Russian there existed a series of neuter collectives in -ье, i.e. substantives which, though singular in grammatical number, denoted a plurality of objects. This, as in the case of the original feminine collectives in -ья, led to their being interpreted as plural in grammatical number. The ending -ье changed to -ья either under the influence of the neuter plural in -а/-я or by analogy with the masculine plural (originally feminine singular) in -ья or, in the opinion of some writers, simply by way of phonetic change[1] and subsequent recognition of this change in spelling, or by virtue of a combination of some or all of these factors.

It was pointed out above that several of the masculine substantives with plural in -ья have alternative plurals with different meanings. Only one neuter substantive with nominative plural in -ья has alternative plural forms: in the

1 By virtue of the centralization of unstressed vowels (a process which affected all except the north Russian dialects between the thirteenth and the sixteenth centuries), such that unstressed [e] became [ə] or [ɪ].

meaning *knee*, коле́но has a plural of the soft masculine type—коле́ни, коле́ней, etc., while in the meaning *passage* (of a song), *generation* it has a normal neuter plural—коле́на, коле́н, etc. In the meaning *bend* (of a river), *elbow* (e.g. of a crankshaft) both коле́нья and коле́на are found as the plural.

The only neuter declension which is almost entirely distinct from the basic neuter declensions is the singular declension of the ten substantives epitomized by и́мя *name*.

nom.	и́мя
gen.	и́мени
dat.	и́мени
acc.	и́мя
instr.	и́менем
prep.	и́мени

Apart from the fact that phonetic changes have affected the instrumental[1] this is almost a direct legacy of the Old Russian consonantal-stem declension. The other substantives of this type are бре́мя *burden*, вре́мя *time*, вы́мя *udder*, зна́мя *banner*, пла́мя *flame*, пле́мя *tribe*, се́мя *seed*, стре́мя *stirrup*, and те́мя *crown of the head*. In the plural, while retaining the element -ен-, substantives of this type have a normal neuter declension: имена́, имён, имена́м, etc. The stress is on the ending in the plural in all except зна́мя— знамёна, etc. Се́мя and стре́мя are slightly anomalous in reinstating the я of the nominative singular in the genitive plural; семя́н, стремя́н. Те́мя has no plural, the plural of вы́мя is rare and the plural of пла́мя is now archaic, the singular meaning either *flame* or *flames*.

In general, there is not in the declension of the neuter substantives as much evidence of a slow process of levelling as was noted in the declension of the masculine substantives.

---

1 Old Russian име́ньмь > и́менем.

In the colloquial language one notes 'regularizations' which the grammarians do not admit to the canon of the literary language. Among these is one which has not been commented on above, namely the declension of neuter substantives which in the grammar of the literary language are indeclinable—бюро́, пальто́, депо́, пенсне́, etc.

Feminine

There are two basic systems of declension for feminine substantives. The first of these, for substantives ending in -a/-я in the nominative singular, has a few variations due largely to the hard-soft alternation.

Hard		*singular*	*plural*
	nom.	гора́	го́ры
	gen.	горы́	гор
	dat.	горе́	гора́м
	acc.	го́ру	го́ры
	instr.	горо́й	гора́ми
	prep.	горе́	гора́х

Soft			
	nom.	неде́ля	неде́ли
	gen.	неде́ли	неде́ль
	dat.	неде́ле	неде́лям
	acc.	неде́лю	неде́ли
	instr.	неде́лей	неде́лями
	prep.	неде́ле	неде́лях

The instrumental singular ending of the soft variety is phonetically [öi̯] when stressed: землёй [z̦ɪmˈl̦öi̯]. The alternative instrumental singular endings -ою ([ˈoju] and [əju]), -ею ([ˈöju] and [ɪju]) are more often found in the written language than in the spoken language. In the latter they may characterize a more formal or bookish style or may be used

for rhythmic purposes. The unstressed -ею ending in particular is rare in speech and has a pedantic ring.

The spelling conventions, whereby certain vowel letters
cannot appear after к, г, х, ш, ж, ч, щ or ц, lead of course to
obvious variations in the spelling (and pronunciation) of
some of the endings. One should remember that ы does
appear after ц in suffixes and that therefore the basic spelling
of feminine case-endings in -ы is retained: овца́ *sheep*—
genitive овцы́, etc. With substantives whose stem-consonant
is ш, ж, ч or щ the instrumental singular is spelt -ей when
unstressed and -ой when stressed. In all except one type of
feminine substantive in -a/-я the prepositional and dative
singular ending is spelt -e (pronounced [ɛ] or [ɪ] according to
the location of stress). In the type which has и before the я
of the nominative singular these two case-endings are spelt
-и: а́рмия *army*—а́рмии.

The (phonetically) zero ending of the genitive plural is
even more characteristic of the declension of feminine substantives in -a/-я than it is of the declension of neuter substantives, where, as we have seen, the endings -ей, -ов and
-ев are also found. This ending, while phonetically zero, is
marked by the presence of the soft sign in those substantives
with nominative singular in -я after a consonant: неде́ля–
неде́ль. However, in substantives ending in -ня preceded by
a consonant (including й) the ending of the genitive plural
is *hard*[1]: пе́сня *song*—пе́сен, бо́йня *slaughter-house*—бо́ен
(where й changes to the mobile vowel e), etc. Дере́вня
village and ба́рышня *young lady* are exceptional in having a
soft ending in the genitive plural: дереве́нь, ба́рышень.

In some instances the phonetically zero ending of the
genitive plural is somewhat 'disguised' by the spelling. In
those substantives with a vowel or soft sign before the
nominative singular ending -я the stem ends, phonetically,

---

1 Some have the ending -ей (see below).

in [j]: струя *jet*—[stru'j-a], áрмия *army*—['armįj-ə], семья́
family—[sị'mj-a]. When the final vowel is removed to form
the genitive plural, one has a form ending phonetically in
[j], which is written й: струй, áрмий. In substantives such
as семья́ the soft sign is replaced by the mobile vowel e,
giving genitive plural семéй,[1] where, in spite of appearances,
the case-ending is phonetically zero. Substantives such as
го́стья *guest* (fem.) with stress on the stem are orthographically unusual in having и as mobile vowel in the genitive
plural: го́стий (cf. мучéний above).

There are, however, some substantives of this declension
which have the genitive plural ending -ей. They are mostly
substantives having a stem ending in л, н or р, usually
(though not always) after another consonant: бу́кля *curl*—
бу́клей, цáпля *crane*—цáплей (and цáпель), клешня́ *nip-
per*—клешнéй, ступня́ *foot*—ступнéй, ноздря́ *nostril*—
ноздрéй, до́ля *portion*—долéй, etc., and some others, such
as дя́дя *uncle*—дя́дей,[2] тётя *aunt*—тётей,[2] ю́ноша *youth*
—ю́ношей,[2] свечá *candle*—свечéй,[3] левшá *left-handed person*—левшéй, ханжá *hypocrite*—ханжéй, во́жжи *reins*—
вожжéй, etc.

The other feminine declension comprises substantives
with the nominative singular ending in the soft sign.
Phonetically therefore, the ending is a soft consonant (including [tʃ] and [ʃtʃ]) or the hard consonant [ʃ] (represented
by -шь or -жь). Here we have a declension which, in the
singular, has come down almost unchanged from the Old
Russian of nine hundred years ago.

1 This is in effect the same process as occurs with many feminine
substantives having two consonants before the ending -a/-я. Cf.
земля́—gen. pl. земéль. It happens that the spelling system of Russian
disguises the fact that there are phonetically two consonants before the
ending in such words as семья́.

2 Identical with the instrumental singular in -ей.

3 Also свеч, as in игрá не сто́ит свеч *the game is not worth the
candle.*

	singular	*plural*
nom.	кость	кóсти
gen.	кóсти	костéй
dat.	кóсти	костя́м
acc.	кость	кóсти
instr.	кóстью	костя́ми
prep.	кóсти	костя́х

There are very few points which call for comment, for the set of substantives which this declension comprises is the most regular of all the large sets. Some substantives have a special form of the prepositional after в and на, i.e. a locative, distinguished from the normal prepositional by having the stress on the ending: на брови́ *on the brow*, на груди́[1] *on the breast*, в грязи́ *in the mud*, на мели́ *on a sandbank, grounded*, в ночи́ *in the night*, на оси́ *on the axis*, на Руси́[2] *in Russia*, в степи́ *in the steppe*, в тени́ *in the shade*, на цепи́ *chained up*, etc. However, there are some such substantives with alternatives with the stress on the stem: Avanesov and Ozhegov[3] admit both на двери́ and на двéри *on the door*, в/на кости́ and в/на кóсти *in/on the bone* and, while giving в/на печи́ *in/on the stove*, point out в дóменной пéчи *in the blast-furnace*. Similarly, while one says в связи́ с *in connection with* and в э́той связи́ *in this connection*, one says on the other hand в неразры́вной свя́зи с *indissolubly bound up with*, and, while both в сети́ and в сéти *in the net* are admitted, one says only в электри́ческой сéти *in the electrical network*. Moreover, it is evident that some of these substantives after в or на form invariable expressions functioning as 'compound prepositions'—в связи́ с—or adverbs—Корáбль был на мели́ *the ship was grounded*, быть в чести́ *to be honoured*. Some such forms, such as вдали́ *in the distance*,

1 This substantive, however, is also stressed on the ending in the genitive and dative after the common prepositions.
2 Русь being the old name for Russia.
3 *Op. cit.*

впереди *in front*, have in fact long since become single-word adverbs. There is therefore some slight evidence, as in the case of the masculine locative in -ý/-ю́, that the feminine locative in stressed -и is in process of being replaced by the normal prepositional in unstressed -и or of becoming fossilized in adverbial expressions.

The two substantives мать *mother* and дочь *daughter* retain in declension the element -ер- which marked them as members of the Old Russian consonantal stem declension: мать, genitive, dative, prepositional—ма́тери, instrumental —ма́терью. Дочь has in fact retained the instrumental plural ending -ьми (дочерьми́), characteristic of the feminine substantives in the Old Russian consonantal stem declension, while having a colloquial alternative дочеря́ми. The instrumental plural ending -ьми was also characteristic of other substantives in -ь in Old Russian. A few still retain it: лошадьми́ (and лошадя́ми), дверьми́ (and дверя́ми), плетьми́ (usually only in such phrases as бить плетьми́ *to flog with whips*) and костьми́ (only in the phrase лечь костьми́ *to die in battle*). It is evident that the form in -ьми is practically dead.

The fact that, since the Revolution, many thousands of women have entered professions which had been largely or entirely the preserve of men has had an effect on the grammar of substantives. Epicene substantives denoting membership of a particular profession are originally masculine, and it is only when women enter the profession that the substantive takes on epicene gender. Formerly, such substantives continued to require masculine agreement, i.e. *She is an outstanding professor*, for example, was Она́ выдаю́щийся профе́ссор. While such usage continues to be correct, there are instances of feminine agreement with substantives which according to their morphological characteristics are apparently masculine, as in Касси́р, немолода́я и полногру́дная Еле́на Ива́новна, заходи́ла в свою́ уединённую клетýшку (V. Lidin) *The cashier, Yelena Ivanovna, full-bosomed and no longer young, went into her secluded little nook*.[1] Many feminine substantives ending in -ша which are derived from masculine substantives used to have the meaning 'wife of . . .', e.g. аптéкарша *pharmacist's wife*, дóкторша *doctor's wife*, профéссорша *professor's wife*. This use of such substantives is now rather old-fashioned, or popular, the 'neutral' idiom being женá аптéкаря, . . . дóктора, etc. The use of these substantives in the sense of 'female pharmacist, . . . doctor', etc. is not old-fashioned but sometimes has a popular nuance and may even on occasion take on a hypocoristic or very slightly condescending nuance. The originally masculine substantives used with reference to women (кассúр, профéссор, дóктор, etc.) are completely neutral in tone, and their use is standard. Some substantives in -ша are also neutral in tone—секретáрша *secretary*, маникю́рша *manicurist* (having no masculine equivalent).

1 Quoted by A. and T. Fesenko, *Русский язык при советах*, p. 164. Cf. also M. V. Panov: 'Теперь говорят и пишут: *Доктор пришел* и *Доктор пришла, Председатель сказал* и *Председатель сказала*' ('Некоторые тенденции в развитии русского литературного языка XX в.', *Вопросы языкознания*, 1, 1936, pp. 3–17).

8

Adjectives

The adjective shows far less variety in declension than the substantive. In fact there is one basic system of declension for the great majority of adjectives, with two variants—hard and soft.

	masc.	*neut.*	*fem.*	*plural*
Hard				
nom.	кра́сный	кра́сное	кра́сная	кра́сные
gen.	кра́сного	кра́сного	кра́сной	кра́сных
dat.	кра́сному	кра́сному	кра́сной	кра́сным
acc.	(as nom. or gen.)	кра́сное	кра́сную	(as nom. or gen.)
instr.	кра́сным	кра́сным	кра́сной/ою	кра́сными
prep.	кра́сном	кра́сном	кра́сной	кра́сных
Soft				
nom.	си́ний	си́нее	си́няя	си́ние
gen.	си́него	си́него	си́ней	си́них
dat.	си́нему	си́нему	си́ней	си́ним
acc.	(as nom. or gen.)	си́нее	си́нюю	(as nom. or gen.)
instr.	си́ним	си́ним	си́ней/ею	си́ними
prep.	си́нем	си́нем	си́ней	си́них

When stressed on the endings the hard variant takes the ending -ой in the nominative singular masculine—молодо́й *young*. The soft variant never has stress on the endings. The alternative accusative forms in the masculine and plural

186

depend of course on whether the adjective refers to an inanimate object or an animate being. Of the alternatives in
the instrumental feminine the ending -ой/-ей is commoner
than the ending -ою/-ею, which either has a bookish
nuance or is used for rhythmic purposes. The so-called
'mixed' types of declension, in which, orthographically,
hard and soft endings are both found, arise partly from the
conventions of Russian orthography and partly from certain features of the phonetic system.

Relative adjectives are derived mostly from the names of
animals. A few are derived from names of persons and the
class also includes Бо́жий and тре́тий. They are distinguished by having a stem ending in [j], orthographically ь,
in all forms except the nominative singular masculine, and
by a monosyllabic ending in the nominative-accusative
neuter, the nominative and accusative feminine and the
nominative plural:

	masc.	*neut.*	*fem.*	*plural*
nom.	ли́сий	ли́сье	ли́сья	ли́сьи
gen.	ли́сьего	ли́сьего	ли́сьей	ли́сьих
dat.	ли́сьему	ли́сьему	ли́сьей	ли́сьим
acc.	(as nom. or gen.)	ли́сье	ли́сью	(as nom. or gen.)
instr.	ли́сьим	ли́сьим	ли́сьей/-ею	ли́сьими
prep.	ли́сьем	ли́сьем	ли́сьей	ли́сьих

Possessive adjectives ending in -ин, derived from names
of persons ending in -а/-я, are distinguished by having substantival type endings in the nominative cases and in the
accusative feminine:

	masc.	*neut.*	*fem.*	*plural*
nom.	ма́мин	ма́мино	ма́мина	ма́мины
gen.	ма́миного	ма́миного	ма́миной	ма́миных
dat.	ма́миному	ма́миному	ма́миной	ма́миным

	masc.	neut.	fem.	plural
acc.	(as nom. or gen.)	ма́мино	ма́мину	(as nom. or gen.)
instr.	ма́миным	ма́миным	ма́миной/-ою	ма́миными
prep.	ма́мином	ма́мином	ма́миной	ма́миных

In an older type of declension such adjectives have substantival endings in the genitive and dative masculine and neuter: ма́мина, ма́мину. Possessive adjectives in -ов/-ев, which are no longer productive, decline in the same way, with substantival endings in the nominative cases, the accusative feminine and the genitive and dative masculine and neuter: отцо́в *father's* отцо́ва, отцо́ву, but отцо́вым, etc.

There are analytical and synthetic forms of both the comparative and superlative. The analytical comparative consists of the appropriate case form of the adjective preceded by бо́лее *more*. Any adjective expressing a quality which can be thought of in degrees of comparison can have this form of the comparative: бо́лее динами́ческий *more dynamic*, бо́лее фотогени́ческий *more photogenic*. A comparative of inferiority is formed in the same way with ме́нее *less* —ме́нее плодоро́дный *less fruitful*, ме́нее морозоусто́й-чивый *less frost-resistant*. The productive suffix for the synthetic comparative is -ee, as in длине́е *longer*, краси́вее *more beautiful*. Only adjectives denoting quality may form the comparative in -ee, but not if they end in -лый, -лой, -овый, -овой, nor if the last consonant before the ending is a dental plosive or a velar consonant (written, д, т, г, к, х). The suffix -ee has the variant -ей in colloquial language and, for metrical purposes, in poetry.

A non-productive monosyllabic suffix is found in over sixty comparatives, some of which are not very frequently used. In most of them the suffix is -e, involving consonant substitution of those consonants which undergo substitution (к > ч, г > ж, etc.). Such are гро́мкий *loud*—гро́мче, лёгкий *light*—ле́гче, дорого́й *dear*—доро́же, бога́тый *rich*—бога́че, etc.[1] The suffix -(ь)ше is found in далёкий *far*—да́льше, до́лгий *long (lasting)*—до́льше, ста́рый *old* ('not young')[2]—ста́рше, то́нкий *fine, thin*—то́ньше, the suffix -же in глубо́кий *deep*—глу́бже, and the suffix -ще (or a unique substitution of щ for д) in сла́дкий *sweet*—сла́ще.

The synthetic comparative may be prefixed with по-, signifying 'a little more . . ., rather more . . .' and sometimes 'as . . . as possible.'

The analytical comparatives may be used either attributively (as modifier of a substantive) or predicatively (as complement). The synthetic comparatives are commoner in predicative function but are also found in attributive function, as in Секрета́рь помоло́же направля́ется к пе́рвому за́му; секрета́рь поста́рше — к председа́телю (Klen.). *The (somewhat) younger secretary goes to the first deputy, the somewhat older one to the chairman.*

The analytical superlative consists of the appropriate case-form of the adjective preceded by the corresponding case-form of са́мый *most*—са́мый динами́ческий *most dynamic*. The synthetic form in -ейший (or -айший after ж, ш, ч, щ) is derived only from those adjectives which have a synthetic comparative. Sometimes it expresses the third term of comparison (i.e. is a 'true superlative'), as in Э́то длинне́йший путь *that's the longest way*, but is most often used as an 'intensive' adjective, indicating a very high degree of a quality without comparative force, as in важне́йшее явле́ние *a most important phenomenon*. The prefix наи- intensifies the synthetic superlative still further—

1 For fuller lists see B. O. Unbegaun, *Russian Grammar*, pp. 105–107, D. N. Ushakov, etc., *Толковый словарь русского языка*, vol. I, pp. LXXI–LXXVI.

2 But ста́рый *old* ('not new') has the comparative старе́е.

наидлиннейший *the very longest*, наиважнейший *extremely important*.

The short form

The short form of the adjective is derived by removing the endings of the long form and adding -а/-я for the feminine, -о/-е for the neuter and -ы/-и for the plural: красивый *beautiful*—красив, красива, красиво, красивы. Short forms of soft adjectives—синь, синя, etc., *blue*—are very rarely used. In the masculine short form the mobile vowel о/е may be inserted between the last two consonants, as in умный *clever*—умён (Chapter 3, Orthography).

Short forms cannot be derived from certain adjectives. These include adjectives with the suffix -ский and -цкий,[1] adjectives denoting time or place, ending in -ий or -шний (e.g.—зимний *winter's*, домашний *domestic*), relative adjectives ending in -ий (e.g. лисий *fox's*), and adjectives denoting material, ending in -янный, -енный, -анный, -аный (e.g. стеклянный *glass*, кожаный *leather*), adjectives ending in -овый/-овой (e.g. массовый *mass*) and some others.[2] No short forms are derived from большой *big* and маленький *small*: the short forms of великий *great* and малый *small* serve also as the short forms of большой and маленький respectively, with stress differentiation in the case of велик, etc., between *big* and *great* (see Chapter 2, Stress).

The adjectives рад *glad* and горазд (colloquial) *clever at* are not derived from any corresponding long forms. In some other adjectives the long and short forms have become entirely or almost divorced in meaning, so that one can no longer say that a particular short form is the short form of a particular long form. Compare the following pairs: Он

---

1 If the -ск- in the ending -ский is *not* a suffix, then adjectives ending in -ский can have short forms, e.g. веский *weighty*—весок, etc., where the root is вес- and the suffix is -к(ий).

2 See Academy Grammar, vol. I, pp. 286–288.

ви́дный учёный *He is an outstanding scholar*—Отсю́да го́род не ви́ден *The town cannot be seen from here;* Он вла́стный челове́к *He is an imperious person*—Он в э́том не вла́стен *He has no authority in this matter;* Э́то не пра́вое де́ло *That is not a just/true cause*—Вы пра́вы *You are (in the) right;* Он сла́вный *He is a fine person*—Он сла́вен *He is famous;* Она́ о́чень жива́я *She is very lively*—Она́ ещё жива́ *She is still alive;* Э́то плохо́й результа́т *That is a poor result*—Он плох *He is ill, 'in a bad way';* Он хоро́ший *He is a fine fellow*—Он хоро́ш собо́й *He is handsome.* Любо́й *any* is now entirely distinct from люб 'liked' and, though Ushakov[1] calls the latter 'archaic-poetic', K. Chukovsky is found using it still[2]: Тот и́ли ино́й речево́й оборо́т быва́ет нам люб и́ли га́док не сам по себе́ *We like or dislike this or that turn of phrase not merely for its own sake.*

In modern Russian the only productive forms of the short adjective are the 'nominative' forms, e.g. кра́сен, красна́, кра́сно, кра́сны, used predicatively. The other case-forms of short adjectives are now found 'fossilized' in adverbs originally derived from adjectives, such as сле́ва *on the left*, спра́ва *on the right*, сно́ва *again*, and in such expressions as средь бе́ла дня *in broad daylight*, от ма́ла до вели́ка (*people*) *of all ages*, на босу́ но́гу *without stockings*, мал мала́ ме́ньше *each one smaller than the other*, по бе́лу све́ту *through the great big world.* Although with these exceptions, the short form is used only predicatively, the long form is used both attributively and predicatively. As we have seen above, there are certain adjectives which can be used predicatively only in their short forms. Since many adjectives can be used predicatively either in their long forms or in their short forms it is necessary to determine what, if any, is the grammatical and semantic difference between the two uses.

1 *Толковый словарь русского языка.*
2 'О соразмерности и сообразности', *Новый мир*, 5, 1961.

Most grammarians who treat the short form at any length are agreed that in Modern Russian there is a tendency to replace it by the long form. This is undeniably true of the colloquial language, whose example is affecting the literary language, but the bald statement might imply that the short form is being replaced indiscriminately by the long form. A brief perusal of contemporary literature will reveal that this is not in fact so, that there is a difference in meaning between the short form and the long form and that when the long form 'takes over' from the short form it is primarily because the difference is felt to be negligible or unimportant. Moreover, there are still many instances, apart from those mentioned above, when the short form is not merely preferable but is essential.

The criterion generally applied in distinguishing between the use of the short form and the long form has been a temporal one: the long form, to put it briefly, is said to describe a permanent characteristic, the short form a temporary characteristic. Thus, V. V. Vinogradov writes: 'permanent, extratemporal properties of objects or persons . . . cannot be expressed by the short form of the adjective'[1] and 'short forms express a qualitative state proceeding in or arising in time, long forms a property thought of outside time, but in the given context attributed to a particular time'.[1] More recently, Galkina-Fedoruk, etc., write: 'The long form of the adjective expresses a permanent characteristic of the object . . . whereas the short form denotes a qualitative state characteristic of the object only at a specific time.'[2]

M. V. Trofimov, having said that the function of the long form is 'the indication of particularity which separates a given individual from others of the same kind, or under the same concept',[3] which in our opinion is a correct assess-

1 *Русский язык*, p. 262 & 263.
2 *Op. cit.*, p. 265.
3 *Op cit.*, p. 69.

ment, then applies a different—a temporal—criterion to the short form and says that its function is 'the indication of a passing state or condition, i.e. one which is attained by a subject at some particular point or points of time'.[1] Borras and Christian, although they ultimately return to Vinogradov's permanent-temporary opposition, apply various criteria, saying[2] that the short form predominates (a) in a generalized statement, even when the quality is permanent, as long as the statement does not identify but defines; (b) when the *degree* of a quality is indicated, emphasized or compared; (c) when the subject is a part of the body and is accompanied by the personal pronouns eró, eë, их; (d) when the adjective is followed by a complement or qualified by an adverb. Here we have a variety of semantic, lexical and grammatical criteria. However, the authors then go on to make the very good point that the long form identifies a quality completely with an object whereas the short form expresses the quality without identification or without attributing it to a person or thing.

This is in fact the fundamental difference between the long form and the short form, from which all other differences in meaning arise. The short form isolates the quality as such, without attributing it to a specific object.[3] The quality is extracted from the context, as it were, and held out for specific attention in itself. The long form, on the other hand, does not isolate the quality as such but presents it as an attribute of the subject. When, for instance, the quality is one of size, the short form represents a point on a scale of size, considered without direct or necessary reference to objects—it is concerned with the degree of size—whereas the long form, associating quality and object, presents us

1 *Op. cit.*, p. 70.
2 *Op. cit.*, pp. 75–78.
3 Whether the short or the long form is used, the quality is of course referred to the subject by virtue of the structure of the clause.
7+

with one of a set of objects graded according to size. It is certainly not the case that the *primary* function of the short form is to express a temporary characteristic. Indeed the short form is usual in generalized statements presenting a permanent or quasi-permanent truth. N. S. Pospelov, for instance, writes[1]: 'the short forms of adjectives in sentences without a copula have a generalized significance of the permanent presence of a quality in an object . . . Счáстье неуловимо . . . Жизнь всё-таки прекрáсна . . . Лéтние нóчи корóтки.' Moreover, Pospelov continues, in such sentences without a copula the idea of *impermanence* is derived from the entire context or 'depends upon the lexical meaning of the adjective—Вагóн комáнды пуст . . . Я брежý. Я несчáстна'.

As far as clause-structure is concerned, two clauses which differ only in respect of the form of the adjective (short or long) have the same structure. Thus, the structure of Тýфли ýзки and Тýфли ýзкие is identical: Subject + Complement, and so is the structure of Тýфли бýли ýзки and Тýфли бýли ýзкие: Subject + Predicator + Complement. In all four cases the complement is occupied by a nominal group but the structure of these nominal groups differs. In the case of the long form the structure consists of a modifier (attributive epithet) while in the case of the short form the structure consists of a head. In other words, the long form is regarded as being a modifier, or 'attribute', even when it is used 'predicatively', but the short form as being a special form of the adjective akin to the substantive in that its only function is to stand as the head of a nominal group which is the complement. It is for these reasons that in Chapter 4 the short form of the adjective was not assigned to a special part of speech, the 'category of state'.

---

[1] 'Соотношение между грамматическими категориями и частями речи', *Вопросы языкознания*, no. 6, 1953, p. 62.

The expression of permanent characteristic by means of the short form is seen in the following examples

Мебель, которую получают школы и детские учреждения, громоздка и неудобна (*Krok.*)	*The furniture which schools and children's establishments receive is clumsy and uncomfortable*
Ему сорок восемь лет, он статен, хорош собой (Arb.)	*He is forty-eight, well-made, handsome*
Жизнь трудна (Klen.)	*Life is hard*

The idea of temporary quality expressed by the short form derives directly from its isolative function, since the isolation and presentation as a quality in itself underlines the fact that it is a temporary or newly arisen quality. However, this temporariness is known, as Pospelov points out (see above), only from the context or the lexical meaning of the adjective. Examples of this are:

Папа был суров и грозен (*Krok.*)	*Papa was* (i.e. 'looked at this particular time') *severe and stern*
Ветер был порывист, изменчив и влажен (G. Nik.)	*The wind was gusty, changeable and damp*
Они были в простых штатских пальто, лица их были жестковаты, твёрды (G. Nik.)	*They were wearing ordinary civilian coats and their faces were stiff, resolute*
Равнина была пустынна и печальна (A. N. Tol.)	*The plain was deserted and melancholy*

В по́лночь Кра́сная пло́щадь строга́ (Klen.)	*At midnight Red Square is forbidding* (also construable as a permanent, generalized characteristic—at midnight on any day)

It is because of the isolative function of the short form that the past passive participle must be in the short form when used predicatively. The quality denoted by the past passive participle is new, has just arisen because of the action performed and is therefore to be isolated and not presented as an attribute of the subject. The short form is obligatory too when the adjective is delimited by an infinitive, a nominal group or a clause, since the addition of the delimiting factor necessarily isolates the quality for specific attention:

Вы недосто́йны быть солда́том революцио́нной а́рмии (A. N. Tol.)	*You are not fit to be a soldier of the revolu- revolutionary army*
Он добр к лю́дям (Arb.)	*He is good to people*
Он был неприя́тен тем, что по утра́м вытряса́л свой штаны́ в дверь (Rom.)	*He was objectionable in that he used to shake out his trousers at the door in the mornings*
К несча́стью, он [дождь] был недоста́точен, что́бы смыть с насти́ла ско́льзкую сля́коть (Kat.)	*Unfortunately, it [the rain] was not enough to wash the slippery slush from the sidewalk*
Он мне мёрзок (Arb.)	*I find him loathsome*
Но́ги челове́ка не ме́нее вырази́тельны, чем ру́ки (Klen.)	*A person's feet are no less expressive than his hands*

Семён Горислáвович был ко мне внимáтелен (Klen.)	*Semyon Gorislavovich paid me some attention*

Similarly, the short form is usual when the adjective in predicative function precedes the subject and is thus positionally isolated for emphatic or contrastive purposes:

Стрáшен был Петербу́рг в концé семнáдцатого гóда (A. N. Tol.)	*Petersburg, at the end of 1917, was terrible*
Был стрáшен Семён на э́той послéдней своéй косьбé (Leon.)	*At this, his last mowing, Semyon was fearful to look upon*
Разноли́ки и разношéрстны посети́тели, пришéдшие по ли́чным делáм, чáще всегó жили́щным (Klen.)	*The people waiting, who have come on personal matters—mostly to do with housing, are of all sorts and types*

It is from its isolative function that there arises the use of the short form of adjectives of size in meanings corresponding to the English 'too . . .', since the quality is presented as such, for comparison with the normal degree, and not simply as a direct attribute of its subject. For instance, in Ту́фли (бы́ли) у́зки the shoes are presented as being narrow with respect to the person wearing them or trying them on, whereas in Ту́фли (бы́ли) у́зкие the narrowness is attributed to the shoes whoever may be wearing them and is therefore, incidentally, a permanent quality.

The long form, however, can be found in structures similar to those of the examples just given. The Academy Grammar[1] quotes an example from the first half of the nineteenth century—

1 Vol. II, part 1, p. 460.

Пан здоро́вый и кре́пкий с виду (Gog.) — *The gentleman is healthy and strong in appearance*

an example from the turn of the century—

А твоя́ ко́мната така́я хоро́шая для ребёнка (Chekh.) — *And your room is so suitable for the baby*

Это я то́лько к тебе́ до́брый ... А, пожа́луй, ве́рно, я ко всем до́брый (Gor.) — *It's only you I am kind to ... but perhaps it's true— I'm kind to everybody*

To these A. Semeonoff[1] adds a more recent example—

Скаме́йка была́ тёплая от со́лнца (Paust.) — *The bench was warm from the sun*

This use of the long form appears to be spreading but there is no data available which would enable one to say at what rate the long form is supplanting the short form here.

The isolative function of the short form also lies at the root of such differentiations as Муж бо́лен *My husband is ill* and Муж больно́й *My husband is an invalid*. In the first sentence the quality as such is presented and a contrast with the normal state is implied, while in the second sentence the quality is presented as an attribute of a substantive—'my husband is a sick person'.

In nineteenth-century Russian the short form could appear in the complement after predicators other than the verb 'to be':

Этот взор показа́лся мне чу́дно не́жен (Lerm.) — *This glance seemed wonderfully tender to me*

Я верну́лся домо́й угрю́м и серди́т (Lerm.) — *I returned home gloomy and angry*

1 *Russian Syntax* (London, 1962), p. 40.

The short form is still occasionally found in such sentences:

Четырнадцатилетний Дэвид Мартин соскочил с рельсов и остался невредим (*Kom. Pr.*)	*Fourteen year old David Martin jumped off the rails and was unhurt*
С войны он возвращается цел и невредим (Arb.)	*He comes back from the war hale and hearty*

The long form is commoner in this function:

Заспанный пришёл есаул Попов (Shol.)	*Cossack-captain Popov arrived looking sleepy*
Вешалка стояла пустая (Rom.)	*The coat-rack stood empty*
А сама ходила всегда нечёсаная (*ibid.*)	*And she herself always used to go about unkempt*

Instances of the long form in the writings of modern authors, where a generation ago the short form would have been more likely, are plentiful. Two plays of A. Arbuzov neatly illustrate the status and recent history of the short form. In this author's Иркутская история, *The Irkutsk Story*, the language is much more colloquial than in his Двенадцатый час, *The Twelfth Hour*, and there are far more examples of predicative long forms in the former than in the latter. Furthermore, the time of Двенадцатый час is the end of the NEP period, the characters were born before the Revolution and some of them are of bourgeois origin, whereas the time of Иркутская история is in the period after the second World War, almost all the characters are 'post-revolutionary', and have been brought up in the Soviet period. The differentiation of the speech of the characters in these two plays is, if only with regard to the use of long and short forms, a clever piece of historical stylization by linguistic means.

In the following examples, taken from A. Arbuzov and A. Klenov, the long form has been used either because the attributive function is required, or the isolative function of the short form is superfluous, or because the difference between the long and short forms is negligible in the context. Examples from A. Arbuzov are:

Ты хра́брый	*You are (a) brave (person)*
Он сли́шком до́брый и че́стный	*He is too good and honest (a person)*
Но ведь ты хи́трый	*But, you know, you're (a) cunning (person)*
Она́ удиви́тельно краси́вая и о́чень, понима́ешь, остроу́мная	*She is (a) surprisingly beautiful and, you know, witty (person)*
А он смешно́й, э́тот машини́ст	*But he's (a) funny (one), that engine-driver*
А вы всегда́ холосто́й бы́ли? —Был и жена́тый	*And have you always been a bachelor?—I've been (a) married (man) too*
Ты на мать похо́жа — краси́вая	*You're like your mother—(a) beautiful (woman)*

From A. Klenov we have:

Ладо́нь Ната́ши лежи́т в мое́й ладо́ни; она́ тёплая и не́жная	*Natasha's palm lies in mine; it is (a) warm and tender (palm)*
Маяко́вский большо́й, и оттого́, что скала́, на кото́рой	*Mayakovsky['s statue] is big and, because the*

он стои́т, сравни́тельно ни́зкая, он вы́глядит ещё бо́льше	*rock on which he stands is comparatively low, he looks even bigger*
До чего́ была́ делика́тна . . . А ты гру́бый	*How refined she was—but you're (a) coarse (person)*
У нас те́сно. Ме́бель громо́здкая, неудо́бная	*We haven't enough room. The furniture is clumsy, inconvenient (furniture)*
Сте́ны в мастерско́й бе́лые и пусты́е	*The walls in the studio are white and empty (walls)*

Instances where the long form is not immediately explicable or is completely unexpected are not so numerous, a fact which testifies to the superfluity of the distinction of long and short forms in many contexts. Here the use of the long form may be a result of the influence of such sentences as those quoted above and also perhaps of such sentences as У́тро све́тлое, я́сное (Klen.), where it is not clear whether the clause structure is Subject + Complement—*The morning is bright, clear*—or Subject only, consisting of a nominal group of substantive and two modifiers—*A bright, clear morning*. Consider in this light the following sentences from A. Arbuzov:

Ты тако́й неспоко́йный сего́дня	*You are so restless (such a restless person?) today*
Что́-то я сего́дня кака́я-то на себя́ не похо́жая	*Somehow I'm not myself today*
Лари́са (вы́пив) — Ещё холо́дное . . .	*Larrisa (drinking): It [the beer] is still cold . . .*
Жизнь о́чень коро́ткая	*Life is very short*

7*

and from A. Klenov:

Ты такóй же, Вáня . . . Тóлько совсéм взрóслый . . . И, как всегдá, небри́тый	You're just the same, Vanya . . . only quite grown-up . . . and as al- ways, unshaven
Он [парапéт] холóдный и сту- ди́т спи́ну; и меня́ зноби́т; а ру́ки жáркие и мóкрые	It [the parapet] is cold and chills my back; and I am shivering; but my hands are hot and damp (hardly '. . . are hot and damp hands' ?)
— Ты непрáва, Натáша, он не серди́тый, скорéе реши́тель- ный и стрóгий. — И ты сей- чáс не серди́тый, — говори́т Натáша.	'You're wrong, Natasha, he's not (an) angry, but rather (a) resolute, stern (person)'. 'And you're not angry now', says Natasha

(In this last sentence it is clear from the context that the meaning is *not* 'an angry person'.)[1]

1 This book was already in print when A. Bogusławski published an article on the long and short forms of the adjective in *Русский язык в школе* (1964, no. 1), under the title "О кратких и полных формах прилагательного в сказуемом". Dr Bogusławski considers that the function of the long form as a complement is to draw an opposition of the object with the property specified to other objects without this property, whereas the short form implies many degrees of the property specified and, so to speak, assigns the property of the object to a place on a scale. Hence the short form approaches in its meaning combinations of adjectives and such adverbs as 'fairly', 'rather', 'very', etc., while the long form approaches in meaning '"not of the opposite quality", i.e. "not above (below) a certain limit"'. The fact that the short form implies many degrees of the quality, says Dr Bogusławski, is confirmed 'by the mutual gravitation of the short form and words indicating gradience, such as "very", "extremely", etc.' The idea of gradience or scale can easily be appreciated where the adjective is one of size, as I have indicated above. In his article, Dr Bogusławski refers to an article, not at present available to me, by Professor A. V. Isačenko—

'Трансформационный анализ кратких и полных прилагательных', (in *Исследования по структурной типологии*, Moscow, 1963)—in which the author considers that the function of the long form is to ascribe an object to the class of other objects having the same property. This appears to be diametrically opposed to Dr Bogusławski's own interpretation of the function of the long form but it is very significant that underlying both authors' views is the idea that when the long form is used the property and the object are closely associated: the property is not isolated as a thing in itself. This, it will be seen, is fundamental to my own view of the function of the long form.

9
The Genitive-Accusative and the Negative Genitive

The phenomena of the genitive-accusative—the use of the genitive to express the direct object of non-negated or negated verbs—and the negative genitive—the use of the genitive to express the direct object of negated verbs—affect not only the substantive but the other nominal parts of speech too. For this reason these two phenomena are dealt with here instead of piecemeal in chapters dealing with various parts of speech. In this chapter remarks on the use of the genitive-accusative of the substantive and the genitive of the substantive after negated verbs are to be understood to apply also to adjectives and participles standing either as modifiers or heads in nominal groups. Where parts of speech (e.g. pronouns and numerals) call for special remarks, these are made separately.

GENITIVE-ACCUSATIVE[1]

Masculine substantives denoting animate beings (other than plant life) have a genitive-accusative in both singular and plural: доктор *doctor*—gen.-acc. sing. доктора, gen.-acc. pl. докторо́в, учи́тель *teacher*—gen.-acc. sing. учи́теля, gen.-acc. pl. учителе́й. It was in the class of masculine substantives that the use of the genitive-accusative, leading to the creation of the animate-inanimate category, arose. In Old Russian the nominative and accusative singular of

1 See in particular F. M. Borras and R. F. Christian, *Russian Syntax*, pp. 5–7, and Ye. M. Galkina-Fedoruk, etc., *Современный русский язык*, pp. 202–204.

masculine substantives other than those ending in -a/-я were originally identical, whether or not they denoted inanimate things. Because of the freedom of word-order, whereby subject or object could come first, sentences in which both subject and object were masculine substantives could be ambiguous. The need to avoid ambiguity was most sharply felt with regard to substantives denoting male persons, since they are most likely to figure as the subject of a transitive verb and hence, if there is no morphological differentiation of subject and object, be confused with the object. Compare for instance, on the one hand, Old Russian отьць любить сынъ, where, out of context—and often enough in context, it is impossible to say which is the subject and which is object, with, on the other hand, modern Russian отéц любит сы́на where subject and object are clearly differentiated, whatever the order of words: сы́на отéц лю́бит, сы́на лю́бит отéц, отéц сы́на лю́бит, лю́бит сы́на отéц, лю́бит отéц сы́на.

A model for the differentiation of subject and object was at hand in those pronouns such as я, мы, ты, онъ, къто, etc., which already had an accusative identical with the genitive, a feature of pre-Russian origin. Moreover, some verbs required the direct object to be in the genitive case, which was also found as the direct object after negated verbs. Apart from these factors, the genitive was of all the oblique cases the least precise or limited in semantic content: it could more easily embrace the function of expressing the direct object than could the more sharply delimited dative, instrumental or locative.

The phenomenon of the genitive-accusative affected proper names first, then common substantives denoting male persons. In the plural there had originally been a distinction between the nominative and accusative of masculine substantives but when, under the influence of the feminine plural declension, this difference was obliterated and the original accusative began to function both as accusative and nominative, then the animate-inanimate distinction began to affect the plural too. This began in the fourteenth century and affected first substantives denoting male persons, later on those denoting female persons too, thus, as it were, compensating for the earlier influence of feminine on masculine substantives. Finally, substantives denoting male animals were also affected by the animate-inanimate distinction, though this process was not completed until the eighteenth century.[1]

In modern Russian the animate-inanimate distinction affects feminine and neuter substantives only in the plural. In the singular, feminine substantives distinguish nominative and accusative by means of the opposition -а/-я ~ -у/-ю irrespective of animateness or inanimateness, or else, in the case of those ending in -ь, do not distinguish nominative and accusative. Masculine substantives of the type ста́роста *elder*, дя́дя *uncle* have accusative in -у/-ю but any accompanying modifier has genitive-accusative: Я ви́дел ва́шего ста́рого дя́дю. Neuter substantives (including adjectival substantives such as живо́тное *animal*, насеко́мое *insect*) denoting animate beings do not distinguish nominative and accusative in the singular and this applies even to существо́ *being*, *creature* and лицо́ *person*. The word подмасте́рье *apprentice*, though neuter in form, is masculine in gender and hence has genitive-accusative singular подмасте́рья and plural подмасте́рьев.

Substantives denoting a group of animate beings, including people (e.g. ста́до, наро́д, полк, во́йско, etc.) do not have a genitive-accusative. Curiously enough, the words поко́йник *the deceased* and мертве́ц *corpse*, *dead man* (and

1 There is one set of instances where the nominative-accusative plural has persisted. This is illustrated by such expressions as произвести́ в офице́ры *to promote to the rank of officer*, идти́ в ня́ни *to become a nanny*, etc., where the genitive-accusative is not permitted.

the adjectival substantive мёртвый) do have genitive-accusative in both singular and plural but труп *corpse, cadaver* does not. Words which denote supernatural beings —бог *god*, чёрт *devil*, бес *demon*, etc.—have genitive-accusative and so do words which denote animate beings when used in a transferred sense: Ви́дели вы тако́го оригина́ла/ти́па? *Have you ever seen such an eccentric/type?* A word like спу́тник has a genitive-accusative when it denotes *fellow-traveller* but a nominative-accusative when it denotes *satellite*. Substantives figuring in the titles of plays, novels, etc., must be put in the appropriate case if governed by some word outside the title, hence in *I have read 'Faust'/'The Three Sisters'*, for example, the genitive-accusative must be used: Я чита́л «Фа́уста»/«Трёх сестёр». This rule does not hold, however, when the title is preceded by some word such as пье́са, рома́н, etc.— Я чита́л пье́су «Фа́уст»/«Три сестры́». A curious extension of the genitive-accusative is to the names of cards and chessmen, presumably because some of them are also names of animate beings. Hence коро́ль *king*, вале́т *jack*, туз *ace*, ко́зырь *trump*, слон *bishop*, ферзь (m.) *queen* have a genitive-accusative. In billiards the word шар *ball* also has a genitive-accusative.

There is some hesitation between genitive-accusative and nominative-accusative for the names of the lowest living organisms, such as микро́б *microbe*, ви́рус *virus* (and, in the plural, баци́лла *bacilla*, бакте́рия *bacterium*, etc.), though modern usage prefers the *nominative*-accusative here. Similarly both genitive-accusative and nominative-accusative are found in, for example, запусти́ть зме́я/змей *to launch a kite*, Я купи́л «Москвича́/Москви́ч» *I have bought a 'Moskvich'* (type of car). When they denote a dish, the names of fishes, etc., have a nominative-accusative—есть шпро́ты/ома́ры *to eat sprats/lobsters* (but лови́ть шпрот/ома́ров *to catch sprats/lobsters*). This applies also to feminine substantives in the plural—есть у́стрицы *to eat oysters* (but разводи́ть у́стриц *to breed oysters*).[1]

The third person pronoun, the reflexive pronoun and the reciprocal pronoun have the genitive-accusative (его́, её, их, себя́, друг дру́га) even when they refer to an inanimate object and in this respect are unique. The word не́чего (*there is*) *nothing* serves apparently as genitive and accusative but its apparent genitive-accusative should probably be construed as the genitive appearing in a negative construction (see below). The negating element is, as it were, contained within the pronoun itself. Notice that when this pronoun occurs with a preposition requiring the accusative case its form is не . . . что, as in не́ за что, не́ на что, не́ во что.

The numeral оди́н, одно́, etc., always behaves like an adjective in agreeing with its substantive and hence, in the appropriate circumstances, has a genitive-accusative— Я ви́дел то́лько одного́ котёнка *I saw only one kitten*. This also applies when оди́н is the last element of a higher numeral—Я ви́дел всего́ два́дцать одного́ котёнка *Altogether I saw twenty-one kittens*. The numerals два/две, три, четы́ре and the numeral pronoun о́ба/о́бе also behave like adjectives in the matter of agreement when the substantive is in an oblique case and hence have a genitive-accusative when referring to animate beings—Я ви́дел двух студе́нтов/трёх де́вочек/четырёх мужчи́н/обо́их друзе́й *I saw two students/three little girls/four men/both friends*. For higher numerals ending in два/две, три or четы́ре the grammarians lay down that the literary language does not admit the genitive-accusative and therefore one has Я ви́дел два́дцать два студе́нта *I saw twenty-two students*, etc. However, educated speakers can be heard to say Я

1 Ye. M. Galkina-Fedoruk, etc., *op. cit.*, p. 202, note 1, record that some names of fungi may be found in the genitive-accusative, but in the phrases quoted the genitive could be interpreted as a partitive genitive.

ви́дел два́дцать двух студе́нтов, etc., thus extending the genitive accusative rule to higher numbers ending in два/две, три and четы́ре. On the other hand the colloquial language offers such examples of the *nominative*-accusative as Я ви́дел два осла́.[1] Numerals other than the ones mentioned above do not share the genitive-accusative feature: Я ви́дел пять де́вушек *I saw five girls*.

Excursus: the grammar of numeral-phrases

The grammar of numeral-phrases in Russian is notoriously complex. A set of rules for canonical usage is given below, followed by a remark on recent developments.

1. *Number:* In all numeral-phrases the grammatical number of the substantive head and any modifiers in the group is always determined by the numeral.

With оди́н and higher numbers ending in оди́н the grammatical number of the substantive head and any adjective modifiers is singular: два́дцать оди́н но́вый рубль *twenty-one new rubles*, три́дцать одно́ дли́нное письмо́ *thirty-one long letters*. Pronominal modifiers are in the plural: за э́ти два́дцать оди́н час *during these twenty-one hours*.

With numbers other than два/две, три, четы́ре and higher numbers ending in these elements the grammatical number of the head and modifiers is plural.

With два/две, etc., the grammatical number of adjectives and pronouns is always plural but that of substantives is singular or plural, according to rules 3 and 4 below.

2. *Gender:* If the numeral has gender-distinctions then the gender is always determined by the head: оди́н ма́льчик, одна́ де́вушка, одно́ живо́тное, два ма́льчика, две де́вушки.

1 M. V. Trofimov, *Handbook of Russian*, II, p. 83, gives an example involving a person—Я ви́дел две де́вочки but A. Mazon, *Grammaire de la langue russe*, p. 88, denies the possibility of this—'dans un pareil cas, pour les noms de personnes, le génitif-accusatif sera toujours employé'.

3. *Case:* If the structure is such that the nominative or nominative-accusative of the head of a non-numeral group in the same place would be correct then the numeral is in the nominative(-accusative) and determines the case of the head and modifiers. With один, etc. and higher numbers ending in один, etc., the case is nominative (see examples under 1). With два/две, три, четыре and higher numbers ending in these elements the substantive is in the genitive singular, the modifiers are in the genitive or nominative plural. The genitive is more usual when the substantive is masculine or neuter, the nominative when the substantive is feminine: два новых друга *two new friends*, три старые книги *three old books*. With certain adjectival pronouns, which *precede* the numeral, the nominative plural is more usual, whatever the gender of the substantive: каждые два часа *every two hours*. Substantivized adjectives are also in the genitive or nominative plural: два рабочих *two workers*, две столовых (or две столовые) *two dining-rooms*.

If the structure is such that some case other than the nominative(-accusative) of the head of a non-numeral group in the same place would be correct then the numeral and any other modifiers agree with the substantive, which thus determines the case of the numeral: к двадцати одному новому рублю *to twenty-one new rubles*, от двух лучших друзей *from (my) two best friends*, с пятью старыми книгами *with five old books*, Я видел двух студентов *I saw two students*. This rule is modified by the rules for the use of the genitive-accusative with numerals given at the end of the preceding section.

Finally, note that words such as тысяча *thousand*, миллион *million*, etc., are substantives and behave as such: тысяча школьников *a thousand schoolboys*, от двух тысяч школьников *from two thousand schoolboys*, с тремя тысячами школьников *with three thousand schoolboys*, etc.

All numerals decline. In a long compound number the

literary canon requires that the last and first elements should
be put into an oblique case where appropriate: с пятью-
десятью двумя бойцами *with fifty-two warriors*, с тремя
стами пятьдесят двумя бойцами *with three-hundred and
fifty-two warriors*, с двумя тысячами триста пятьдесят
двумя бойцами *with two thousand three hundred and fifty
warriors*. In modern colloquial usage only the last element is
put into the appropriate oblique case and this usage is also
found in written Russian: с пятьдесят двумя бойцами, с
триста пятьдесят двумя бойцами, с две тысячи триста
пятьдесят двумя бойцами. The grammar of numerals is
thus being simplified but it still remains very complex.

NEGATIVE GENITIVE AND
NEGATIVE ACCUSATIVE

Both the genitive and accusative are used as the direct object
of a negated verb. The genitive in such use will be referred
to here as the 'negative genitive', the accusative as the
'negative accusative'. Popular grammars usually state cate-
gorically that the genitive is used with negated verbs.
M. V. Trofimov writes[1]: 'the tendency [to use the negative
genitive] is formulated in popular Russian grammars as an
imperative rule running as follows: "after a negative use the
genitive".'

Before going on to examine this problem further, it is as
well to look briefly at those instances where the genitive is
obligatory and is not conditioned by the presence of negation. These are the genitive-accusative (see above), the genitive controlled by a preposition, the genitive controlled by a
verb which always requires the genitive case (such as бояться, лишить, достигнуть, etc.), the partitive genitive, and,
of course, the genitive after numerals and such words as
сколько, много, etc. In other words, in all instances where
the genitive is required in a positive sentence, it also appears

1 *Handbook of Russian*, vol. II, p. 50, note 1.

in a negative sentence.

To this one must add that the genitive is obligatory with нет *there is/are not*, не́ было, *there was/were not* and не бу́дет *there will not be* and here the genitive *is* conditioned by the presence of a negative. Here we have in fact a negative partitive idea ('zero quantity') and it is probably from the use of the genitive with нет, не́ было and не бу́дет that the use of the genitive with negated verbs arises.

Some authors try to distinguish negative genitive and negative accusative on stylistic grounds. A. Mazon,[1] for instance, says: 'the accusative is also possible in this instance but is less literary', while I. M. Pulkina[2] says: 'in *colloquial*[3] speech transitive verbs preceded by the negative particle are sometimes followed by the accusative case'. However, one has only to read a few pages of contemporary Russian to find both negative genitive *and* negative accusative in the literary language—and the latter not by any means only in dialogue, where one would expect to find colloquial usage represented. It is not unusual to find in grammars statements on the following lines: 'the negative accusative means that the speaker is thinking of a definite object [a particular, specific object], while the negative genitive does not mean this'.[4] Again, a perusal of a few pages of contemporary Russian soon reveals that this very imprecise formulation is constantly contradicted by usage. Compare, for instance, the following pairs[5]:

1 *Grammaire de la langue russe*, p. 96.
2 *A Short Russian Reference Grammar*, p. 62.
3 My italics.
4 E.g. I. M. Pulkina, *op. cit.*, p. 62: 'the accusative case is generally used when the speaker wants to stress the fact that the object in question is a definite one', and M. V. Trofimov, *op. cit.*, p. 50: 'the accusative persists, however, in relational expressions exhibiting the second term as a determinate whole [=definite, particular object?], e.g. не забу́дем мы никогда́ э́ту пое́здку'.
5 Quoted by P. A. Restan in 'The objective case in negative clauses in Russian', *Scandoslavica*, VI, pp. 92–112.

не снимая фуражку (Gor.) *not taking off his cap*	не скинув фуражки (Shol.) *not taking off his cap*
Не понимаю я Соню (Ehr.) *I don't understand Sonya*	Он не видел Сони (Ehr.) *He did not see Sonya*
Школу она среди года не бросит (Ehr.) *She will not leave school in the middle of the year*	Школы Лёна не бросит (Ehr.) *Lena will not leave school*

F. M. Borras and R. F. Christian[1] quite rightly consider that this phenomenon is worthy of close attention and devote several hundred words of explanation and illustration to it. Beginning with the statements that 'there is considerable confusion in modern Russian' and 'the broad distinction between abstract object (genitive) and concrete object (accusative) is a useful working one[2] but does not go far enough', they then give a set of rules and recommendations for the use of the negative-*accusative*. In arriving at these rules, however, they have applied varying criteria, some lexical, some grammatical, some which are both lexical and grammatical and at least one which is stylistic. There could and indeed must be not infrequent overlap of these rules, and this would explain the apparent 'considerable confusion'. Similarly, the statistical tables compiled by P. A. Restan in the article referred to above, in which he summarizes the results of his doctoral dissertation on the subject, include, without discrimination, both grammatical (types of structure) and lexical items (types of words). Here too, therefore, considerable overlap of apparently conflicting criteria is admitted. Restan's statistics are of interest: having examined 2,119 negative sentences covering the

---

1 *Russian Syntax*, pp. 25–27.
2 Cf. Pulkina and Trofimov above.

period from 1918 to 1959, he finds that the accusative is used in 31%, the genitive in 69% of his examples. Furthermore, the occurrence of the negative accusative is higher in dialogue (36.4%) than in narrative (28.1%) and in the newspapers which he examined the occurrence of the negative accusative has increased from 21.7% in 1918–1923 to 38.3% in 1959. These statistics tend to give support to the claim that the negative accusative has a colloquial nuance, but Restan himself thinks that the frequency of the negative accusative in dialogue is only an 'indirect result' of the use of a colloquial style, the 'direct reason' being the structure or form of the clauses in which the negative accusatives occur. In general, Restan elicits no general principle[1] apart from the rather vague one that stylistic factors often determine the choice between negative accusative and negative genitive. B. O. Unbegaun[2] gives a single, precise formulation: 'in negative statements this accusative [= direct object] is replaced by the genitive, provided that the purpose of the negation is, as it usually is, to preclude the action of the sentence and to suppress the transitivity of the verb: я не вижу дороги "I don't see any road" ... If the negation does not preclude the action of the sentence, the verb continues to be transitive and takes the accusative: я не люблю свою тётку "I do not like my aunt".' Although the terminology is different, the meaning of Unbegaun's formulation accords with the formulation given below.[3]

The difference in meaning between the negative accusative and negative genitive is explained most neatly and clearly by W. A. Morison[4]: 'The Negative Accusative is used if the

---

1 No general principle is deduced by Zinaida Uglitsky in her 'Accusative and genitive ... in contemporary Russian', *Slavonic Review*, XXXIV, 83, pp. 377–387.

2 *Russian Grammar*, p. 295.

3 I do not agree, however, that the effect of the negative genitive is 'to suppress the transitivity of the verb'.

4 *Studies in Russian Forms and Uses*, p. 23.

sentence expresses *what was* (*is*, etc.), *not done*, whereas the negative genitive appears if the idea emphasized is *TO what* (*whom*) *was* (etc.) *it not done*. Thus, "I did not READ the book" ("book" in Negative Accusative) *versus* "I did not read the BOOK" ("book" in Negative Genitive).' A variant of the formula *to what was it not done* is 'WHAT *was not x'd?*, *x* representing any verb.'[1] 'Thus, он не купи́л маши́ну means *he didn't BUY the car* (though he may have examined it, hired it or what not) . . . while он не купи́л маши́ны means he didn't buy the CAR (though he may have bought something else).' 'One frequently has the accusative of feminine names because in so many of these cases one *knows* that it is a question of Mariya Fedorovna; what is being pointed out is what doesn't HAPPEN to her.'

The structure of both clauses, он не купи́л маши́ны and он не купи́л маши́ну, is identical: subject+(negated) predicator+complement, but the complements are grammatically differentiated and it is this grammatical differentiation of the complements which, as we have just seen, expresses the difference between what was not done (accusative) and to what was it not done (genitive). The use of brackets will demonstrate graphically this difference in meaning arising from the grammatical differentiation.[2] Thus:

He did not (do what?—) *buy the car*
Он [не]   [купи́л маши́ну]

He did not buy (what?—) *the car.*
Он [не купи́л]   [маши́ны]

---

1 This and further quotations of Dr Morison's words in this paragraph are from letters written to me.
2 Note particularly that the insertion of square brackets in the Russian both here and below is not to be taken as meaning that the clauses differ in structure from one another. It is merely a device to show how the difference in meaning, which can rarely be expressed in English, arises from the differentiation of the complements.

It happens that this differentiation of the complement can sometimes express the 'concrete-abstract' or 'definite-in-definite' contrast which some grammarians consider is the basic function of the negative accusative/negative genitive opposition, but this, as we have seen, is at best a vaguely formulated contrast and is by no means always present.

With не ви́дно and не слы́шно the accusative is very rare, since не ви́дно and не слы́шно are, so to say, 'extensions' of нет—'there is/are not (visible/audible)'—and with нет, as we know, the genitive is obligatory. Similarly, in such colloquial turns as пра́вды не существу́ет the genitive is expected since не существу́ет says little more than нет—*there is no truth*. The following examples, requoted from P. A. Restan's article, contain negated *transitive* verbs taking now the accusative, now the genitive.

Accusative

Шу́рочка [не] [узна́ла ба́бушку]   *Shurochka did not recog-*
(Ehr.)   *nize her grandmother*

Одна́ко, э́ти ко́зни [не] [оста-   *However, these machina-*
нови́ли ира́кский наро́д]   *tions did not stop the*
(*Izv.*)   *Iraki people*

In both instances what might have been expected to happen did not in fact happen. The sentences express, in W. A. Morison's words, 'what did not *happen*,' hence the accusative is used. Similarly in the following sentences or phrases:

[Не] [сняла́ с головы́ плато́к]   *She did not remove the*
(Ehr.)   *kerchief from her head*

Нет, шко́лу она́ среди́ го́да   *No, she will not leave*
не бро́сит   (Ehr.)   *school in the middle of*
(=Нет, она́ [не] [бро́сит   *the year*
шко́лу], etc.)

Не понимаю я Сóню   (Ehr.)   *I don't understand Sonya*
(= Я [не] [понимáю Сóню]

[не] [снимáя фурáжку]   (Gor.)   *not taking off his cap*

Полину Николáевну на   *You didn't see Paulina*
мúтинге не видáли?   (Kat.)   *Nikolaevna at the meet-*
(= [не] [видáли Полину, etc.])   *ing?*

[не] [считáя квартúру и про-   *not counting the board*
довóльствие]   (*Izv.*)   *and lodging*
(a clear contrast with считáя квартúру, etc.)

Genitive
[Платкá] у негó тóже [не на-   *They didn't find the ker-*
шли]   (Zoshch.)   *chief at his place either*
(and there were other
things which they did
not find)

[Шкóлы] Лéна [не брóсит]   *Lena will not leave school*
(Ehr.)
(This sentence tells us what Lena will not give up, whereas
the similar sentence above, with the negative accusative,
tells us what she will not do.)

Он [не вúдел] [Сóни]   (Ehr.)   *He did not see Sonya* (but
he may have seen
others)

[не скúнув] [фурáжки]   (Shol.)   *not taking off his cap*

[Грúшки] онá пoчтú [не вú-   *She hardly saw Grishka*
дела]   (Shol.)   *(but presumably saw*
others)

[не считáя] [чугунá]   (*Izv.*)   *not counting pig-iron* (but
counting other things)

The differentiation of the complement (genitive *versus* accusative) is also found in clauses where there is 'indirect negation' of the verb which has a direct object, i.e. where the verb with complement is a predicator in the form of an infinitive which is itself dependent on a negated verb, adverb, etc. Here too the difference in meaning can be shown by the insertion of brackets.

Genitive

Я э́того письма́ прочёсть не могу́! (Zoshch.)	*I can't read this letter*

(=Я [не могу́ прочёсть] [э́того письма́])

. . . [не могу́ пода́ть] вам [ру-**ки́**] (Leon.)	*I can't offer you my hand*

Accusative

[Нельзя́ же] дире́ктору заво́да [устра́ивать рома́ны] (Ehr.)	*The manager of a factory cannot arrange romances*

. . . неу́чи, [не уме́вшие] иногда́ [подписа́ть да́же и со́бственное и́мя] (*Izv.*)	*. . . ignoramuses who are sometimes incapable of signing their own names*

Similarly when the infinitive predicator is itself negated:

Genitive

. . . не мо́жет не вызыва́ть трево́ги и озабо́ченности (*Izv.*)	*. . . cannot but evoke alarm and concern*

(=[не мо́жет]: что?—[не вызыва́ть]: чего́?—[трево́ги, etc.])

Нельзя́ не отме́тить глубоко́ реалисти́ческих панно́ худо́жника Пу́хова (Ehr.)	*One cannot pass over the deeply realistic panneaux of the artist Pukhov*

(=[нельзя́]: что?—[не отме́тить]: чего́?—[. . . реалисти́ческих панно́])

Accusative

. . . не мо́гут не вызыва́ть та́кже серьёзную трево́гу (*Izv.*)	*. . . cannot but evoke serious alarm too*

(=[не мо́гут]: [не] [вызыва́ть . . . трево́гу])

Нельзя́ не отме́тить ту то́чность и аккура́тность с како́й . . . (*Izv.*)	*One cannot pass over the precision and accuracy with which . . .*

(=[Нельзя́]: [не] [отме́тить ту то́чность, etc.])

It follows logically from the criterion applied here that one would not expect to find the accusative very often, if at all, when a transitive verb has a complement consisting of an 'intensive' negative modifier such as никако́й and substantive. For example, in such a sentence as Я никако́го звонка́ не слы́шал *I heard no bell/I did not hear any bell* the negative modifier underlines, so to speak, the 'non-occurrence' of any object—it serves to emphasize 'to what was it not done'. Conversely, one would not expect to find the genitive in such a sentence as Я не счита́ю э́то обяза́тельным *I do not consider this obligatory*, for the emphasis is not on *what* is not considered obligatory but on what is not *done*. The genitive is not impossible, however, in such structures, for if one says Э́то я счита́ю обяза́тельным, а э́того я не счита́ю обяза́тельным *This I consider obligatory but this I do not consider obligatory*, the emphasis in the second clause is not on what is not *done* but on *what* is not considered obligatory. In this sentence the word-order serves to contrast one 'this' with another 'this'. Such devices of contrast and emphasis work independently of the negative genitive/negative accusative contrast, since they are found in non-negated sentences, but, as the example shows, they can serve the same ends as the negative genitive/negative accusative contrast.

Without considerably more statistical information it is impossible to be categoric with regard to the historical status of the negative genitive/negative accusative contrast, but it seems that it is not yet fully consolidated. This would account for the occasional dubious use of one case or the other. Restan's discovery that the negative accusative in newspapers has almost doubled in proportionate frequency in fifty years (see above) lends weight to the suggestion that usage is not yet entirely settled. It may also be that the occasional unexpected use of one case instead of the other occurs in 'marginal' instances, where the difference between the two meanings is very small or negligible in the particular context. In any event—in spite of what has been said by some grammarians—the negative genitive is *not* the rule and there is not considerable confusion in the use of the negative genitive and negative accusative.

10
Verbs

Conjugation and classification

Although the morphology of the verb is complicated, it is much less irregular than the morphology of the substantive, where the mutual influence of paradigms has been considerable and where some regularization is still going on. The system of personal forms (embracing the present and future tenses) is very simple and presents very few irregularities, but the classification of Russian verbs is complex. The Academy Grammar, for instance, deduces four productive classes, one of them with two sub-classes, and eleven non-productive classes, several of them having two or three sub-classes. M. V. Trofimov[1] sets up seven main classes, some of which have sub-classes which themselves may have sub-divisions. A. Mazon[2] has five main classes, embracing ten sub-classes, which, with further sub-division, produce fifteen groups. B. O. Unbegaun[3] has four classes, embracing nine sub-classes and twenty-five sub-groups. In addition, there are several anomalous verbs, which do not fit into any classification.

The reason for this complexity and variety of classification lies partially in the variety of the stems and partially in the complex relations of the present-future stem and the infinitive-preterite stem. As B. O. Unbegaun says[4], 'any

1 *Handbook of Russian*, Vol. II, pp. 129–139.
2 *Grammaire de la langue russe*, Ch. XI.
3 *Russian Grammar*, Ch. XI.
4 *Op. cit.*, p. 181.

221

system of classification of Russian verbs must aim at establishing groups which present a constant relationship between the two stems'. Hence, according to the criteria adopted, the variation in detail of the classifications of different authors. A detailed classified list of Russian verbs is outside the scope of this small book but we shall examine below the criteria which may be applied in devising a classi-fication.

The person-number markers are -у/-ю for the first person singular, -шь for the second person singular, -м for the first person plural, -те for the second person plural and -т for the third person. The vowels e and и before all of these markers except the first person singular and the third person plural distinguish two conjugations—'first' (with e) and 'second' (with и). In the third person plural the -т is preceded by a vowel which at one and the same time indicates plurality and the type of conjugation. Thus the full endings are:

	First conjugation	*Second conjugation*
1st pers. sing.	-у/-ю	-у/-ю
2nd pers. sing.	-ешь	-ишь
3rd pers. sing.	-ет	-ит
1st pers. pl.	-ем	-им
2nd pers. pl.	-ете	-ите
3rd pers. pl.	-ут/-ют	-ат/-ят

Examining the personal forms of the Russian verb from a phonological point of view, A. K. Albrow[1] establishes five classes of verbs, which may be exemplified by the following paradigms:[2]

1 'The phonology of the personal forms of the verb in Russian', *Archivum Linguisticum*, XIV, 2, pp. 146–156.
2 The order in which the classes are put is not significant.

1	2	3	4	5
m̩ɪˈtu	ˈpr̩ætʃu	l̩ɪˈtʃu	nʌˈʃu	tʃɪˈtaju
m̩ɪˈtoʃ	ˈpr̩ætʃɪʃ	l̩ɪˈtiʃ	ˈnoʂɪʃ	tʃɪˈtajɪʃ
m̩ɪˈtot	ˈpr̩ætʃɪt	l̩ɪˈtit	ˈnoʂɪt	tʃɪˈtajɪt
m̩ɪˈtom	ˈpr̩ætʃɪm	l̩ɪˈtim	ˈnoʂɪm	tʃɪˈtajɪm
m̩ɪˈtöti	ˈpr̩ætʃɪti	l̩ɪˈtiti	ˈnoʂɪt̩	tʃɪˈtajɪti
m̩ɪˌtut	ˈpr̩ætʃut	l̩ɪˈtat	ˈnoʂət	tʃɪˈtajut

(Infinitive:

   m̩ɪˈʂti   ˈpr̩atət̩   l̩ɪˈtet̩   nʌˈʂit̩   tʃɪˈtat̩)

Classes 3 and 4 are distinguished by the occurrence of stress-shift in Class 4 but not in Class 3. Stress-shift in second conjugation verbs, of which Classes 3 and 4 are examples, cannot be predicted and therefore it is necessary to take stress-shift into account in such a phonological classification. In Class 2 (first conjugation) stress-shift *is* predictable, the rule being that verbs with stress on the last syllable of the first person singular have stress on the preceding syllable in all the other forms: p̩ɪˈʃu, ˈp̩ɪʃtʃ, ˈp̩ɪʃɪt, etc. (infinitive p̩ɪˈsat̩). Thus the occurrence of stress-shift in verbs of this type does not lead to the setting up of two phonologically distinct classes here.

From a purely orthographical stand-point, stress would not, of course, be taken into account, so that Albrow's Classes 3 and 4 would be one class, embracing all second conjugation verbs, including those with, orthographically, a vowel-letter before -ю, -ишь, etc. Again from an orthographical stand-point, Albrow's Class 2 would probably have to be divided into two classes to account for such verbs as берегу́, бережёшь . . . берегу́т. Thus one would also have five classes of verbs in a classification which is based on the orthography and starts from the personal forms of the verb.

Consideration of the infinitive-preterite group of forms now leads to further sub-divisions. Thus, while the majority of second conjugation verbs have an infinitive with the stem-vowel, и, some have an infinitive with the stem-vowel a or я (e.g. кричáть, стоя́ть) and some have an infinitive with the stem-vowel е (e.g. ви́деть).

The classification of first conjugation verbs is much more complicated, because of the intricate relationships of the present-future stems and the infinitive-preterite stems. A large (and productive) class of verbs is that with a stem-vowel a/я or e in both present-future and infinitive-preterite. This class with constant stem-vowel falls then into two sub-classes: (a) читáю–читáть, стреля́ю–стреля́ть, etc., etc., and (b) краснéю–краснéть, etc. Verbs with the stem-vowel у in the present-future, such as образу́ю, have a two-fold stem element in the infinitive—образ-ов-а-ть—and thus comprise a second class, which is also productive. Verbs such as кую́–ковáть, though they are orthographically similar to the образу́ю–образовáть class, form a separate class(see below).

No other first conjugation classes have stem-vowels in the present-future group of forms. Such verbs as those typified by мёрзну on the one hand and сту́кну on the other hand have a stem-consonant н in the present-future group of forms. The сту́кну-type has a stem-element ну in the infinitive-preterite group (сту́кнуть, сту́кнул) whereas the мёрзну-type has this stem-element only in some of the infinitive-preterite forms (infinitive мёрзнуть but past tense мёрз). There are therefore two classes of verbs here.

No other verbs have consonantal stem-elements, either in the present-future or in the infinitive-preterite. Such verbs as are typified by несу́, сосу́, рву, зову́, колю́, бью, пойму́, начну́, жму, etc., have neither stem-vowel nor stem-consonant: the root alone is the stem. One class has no stem-element in the infinitive-preterite: несу́–нести́. Another class has the stem-vowel a in the infinitive-preterite: сосу́–сосáть, рву–рвать, зову́–звать. If alternances within the root are to be admitted as criteria for classification purposes, then зову́–зва́ть is a member of a sub-class which also includes беру́–бра́ть, гоню́–гна́ть, деру́–дра́ть and стелю́–стла́ть. Other small classes comprise the five verbs with a stem vowel o in the infinitive-preterite: колю́–коло́ть, полю́–поло́ть, борю́сь–боро́ться and мелю́–моло́ть; the verbs with a stem-vowel e in the infinitive but not in the preterite: тру–тере́ть–тёр, умру́–умере́ть–у́мер, запру́–запере́ть–за́пер, простру́–простере́ть–простёр, etc. The verbs with a present-future root ending in a nasal consonant which does not appear in the infinitive-preterite may be considered to be members of various classes or members of one class with sub-classes. They include начну́–нача́ть, зачну́–зача́ть, жму–жать, жну–жать, мну–мять, де́ну–деть, ста́ну–стать, кляну́–клясть, распну́–распя́ть, сты́ну–сты́ть. A separate class comprises the verbs with future in -йму (after vowels) or -ниму (after consonants) but infinitive in -нять (пойму́–нопя́ть, сниму́–снять) and the verb приму́–приня́ть. A very small class comprises живу́–жить, плыву́–плыть and the archaic verb слыву́–слыть. Finally, in this set of first conjugation classes, there is the small class ушибу́–ушибёшь–ушиби́ть, etc., and the one-member class реву́–ревёшь–реве́ть. The latter might be included in the сосу́–соса́ть class as a member which has an anomalous stem-vowel in the infinitive-preterite group.

A quite distinct class of first conjugation verbs having no stem-element in the present-future is exemplified by берегу́—бережёшь ... берегу́т. The infinitive-preterite has no stem either, and the final consonant of the root is not present in the infinitive, though it is in the preterite: бере́чь–берёг. This class includes all verbs with the infinitive ending in -чь, some of them having root-internal modifications (ля́гу–лечь, толку́–толо́чь, жгу–жечь), and, as an anomalous member or appendage, лгу–лжёшь ... лгут–лгать.

A larger class comprises the sixty or seventy verbs which
8+

have a stem-vowel a in the infinitive-preterite group, no stem-element in the present-future and an alternation of the root-final consonant between present-future and infinitive-preterite. Examples are пишу́–писа́ть, пла́чу–пла́кать, пря́чу–пря́тать, вяжу́–вяза́ть, сы́плю–сы́пать. In this class the infinitive-preterite form of the root is the basic form, from which the present-future root is derived according to the set of rules for those consonant alternations which are not phonetically conditioned.[1]

Another set of classes comprises verbs which, from an orthographical standpoint, have no stem-element in the present-future, the root of which ends in a vowel-letter. They are apportioned to classes firstly according to the presence or absence of a stem-element in the infinitive-preterite. Thus, those classes with a stem-element in the infinitive-preterite include даю́–дава́ть, etc., кую́–кова́ть, etc., ла́ю–ла́ять, смею́сь–смея́ться, and those without a stem-element in the infinitive-preterite include the class мо́ю–мыть, кро́ю–крыть, во́ю–выть, ро́ю–рыть, но́ю–ныть and the one-member class ду́ю–ду́ть. The verbs пою́–петь and гнию́–гнить also form one-member classes and the five verbs бью–бить, вью–вить, лью–лить, пью–пить, шью–шить form another class.

A phonologically based classification results in a smaller

1 The 'non-automatic' (i.e. not phonetically conditioned) consonantal alternations affect various parts of speech. With the basic consonant or consonants (i.e. the one(s) from which the other alternating member(s) can be known) in the left-hand column, they are, orthographically:

п	—	пл	з	—	ж
б	—	бл	ст	—	щ
м	—	мл	ск	—	щ
ф	—	фл	к	—	ч
в	—	вл	г	—	ж
т	—	ч ог щ	х	—	ш
д	—	ж ог жд	ц	—	ч
с	—	ш	к	—	ц

The last two do not occur in the verb.

set of classes, since all first conjugation verbs which do not have a stem-element in the present-future have as stem the root and this root ends in /j/ or some other consonant. The verbs then subdivide firstly according to the phonological features deducible from the paradigms at the beginning of this section and then according to the relationship between present-future and infinitive-preterite. A teaching method based on the phonological analysis but devised so that the verbs are presented orthographically has the advantage that the apparently bewildering variety of present-future stems is much simplified.

As far as *productivity* of verbal classes is concerned, the situation is much more straightforward. The only productive classes are the second conjugation class with infinitive in -ить and the following first conjugation classes: those with the stem-vowel a/я or e in both present-future and infinitive-preterite (classes чита́ю–чита́ть, красне́ю–красне́ть), those with the suffix (stem-element) н(у) in both present-future and infinitive-preterite (class сту́кну–сту́кнуть–сту́кнул) and those with the alternating stem-elements у/ова (об-разу́ю–образова́ть). In Chapter 5, 'Sources of Words I', it was pointed out that these classes are not equally productive.

Aspect

The productive processes of deriving aspectual forms are prefixation and suffixation. Some prefixes are no longer productive in this connection (see Chapter 5). The suffix -ну- produces perfective verbs and these are usually semelfactive, i.e. verbs of 'instantaneous action', such as сту́кнуть *to give a knock*, ду́нуть *to give a puff*, etc. The suffix -ыва-/-ива- produces imperfective verbs, such as спи́сывать *to copy*, осма́тривать *to inspect*, etc. Although this suffix originally produced iterative verbs, i.e. imperfective verbs with the special meaning of 'repeated action', it is now used almost exclusively to produce plain imperfectives. It is only in conjunction with the prefix по- that the suffix -ыва-/-ива- can produce iterative verbs and then the iterative verb so produced is not correlated with a perfective verb—it is not a member of an imperfective-perfective pair.[1] Examples of such iteratives are:

Отéц с удивлéнием посмáтривал на негó (Klen.)	*Father kept glancing at him in surprise*
Улыбáлся и Тéтькин, помáргивая испýганно (A. N. Tol.)	*Tetkin too was smiling and blinking timidly at the same time*
Седóй большевѝк Орлóв — тот задóрно махáл рукáми, поплёвывая под нóги казакóв (Shol.)	*The grey-haired bolshevik Orlov—he waved his arms mockingly and kept spitting at the cossacks' feet*

Not all such unpaired imperfectives are iterative in meaning:

Тут и партѝйными взыскáниями попáхивает (Arb.)	*It smacks a bit of a reprimand from the party*

Moreover, some verbs which do have iterative meaning can also function as plain imperfectives. Otherwise, verbs with the suffix -ыва-/-ива- are plain imperfectives which may appear in contexts implying repeated action. The greatly diminished and still diminishing iterative meaning of the suffix -ыва-/-ива- is part of the general process, which

1 Some verbs suffixed with -ыва-/-ива- and prefixed with при-, such as приплясывать *to execute a few dance-steps* or прихрáмывать *to limp slightly* (as one walks along), are sometimes called 'iteratives'. In fact they are not iteratives: they denote the performance of an action which necessitates repeated movements (of the limbs, etc.) but *not*, of themselves, repeated performances of the same action. Similarly, прихлёбывать means *to sip*, 'to drink by taking repeated sips' and not 'to sip on different occasions'.

has been going on for centuries, towards the elimination of sub-aspectual categories (*Aktionsarten*, спо́собы де́йствия, see below).

Though the great majority of verbs are *either* imperfective *or* perfective, a few are bi-aspectual—they can function as imperfectives or perfectives. These include ра́нить *to wound*, веле́ть *to order*, роди́ть *to give birth*, жени́ть(ся) *to marry*, казни́ть *to execute*, крести́ть *to baptize*, and a few others. Some of these, however, have correlated verbs which are purely imperfective—рожда́ть *to give birth*, or purely perfective—пожени́ть(ся) *to marry*. Many verbs ending in -овать are bi-aspectual but here too the language slowly eradicates the anomaly by suffixation or prefixation. Thus, while организова́ть *to organize*, and образова́ть *to form*, are bi-aspectual, the correlated verbs организо́вывать and образо́вывать are imperfective only, and while телеграфи́ровать and телефони́ровать are bi-aspectual, протелеграфи́ровать and протелефони́ровать are perfective only.

An examination of Russian might lead one to suppose that there were several, or indeed many aspects. There are, for instance, semelfactive verbs, such as сту́кнуть *to knock (once)*, inceptive verbs, such as застуча́ть *to begin knocking*, attenuative verbs, such as постуча́ть *to knock (a little)*, terminative verbs, such as дописа́ть *to write to the end*, 'quantitative' verbs, such as начита́ться *to have one's fill of reading*, inchoative verbs (describing a change in state), such as со́хнуть *to be in process of becoming dry*, resultatives, such as вы́сохнуть *to dry up*, and so on.[1] A deeper examination, however, reveals first that some of these apparent 'aspects', are lexical classes and secondly that all of them may be put into one or the other of two categories,

1 The number of such 'aspects' will vary according to the criteria adopted. See S. Živković, 'Podjela glagola po vidu (aspektu)', *Jezik*, 1959–60, no. 2, 41–46.

according to the presence or absence of a single feature. In other words, there are only two aspects, known in English as 'perfective' or 'imperfective' and in Russian as совершённый and несовершённый, and all the apparently different 'aspects' are examples of one or the other aspect: they are 'sub-aspects' or 'modes of action' (Russian: спóсобы дéйствия, German: *Aktionsarten*).

What perfective verbs have in common is that they present the action as delimited, while imperfective verbs do not present the action as delimited. The perfective notion may be represented diagrammatically thus:

Another way of putting it is to say that perfective verbs present the action as an undifferentiated whole or an indivisible unit.[1] This may be represented diagrammatically thus:

◯

This means that the perfective presents the action as having not merely a definite end but a definite beginning and a definite end: the action is presented as a delimited unit. Other meanings within the perfective arise from the lexical content of the verbs themselves or are expressions of the concepts of various *Aktionsarten*. Variations in the diagrams above will convey some of these sub-aspectual meanings of the perfective. Thus

---

1 Cf. Yu. S. Maslov, Роль так называемой перфективации . . . p. 38. See also H. C. Sørensen, *Aspect et temps en slave*, esp. pp. 109–121.

постучáть—action restricted to a small space of time—

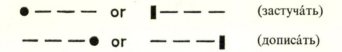

стýкнуть—a single act occupying no more than an instant—may be represented by the circle reduced to its smallest dimension, a dot •, or by the two vertical bars brought very close together ⊢⊣ or even superimposed │.

застучáть—inceptive, the delimited act of beginning an action, but implying that the action goes on thereafter, and

дописáть—terminative, the delimited act of concluding an action, but implying that the action went on for some time beforehand, are both special instances of reduction to the smallest dimensions—

● — — — or ▌— — —	(застучáть)
— — —● or — — —▐	(дописáть)

написáть—a 'plain' perfective, devoid of any of the above meanings, but an action that had a beginning and an end and occupied some unspecified extent of time:

⊢⊣   or   ⭕

From what has been said it is evident that aspect—the way in which the action is presented—has something to do with time. It is not concerned, however, with location in time, for that is the concern of tense, but with progress in time.

Since the imperfective does not present the action as delimited it can present the action as going on, with no specific limits at either end. This, the expression of duration, may be thought of as the basic function of the imperfective but it is not the only function of the imperfective and it is, moreover, a *derived* function—one which follows logically from the fact that the imperfective does not present the action as delimited. The other functions of the imperfective also follow logically from its fundamental meaning.

The imperfective may express the idea of the action in general. This is to say that attention is concentrated on the 'business' in hand, the process that the verb denotes:

Куха́рка спра́шивает, когда́ у́жин подава́ть бу́дем? (Arb.)	*Cook is asking when are we going to be serving supper?*
Недо́лго собира́лась (Arb.)	*She wasn't long in getting ready*
. . . у меня́ не хва́тит де́нег, придётся иска́ть сберка́ссу и брать с аккредити́ва (Klen.)	*I shall not have enough money, so I shall have to look for a savings bank and make use of my letter of credit*
Ты опя́ть пил? (Arb.)	*Have you been drinking again?*
. . . я стреми́лся сде́лать из вас хоро́ших люде́й. Вы, в свою́ о́чередь, дава́ли смысл мо-е́й жи́зни. Я молоде́л с ва́ми (Paust.)	*I have tried to make good people of you. You, in your turn, have given meaning to my life. I have grown young with you*
Но лю́ди стреми́лись к звёз-дам и хоте́ли ве́рить. Гал-лиле́й обраща́л к не́бу свой телеско́п. Ке́плер вычисля́л зако́ны движе́ния плане́т	*But people strove towards the stars and wanted to believe. Galileo turned his telescope to the sky. Kepler calculated the*

| Ломоно́сов открыва́л ат-мосфе́ру на Вене́ре (*Sov. Sojuz*) | *laws of motion of the planets. Lomonosov discovered an atmosphere on Venus* |

The use of the perfective aspect in the last three sentences of this example would simply have meant the presentation of three steps in the history of astronomy, carried out in the sequences given, without particular attention to the processes themselves. It is noteworthy that, whereas a series of perfectives necessarily means that the acts were carried out in the sequence given, a series of imperfectives does not necessarily mean that the actions were performed in that sequence:

| Пока́ ма́ма открыва́ла и за-крыва́ла две́рцы [шка́фа], кла́ла на по́лки бельё, сни-ма́ла и ве́шала пла́тье, он был свой, до́брый шкаф (Klen.) | *As long as mother was opening and closing the [cupboard] doors, putting linen on the shelves, taking down and hanging up clothes, it was our own dear cupboard* |

In the last example the imperfectives express repeated or habitual action. We have already noted above that, with very few exceptions, the iterative function derives from the context and is simply immanent in the imperfective aspect:

| . . . два́жды в ме́сяц, по́сле по-лу́чки, он выпива́л . . . «Ма́-ленькая» выпива́лась в пив-но́й и́ли в столо́вой (Klen.) | *Twice a month, after he had received his wage-packet, he would have a drink . . . The 'little drop' was drunk in a pub or an eating-house* |

Here the adverbial phrase of time elicits the iterative

8*

function of the imperfective, whereas in the following example the iterative function becomes clear from the general context:

. . . колокола́ выта́скивались со зво́нниц, повиса́ли над землёй, тогда́ их броса́ли вниз (Piln.)	. . . *the bells were pulled out of the bell-towers, they hung over the earth and then they were cast down*

Earlier in the same sentence from which this example is taken the whole process is summed up in a perfective iterative:

. . . в 1928-ом году́ со мно́гих церкве́й колокола́ поснима́ли для тре́ста Рудметаллто́рг	. . . *in* 1928 *the bells were removed from many churches for the Rudmetalltorg combine*

Such perfective iteratives, derived by prefixation of an already prefixed imperfective (по-снима́ть, по-выта́лкивать *to push out one after another*), are regarded by grammarians as colloquial. In the following example of iterative function the sequence of imperfectives *is* the sequence in which the actions were carried out:

В реда́кцию Севастья́нов приходи́л, что́бы сдать материа́л и получи́ть зада́ние от Акопья́на. На́скоро просма́тривал газе́ты, выпива́л стака́н ча́я и уходи́л (Pan.)	*Sevastyanov would come to the editorial office to hand in his copy and get an assignment from Akopyan. He would glance through the papers, drink a glass of tea and leave*

The fact that iterative function usually derives from the context is underlined by the use of the *perfective* in contexts which imply iteration: В обы́чной шко́ле дал уро́ки и пошёл домо́й (*Kom. Pr.*) *In an ordinary school, once you have given your lessons you can go home.* Here, in effect, the past perfective is devoid of temporal function. The future perfective is used in a similar way and this will be dealt with below.

The imperfective may also present the action as a state: И вдруг Ната́ша остыва́ла к бале́ту и увлека́лась симфони́ческой му́зыкой (Klen.) *And suddenly Natasha was indifferent to ballet and was carried away by symphony music;* or it may present the action as attempted but not brought to a successful conclusion: Меня́ расстре́ливали по прика́зу Хо́йзингера (*Izv.*) *I was shot on Heusinger's orders.* The perfective would be impossible here, because расстреля́ли would mean 'successfully carried out execution by shooting' and the subject is obviously still alive. The negated imperfective usually means that in general the action is not performed:

Сейча́с об э́том расска́зываю, а тогда́ бы рассказа́ть не могла́. Никому́ и не расска́зывала (Klen.)	*I am talking about it now but at that time I could not have talked about it. And I did not talk about it to anybody*

This generalized negation of the action is often extended to single, specific occasions: А пасья́нсы я ещё не раскла́дывал (Arb.) *But I haven't laid out my patience-hand yet.*

The contrasting functions of the imperfective and perfective are brought out in the following examples. In the first set of examples the contrast is between action in general, the process itself (imperfective) and the single, specific act (perfective):

На́до сади́ться, все уже́ се́ли; собира́юсь то́же сесть, но	*I ought to be taking my place; everybody has*

дверь вагóна ужé захлóпы-
вается (Klen.)

*already taken his place;
I too am preparing to
take my place, but the
carriage door is
slammed shut*

. . . а я роди́лся и воспи́тывал-
ся здесь, в Петербу́рге
(Arb.)

*. . . and I was born and
brought up here, in St
Petersburg*

Лари́са: А кто написа́л [пись-
мó] . . . не зна́ешь?—*Ва́ля:*
Кто писа́л не зна́ю, а я ду-
ра́к чита́ю (Arb.)

*Larissa: And who wrote
[the letter] . . . do you
know? . . . —Valya:
Who wrote it, I don't
know, but I, like a fool,
am reading it* ;

In this last example the contrast between (the business of)
writing and (the business of) reading makes the use of the
imperfective necessary. In the next set of examples the contrast is between iteration, a series of acts, or habitual
action (imperfective), and a single, specific act (perfective):

Ужé в пéрвый мéсяц он зара-
бóтал вдвóе прóтив тогó,
что зараба́тывал в отделé-
нии (Pan.)

*In the first month alone he
earned twice what he
had been earning in the
department*

Не скрóмничай — мать не за-
быва́л, и мать тебя́ не за-
бы́ла (Klen.)

*Don't be modest—you
used to remember your
mother, and your
mother has remembered
you*

Ма́ма открыва́ла óкна нака-
ну́не ма́йских пра́здников.
Вну́тренние ра́мы вынима́-
лись, и я относи́л их на чер-

*Mother used to open the
windows just before the
May holidays. The in-
ner frames were taken*

да́к. В э́том году́ не откры́ла (Klen.)	*out and I would take them up to the loft. This year she did not open them*
Мы прошли́ че́рез алле́ю сме́ха и превраща́лись то в кривоно́гих коро́тышек, то в длинноше́их, с кро́хотными голо́вками жира́фов (Klen.)	*We went through the hall of mirrors and turned now into bowlegged midgets, now into long-necked giraffes with minute heads*

Here the passage through the hall of mirrors is presented as a single, delimited act—therefore perfective—whereas their different transformations while in the hall of mirrors are presented as a non-delimited series of acts—therefore imperfective. The imperfective acts, as it were, take place within the perfective act:

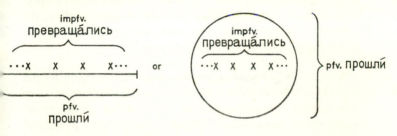

Исчеза́ли да́же при́мусы, и тогда́ все говори́ли, что э́то сын бы́вшей хозя́йки укра́л (Rom.)	*Even the primus stoves disappeared/kept disappearing and then everybody said it was the son of the former owner [of the house] who had stolen them.*

Here again the imperfectives исчеза́ли and говори́ли express the non-delimited series of acts, while the perfective

укра́л expresses the single, delimited act of stealing on each occasion, for what they said on each occasion was: Это сын . . . укра́л.
Hence:

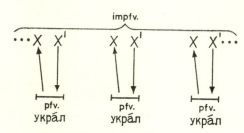

(where ХХХ = исчеза́ли
and X'XX' = говори́ли)

The perfective is 'kinetic' or narrative—each perfective verb in a passage moves the action forward a step. The imperfective, in its frequent concentration on the process or state as such, is often 'static' or descriptive and in this respect it may, so to speak, hold up the flow of the narrative. An extended illustration of this contrast is provided by the following passage from A. N. Tolstoy:

У́тром 25 февраля́ Зна́менская пло́щадь была́ полна́ войска́ми и поли́цией. Пе́ред Се́верной гости́ницей сто-я́ли ко́нные полице́йские на золоти́стых, тонконо́гих танцу́ющих лоша́дках. Пе́шие полице́йские, в чёрных шине́лях, расположи́лись вокру́г па́мятника Алекса́ндру III и — ку́чками по пло́щади. У вокза́ла стоя́ли казаки́ в зало́мленных папа́хах, с торока́ми се́на, борода́тые и[1]

1 On the morning of the twenty-fifth of February Znamensky Square was full of troops and police. In front of the Hotel Severny were mounted policemen on slender-legged little horses, prancing and gleaming like gold. The unmounted policemen, in their black great-coats, were drawn up around the monument to Alexander III or were distributed in groups about the square. By the station were the cossacks—bearded, in high spirits, their fur hats at a rakish angle. They had bundles of hay strapped to the back of their saddles. In the direction of

весёлые. Со стороны́ Не́вского видне́лись гря́зно-се́рые шине́ли па́вловцев.

Ива́н Ильи́ч с чемода́нчиком в руке́ взобра́лся на ка́менный вы́ступ вокза́льного въе́зда, отсю́да хорошо́ была́ видна́ вся пло́щадь.

Посреди́ её на крова́во-кра́сной глы́бе грани́та, на огро́мном коне́, опусти́вшем от гру́за седока́ бро́нзовую го́лову, сиде́л, тяжёлый, как земна́я тя́га, импера́тор — угрю́мые пле́чи его́ и кру́гленькая ша́почка бы́ли покры́ты сне́гом. К его́ подно́жию на пло́щади напира́ли со стороны́ пяти́ у́лиц то́лпы наро́да с кри́ками, сви́стом и ру́ганью.

Так же, как и вчера́ на мосту́, солда́ты, в осо́бенности казаки́, попа́рно ша́гом подъезжа́вшие к напира́ющему со свех сторо́н наро́ду, перебра́нивались и зубоска́лили. В ку́чках городовы́х, ро́слых и хму́рых люде́й, бы́ло молча́ние и я́вная нереши́тельность. Ива́н Ильи́ч хорошо́ знал э́ту трево́гу в ожида́нии прика́за к бо́ю — враг уже́ на плеча́х, всем я́сно, что́ ну́жно де́лать, но с прика́зом ме́длят, и мину́ты тя́нутся мучи́тельно. Вдруг

the Nevsky Prospekt could be seen the dirty-grey coats of the Pavlovsky Regiment.

Ivan Ilyich, with his attaché-case in his hand, climbed up on to the jutting stone ledge of the station entrance, from where he had a good view of the entire square.

On a blood-red block of granite in the middle of the square, mounted on an enormous horse, whose bronze head sagged from the weight of its rider, sat the emperor, heavy as the pull of the earth—his despondent shoulders and his little round cap were covered in snow. On the square, crowds of people, shouting, whistling and swearing, pressed forward from the five streets towards his pedestal.

Just as on the day before on the bridge, the soldiers, in particular the cossacks, who ambled up to the crowd pressing forward from all sides, were exchanging abuse with the people and jeering at them. The groups of tall, sullen policemen stood silent, obviously undecided. Ivan Ilyich was very familiar with this feeling of anxiety which you have when waiting for the order to give battle—the enemy is already on you, everybody can see what has to be done, but the order is slow in coming and the minutes drag agonizingly by. Suddenly the station door

звя́кнула вокза́льная дверь, и появи́лся на ле́стнице
бле́дный жанда́рмский офице́р с полко́вничьими пого́-
нами, в коро́ткой шине́ли. Вы́тянувшись, он огляну́л
пло́щадь — све́тлые глаза́ его скользну́ли по лицу́ Ива́на
Ильича́. Легко́ сбежа́в вниз ме́жду расступи́вшихся ка-
зако́в, он стал говори́ть что́-то есау́лу, подня́в к нему́
боро́дку. Есау́л с криво́й усме́шкой слу́шал его́, разва-
ля́сь в седле́. Полко́вник ки́внул в сто́рону Ста́рого
Не́вского и пошёл че́рез пло́щадь по сне́гу подпры́ги-
вающей похо́дкой. К нему́ подбежа́л при́став, ту́го пере-
поя́санный по огро́мному животу́, рука́ у него́ трясла́сь
под козырько́м. А со стороны́ Ста́рого Не́вского увели́-
чивались кри́ки подходи́вшей толпы́, и, наконе́ц, ста́ло
различи́мо пе́ние. Ива́на Ильича́ кто́-то кре́пко схвати́л
за рука́в, ря́дом с ним вскара́бкался возбуждённый чело-
ве́к, без ша́пки, с багро́вой сса́диной че́рез гря́зное лицо́.

One senses, in reading such passages as this, the greater
'intensity' of the perfective, as compared with the imperfective. The perfective is like a sharp, brilliant flash of light,
the imperfective like a steady, diffuse glow.

Among finite verb forms it is the future perfective where
the aspect system attains, as it were, its highest development.
The normal temporal function of the future perfective is of

clanged and a pale-faced officer of gendarmes with colonel's insignia on
his shoulder-straps and wearing a short great-coat appeared on the
steps. Drawing himself up, he looked round the square—his bright eyes
slid over Ivan Ilyich's face. He ran lightly down between the cossacks,
who parted to make way for him, and began to say something to the
cossack-captain, his little beard upturned towards the latter's face.
Slouched in his saddle, the captain listened to him with a wry sneer on
his face. The colonel nodded towards Old Nevsky Prospekt and with a
springy step went across the snow-covered square. A police-inspector
with his belt stretched tight across his fat belly ran up to him, his hand
quivering at the salute. Meanwhile from the direction of Old Nevsky
Prospekt the shouts of the approaching crowd were becoming louder
and finally the sound of singing could be distinguished. Somebody took
a firm hold on Ivan Ilyich's sleeve and an excited man, hatless, with a
blood-red abrasion across his dirty face, scrambled up beside him.

course the presentation as delimited of an action taking place
in the future. This function includes that of 'immediate
realization', as in я вам скажу *I'll tell you* (*now*), попрошу
вас сделать это для меня *I would* ('*I will*') *ask you to do
that for me.* In some functions, however, the future perfective is devoid of future meaning. In the following examples
the future perfective acts as a 'generalized present', i.e. it
expresses not something which is actually occurring at the
moment of speaking but something which is in general so.
What is expressed here by the future perfective is simply a
delimited action. Thus:

Ты идёшь мимо, и ни один не крикнет тебе «Мама!» (Arb.)	*You go past and not one of them calls out/will call out 'Mummy' to you*
Герой спектакля — иногда тот, который высидит в зале до конца (Krok.)	*The hero of a play is sometimes the person who sits/can sit it out in the auditorium to the end*
Загрустил, затосковал человек, сидит дома, раз в году пройдёт по деревне (Kom. Pr.)	*The man has become sad and melancholy, he sits at home and once a year he walks/will walk through the village*
Пока он [огурец] доберётся до Верхней Масловки, он уже не пахнет и не хрустит (Klen.)	*By the time it [the gherkin] gets to Verkhnyaya Maslovka it is no longer crisp and aromatic*
Мама даст рубль — хватает на два билета (Klen.)	*Mother gives me a ruble and that is enough for two tickets*
Я, когда в консультацию приду, всегда радуюсь (Arb.)	*Whenever I come to see the doctor I always feel glad*

Clearly, this 'generalized present' function of the future perfective is in fact an iterative function deriving from the context. It is probably from this function that the iterative function of the future perfective in the context of verbs in the *past* tense has arisen;

С четырёх лет он пас гусей. Гуси уйду́т в рожь, в ярово́е, а Сте́нка сто́я в по́ле крича́л: Ба́бушка, гу́си во ржи! (Zur.)

From the age of four he tended the geese. The geese would go off into the rye, the spring-sown crop, and Stenka, standing in the field, would shout: 'Grannie, the geese are in the rye!'

. . . ру́сский язы́к . . . подчиня́л свои́м со́бственным зако́нам и тре́бованиям любо́е иноязы́чное сло́во, како́е ни войдёт в его́ орби́ту (Chuk.)

. . . the Russian language . . . has subjected to its own laws and requirements any foreign word which has come into its orbit

Быва́ло, зайдёт со́лнце, про-льются в небеса́х о́гненные ре́ки и сгоря́т, ниспадёт на ба́рхатную зе́лень са́да зо-лоти́сто-кра́сный пе́пел (Gor.)

The sun would set, rivers of fire would be spilled across the heavens and burn out, a golden red ash would descend upon the velvet greenery of the garden

The iterative function of the future perfective is possible only in the context of other verbs, either in the same sentence or in other, preceding sentences, which specify the time to which the future perfective refers. The context which specifies the time may be quite extensive. For instance, the preceding hundred or more words make it clear that in the following sentence from A. Klenov the future perfectives have the function of generalized (iterative) present:

С пе́рвым зво́ном кура́нтов карау́льные взойду́т на грани́тные ступе́ни Мавзоле́я, вста́нут лицо́м к лицу́ пе́ред двумя́ часовы́ми, стоя́вшими на почётном посту́ до них; дво́е сде́лают шаг в сто́рону, дво́е — шаг вперёд; пе́рвые пойду́т на вы́ход; вторы́е разверну́тся и засты́нут у вхо́да в Мавзоле́й — и всё э́то произойдёт так сла́женно и бы́стро, что лю́ди, стоя́щие у барье́ра, не успе́ют вздохну́ть . . .

At the first sound from the chimes the sentries come up on to the granite steps of the Mausoleum, stand face to face in front of the two sentries who have been occupying the post of honour before them; two of them take a pace to the side, two of them —a pace forward; the first go to the exit, the second turn outwards and stand immobile at the entrance to the Mausoleum—and all this happens so smoothly and swiftly that the people standing at the barrier do not have time to draw breath . . . .

A quasi-iterative function is found when the future perfective retains its temporal meaning, as in Исто́рия ещё не раз вернётся к э́тому дню (*Sov. Sojuz*) *History will return again and again to this day*. Here the single event stands for several like events, or a whole series is 'reduced to unity'.

It is probably from the expression of immediate realization (see above) by the future perfective that there arises the expression of 'possibility' or 'feasibility':

Не попро́бовать ли и нам, а? *What about our having a*

Вдруг это развлечёт нас (Arb.)	go too? You never know —it might amuse us
Замуж хочу выйти. А сейчас разве выйдешь замуж без денег? (*Krok.*)	I want to get married. But can you really get married these days without money?

When negated, the future perfective in this function expresses the impossibility of realization:

Ой ... совсем вас не пойму (Arb.)	Oh ... I just cannot understand you
Мамочка, я что-то не пойму: кто из них жена, а кто — любовница? (*Krok.*)	Mummy, there's something I can't understand: which of them is the wife and which is the mistress?
И не узнаешь вас, Яша! (Chekh.)	Why, I wouldn't have recognized you, Yasha!
Они разговорились. Женщины всегда общий язык найдут (B. Rakhmanin)	They fell into conversation. Women will/can always find a common language

Although aspect is a verbal category it has penetrated the realm of the substantive. Deverbal substantives may retain a nuance of the aspect of the verb from which they have been derived. This is particularly evident in substantives derived by means of the suffix -ние from different aspects of the same verb: решение *decision, solution*, решание *solving;* излечение *cure*, лечение *treatment;* произнесение *pronunciation* (act of pronouncing), произношение *pronunciation* (system of or manner of); соотнесение *correlation* (act of correlating), соотношение *(inter)relationship*, *correlation* (state of being correlated). In Chapter 4 it was decided to regard such pairs as lexically separate items rather than as grammatically differentiated forms of one and the same lexical item.

Gerunds and participles

The gerunds, designated 'present' and 'past' in most popular grammars, do not in fact have the grammatical category of tense. That which is called the 'present gerund' (e.g. читая) is in fact an imperfective gerund and may be associated with a verb in any tense. Similarly, that which is called the 'past gerund' (e.g. прочитав) is in fact a perfective gerund and may also be associated with a verb in any tense.

Usually the imperfective gerund describes an action concomitant with that of the associated finite verb but it may also express an action preceding the main one: Вставая на рассвете, она спускалась в кухню и вместе с кухаркой готовила закуску к чаю[1] (Gor.) *Rising at dawn, she would go down into the kitchen and, together with the cook, prepare a light breakfast.* Since the action is repeated, the author has preferred the imperfective to the perfective gerund. The same consideration leads to the use of the imperfective gerund in the example quoted by W. A. Morison:[2] Он иногда исчезал на месяцы и, возвращаясь, бывал встречаем опять той же улыбкой. *Sometimes he would disappear for months at a time and, on returning, would be met by the same smile.*

The perfective gerund usually describes an action prior to that of the associated finite verb. This is not because the perfective gerund then has the grammatical category of tense ('perfect' or 'pluperfect') but simply because one of the derived functions of the perfective aspect is to express 'action

---

1 Example quoted by Galkina-Fedoruk, etc., *op. cit.*, p. 366.

2 *Studies in Russian Forms and Uses: The Present Gerund and Active Participle*, p. 43.

already performed'. The fact that tense is not present in the perfective gerund is underlined by its occasional use to describe an action that does *not* precede that of the associated finite verb: Алексéй обратился к Баймáновой, предложив ей продáть емý дом (Gor.) *Alexei approached Baimanova with the proposal that she sell him her house;* Тяжёлая весть облетáла полки, нагнáв на всех уныние (Fur.) *The sad news flew round the regiments and threw everyone into despondency.*[1] In such a sentence as Кóнчив разносить бýлки, я ложился спать (Gor.) *When I had finished delivering the buns, I would go to bed*[2] the perfective gerund does not have iterative meaning of itself: it remains perfective and implies 'I had already finished, etc., when I went to bed (and I went to bed repeatedly)'.

The past imperfective gerund, i.e. the gerund in -в/-вши from imperfective verbs, which is found in nineteenth-century authors (e.g. не быв, не имéв), is a very rare form as far as prose and the spoken language are concerned.[3]

In the participles too, with one notable exception, which will be discussed below, the category of tense is absent. That which is often called the 'present active participle' (e.g. читáющий) is in fact simply an imperfective active participle, that which is called the 'present passive participle' (e.g. читáемый) is an imperfective passive participle, that which is called the 'past perfective active participle' (e.g. прочитáвший) is a perfective active participle and that which is called the 'past passive participle' (e.g. прочитанный) is a perfective passive participle. One thus has a system of four

1 Examples and translations from Borras and Christian, *op. cit.,* p. 184.
2 Borras and Christian, *op. cit.,* p. 183.
3 It is pointed out in the Academy Grammar, p. 532, that this form is not uncommon in Mayakovsky's poetry but one must bear in mind that the grammar of the language of poetry is frequently not identical with the grammar of prose and the spoken language—and the grammars of the latter two often differ, for that matter.

participles based on the two polarities of aspect and voice:

	imperfective	perfective
active	читáющий	прочитáвший
passive	читáемый	прочи́танный

Like the perfective gerund, the perfective participles usually describe prior actions or states arising from prior actions. Again, this is a result of their perfectivity and not of the presence of the category of tense. An illustration of the use of the perfective active participle to describe an action which is *not* prior to that of the finite verb is: . . . ужé на поля́х Пéрвой мировóй войны́ взошли́ ростки́ нóвого языкá, вскóре почти́ заглуши́вшего язы́к клáссиков (A. and T. Fesenko) . . . *it was on the battlefields of the First World War that there sprang up the shoots of the new language, which soon almost overran the language of the classics.*

In addition to this system of four participles there is a fifth participle, in which the category of tense *is* present. This is the past imperfective active participle, which presents an action in the past as imperfective. This participle usually describes an action which is concomitant with that of the finite verb in the clause or against the background of which the action of the finite verb occurs.

Тёмные ру́ки отта́лкивали бéлую шéю и лошади́ную мóрду, дыша́вшую в человéчьи ли́ца (G. Nik.)	*Dark hands thrust back the white neck and the horse's muzzle, which was breathing into people's faces*
Вáря гла́дила матéрчатую, исходи́вшую пáром гимнастёрку (Leon.)	*Varya was ironing a steaming cloth tunic*

То же са́мое получи́лось и у всех шко́льников четвёртых кла́ссов, реша́вших э́ту зада́чку   (*Krok.*)

The same thing happened with all the fourth-formers who tried to solve this little problem

Го́лос принадлежа́л выступа́вшему у микрофо́на руководи́телю фаши́стской гру́ппы (*Krok.*)

The voice belonged to the leader of a fascist group who was making a speech at the microphone

This participle may also describe a prior action:

На вы́ставке — са́мой большо́й из устра́ивавшихся А́нглией за рубежо́м — 600 фирм пока́зывают о́коло 1000 катего́рий това́ров   (*Sov. Sojuz*)

At the exhibition—the largest ever organized abroad by England — six hundred firms are showing about one thousand types of product

Иссле́дователи, изуча́вшие э́ти проце́ссы . . ., установи́ли разновреме́нность укрепле́ния но́вых форм в ра́зных падежа́х   (V. V. Ivanov)

Researchers who have studied these processes have determined that the new forms were established in different cases at different times (where the 'studying' preceded the 'determining')

Несомне́нно, что уже́ на поля́х Пе́рвой мирово́й войны́ взошли́ ростки́ но́вого языка́, вско́ре почти́ заглуши́вшего язы́к кла́ссиков, создава́вшийся в тече́ние столе́тий путём тща́тель-

There is no doubt that it was on the battlefields of the First World War that there sprang up the shoots of the new language, which soon almost overran the lan-

ного отбóра и культивúро-
вания речевóго материáла
(A. and T. Fesenko)

*guage of the classics,
created* ('which was be-
ing created') *over the
centuries by the careful
selection and cultivation
of linguistic material*

Though such occurrences are not at all common, they are
the only ones where the past imperfective active participle
is essential, if a participle is to be used. In other instances
this participle can often be replaced by the imperfective
active participle ('present active') with little or no change in
meaning. However, the past imperfective active participle is
still used very frequently both in literature and in journalistic
prose. W. A. Morison has expressed the view[1] that, in identical contexts in literary narrative and description, where
the finite verbs are in the past, there is a difference in
meaning between the past imperfective active participle and
the imperfective active participle ('present active'), and that
this difference lies in the fact that the past imperfective
participle is used 'if no logical emphasis falls on the activity'.
'Thus дéвушка сидéвшая на скамéйке would imply
"the girl who, as we know, was sitting on the bench",
whereas дéвушка стоя́щая на скамéйке would imply "the
girl, who, it appears, *was standing* on the bench (and not, as
one would expect, sitting)".' Morison's description satis-
factorily explains many instances of differentiation between
these two participles but it will be necessary to collect much
more data before a definitive statement can be made. As we
see it at present, the difference in meaning or emphasis is
clearly attributable to the differences in grammatical content: since the imperfective active participle ('present
active') lacks the category of tense, the action it describes is,

1 In letters to me. I understand that Dr Morison hopes to expand
his idea in a future volume on the past gerund and past active participle.

so to speak, freed of all references to time and thus more attention is concentrated on the action as such than in the case of the past imperfective participle.

Verbs of motion

The so-called 'verbs of motion' do not include all verbs which denote motion but only certain pairs of verbs and some single verbs. In any one pair both members have the same lexical meaning of motion or of causing to move in some sense, and both members are imperfective. There is, however, a difference in grammatical meaning between the members of a pair and this difference is discussed below. Some individual prefixed verbs are also included in this category but the imperfective-perfective pairs such as уходи́ть–уйти́, прилета́ть–прилете́ть, etc., are not counted as verbs of motion in the restricted sense in which the term is used here. The paired imperfectives are:

бе́гать	бежа́ть	*to run*
броди́ть	брести́	*to wander*
води́ть	вести́	*to lead*
вози́ть	везти́	*to convey*
гоня́ть	гнать	*to drive*
е́здить	е́хать	*to go* (in a vehicle)
ката́ть	кати́ть	*to roll*
ла́зить	лезть	*to climb*
лета́ть	лете́ть	*to fly*
носи́ть	нести́	*to carry*
пла́вать	плыть	*to swim, to sail*
по́лзать	ползти́	*to crawl*
таска́ть	тащи́ть	*to drag*
ходи́ть	идти́	*to go*[1]

1 The verbs сажа́ть, сади́ть *to put, to plant*, listed in the Academy Grammar, p. 460, as verbs of motion do not in fact belong to this category. Nor any longer do лома́ть–ломи́ть and валя́ть–вали́ть, listed as such by A. Mazon in his *Morphologie des aspects du verbe russe*.

The reflexive forms of transitive verbs in this list are also verbs of motion.

A. V. Isačenko[1] considers that бродить–брести should not be counted as verbs of motion because there is a difference in lexical meaning between them, for брести, though it can mean *to wander* (to go along slowly, aimlessly), usually has the connotation of going along with difficulty,[2] whereas бродить does not have this connotation. Similarly, while катать–катить and the reflexive кататься–катиться are paired verbs of motion in the sense of *to roll* and *to be rolled* respectively, they are not, according to Professor Isačenko, paired in the sense of *to drive, to ride, to move along swiftly*. Nor are the verbs лазить–лезть paired in any sense other than *to climb*, for one can say лезть в драку *to be spoiling for a fight* but not лазить в драку. The verbs таскаться–тащиться are paired—and are verbs of motion— only in the sense of *to be dragged*, whereas таскаться in the sense of *to frequent, to hang about* (таскаться по кабакам *to hang around pubs, to pub-crawl*), is not paired with тащиться *to drag oneself along* (*with difficulty*).

It is true that the members of the pairs of verbs which Isačenko excludes from his list of verbs of motion are no longer completely identical in *lexical* meaning. However, they retain the grammatical distinction which other paired members have—indeed their different lexical meanings have become possible precisely because of their different grammatical meanings—and they should therefore be included in the list of verbs of motion, if only as non-paired, individual verbs.[3] For the same reason, certain verbs which are counted

---

[1] 'Глаголы движения в русском языке', *Русский язык в школе* 1961, 4.

[2] 'идти с трудом, волоча ноги', D. N. Ushakov, etc., *Толковый словарь русского языка*.

[3] One does not exclude, for example, очутиться *to (suddenly) find oneself*, очнуться *to come to, to recover consciousness*, and other verbs from the category of aspect simply because they have no paired imperfectives.

as verbs of motion by all grammarians continue to be verbs of motion when they are used in certain 'idiomatic' ways (see below), where their counterparts cannot be used. It is possible that other verbs besides валя́ть–вали́ть, etc. (see footnote 1, p. 250) may in time become restricted to certain lexical combinations and thus be removed from the determinate-indeterminate category. Indeed the removal of these verbs and the lexical differentiation of members of other pairs clearly implies that the category is slowly becoming smaller.

The verbs of motion, while participating in the imperfective-perfective aspect system, also participate in another aspect system, which is unique to them. Terms commonly used to distinguish them are 'indeterminate' (ходи́ть-type) and 'determinate' (идти́-type) and we shall use those terms here. The only meaning which is common to the determinate verbs on all occasions is motion in one direction.[1] All other meanings derive from this. The goal may be specified or implied but need not be (e.g. Он идёт по у́лице *He is walking along the street*). The only meaning common to the indeterminate verbs on all occasions is absence of the idea of motion in one direction[2] and all other meanings derive from this, for if a verb does not express motion in one direction then it can express motion in several directions or habitual motion or the faculty of motion or the abstract idea of motion. The members of the verbs of motion category might therefore be called, on the one hand, 'unidirectional' (идти́) and 'non-unidirectional'[3] (ходи́ть), but these are rather

1 Cf. Isačenko, *op. cit.*, p. 13—'Еди́нственным о́бщим, неизменя́емым значе́нием, сохраня́ющимся за глаго́лами движе́ния во всех конте́кстах, явля́ется значе́ние однонапра́вленности (тип *идти*) и ненапра́вленности (тип *ходить*).'

2 Cf. note 1

3 N.B.—*not* 'multidirectional', for this is one of the derived functions of 'non-unidirectionality', the latter simply being the negation or absence of 'unidirectionality'. Cf. the definition of 'imperfectivity' above as being simply the absence of 'perfectivity'.

cumbersome terms and therefore the more or less traditional
terms 'determinate' and 'indeterminate', as defined above,
are perhaps preferable.

The notion of unidirectional movement, however, is a *derived* notion, for what a verb such as идти́ actually does is to
present the action *as observed at a particular moment in its
progress*.[1] Thus, if a man is walking or riding or carrying,
etc., then at any one observed moment he can be moving in
only one direction. A simple diagram will suffice to illustrate
this:

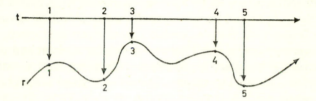

Here a man is following a circuitous route *r*. At any moment
in the time-continuum *t* his action may be observed, so that
at t^1 he is at r^1, at t^2 he is at r^2, and so on, and at each of
these moments and in each of these places he appears in-
evitably to be proceeding in one direction, although over any
section of, or all of the route *r* his direction in fact changes.
At any moment we can say of him Он идёт . . ., and we need
not specify or even imply a goal. Thus идёт means 'proceeding in one particular direction because observed at a particular moment'.

Similarly, if a path, for example, is described as leading to
a particular goal then obviously at any one moment it is

1 I have come to this conclusion, having started from a purely
spatial concept, after a discussion and correspondence with Mr J.
Forsyth, Senior Lecturer in Russian at the University of Aberdeen,
some of whose ideas are used here. See his 'The Russian Verbs of
Motion', *Modern Languages*, XLIV, 4 Dec. 1963, pp. 147–152.

leading in one direction—towards the goal stated: Тропи́н-
ка ведёт/идёт в лес. If the goal stated is the other end of the
path, or if the path is leading from a starting-point, then
again the path is at any moment leading in one direction:
Тропи́нка ведёт/идёт из ле́са. A path is spatially fixed: no
matter when one looks at it it is still there and still leading in
one direction, and one cannot say therefore *Тропи́нка
во́дит/хо́дит. A man, on the other hand, moves about and
if one wants to express the whole of or a stretch of a complex motion then one cannot say Он идёт . . . for one is no
longer observing the action at a particular moment. Hence:
Он ходи́л по у́лице *He walked/was walking up and down the
street*, Он хо́дит по ко́мнате *He walks/is walking up and
down the room*. But this complex motion can be stopped, as
it were—it can be observed at a particular moment and one
can say (Он хо́дит по ко́мнате: сейча́с) он идёт к окну́,
(сейча́с) он идёт к две́ри . . . (*now*) *he is going towards the
window*, (*now*) *he is going towards the door*. Thus, although
the determinate verbs express movement in one direction—
a fundamentally spatial concept—this notion has a temporal
(but not a tense) basis. The length of time devoted to the
action is irrelevant: compare Они́ е́хали весь день *They
were driving all day* with Весь день они́ е́здили по го́роду
All day they drove around the town. In the first example the
entire day is reduced to a moment of observation, or the
moment of observation is *any* moment during the day. In
the second example the day is not reduced to a single
moment of observation, nor is a single moment extracted
from the day and observed in isolation. Hence the action
cannot be perceived as proceeding in one direction: it is
therefore a "complex", non-unidirectional action—as it
happens, a multidirectional action.

Below are examples of the use of some of the verbs of
motion. In some examples the verbs do not have the meaning of physical motion but their determinate or inde-

terminate meaning is still present. In most of the examples the notions of unidirectionality or non-unidirectionality are clearly discernible, in others it may be necessary to look for the presence or absence of the idea of the action observed at a particular point in order to understand why the determinate or indeterminate aspect has been used.

идти–ходить

| Мы шли из кино (Klen.) | *We were coming from the cinema* |

| Охломóн Ожóгов шёл тёмными переýлками к Вóлге (Piln.) | *Okhlomon Ozhogov made his way through dark alleys towards the Volga* |

The alleys may have run in various directions but the subject was moving at any one time in one direction.

| Люди на смéжных ýлицах шли и шли к цéнтру (G. Nik.) | *People were pouring towards the centre on the adjoining streets* |

The groups of people were obviously moving in different compass directions but each group is observed at this particular moment moving in its own single direction.

| Словá не шли к немý (Piln.) | *The words would not come to him/He could not find the words* |

| Рóслый ỳнтер-офицéр . . . ходил от перил до перил (A. N. Tol.) | *The tall N.C.O. kept going back and forth from parapet to parapet* |

| Ходить по коридóрам бы́ло неудóбно (Arb.) | *It was awkward to walk up and down the corridors* |

А сама ходи́ла всегда́ нечёсаная (Rom.)	*She herself always went about unkempt*
Он . . . всегда́ ходи́л в шля́пе (Rom.)	*He . . . always wore a hat*
Ходи́л ба́рин Кара́зин в дворя́нской фура́жке (Piln.)	*Mr Karazin went about in/ wore a gentleman's cap*

The last two examples show the use of ходи́ть в in the sense of *to wear*, from the meaning 'to go about in'. Идти́ cannot be used in this sense, because of its strictly unidirectional meaning. If one says, for example, Вот он идёт, в фура́жке, the meaning is *Here he comes, in/wearing a forage cap*, but the idea of 'wearing' is not expressed by идёт. Similarly носи́ть, besides meaning *to carry* (indeterminate), also means *to wear*—habitually, because one goes about, in all directions, as it were, carrying the garment on one—whereas нести́ *to carry* (determinate) cannot have this meaning.

лете́ть–лета́ть

Ду́мал лете́ть да́льше — самолёты на Москву́ не шли, пого́ды не́ было (Klen.)	*I thought of flying on—but no planes were leaving for Moscow, as the weather was too bad*
— Зна́чит, ты лета́ла? — Коне́чно, не раз (Klen.)	*—So you have flown? — Of course, more than once*

Here the indeterminate verb is used to denote flying in general.

е́хать–е́здить

Они́ е́хали из а́рмии спо́собом «голосова́ния», переса́живаясь из маши́ны в маши́ну (Pol.)	*They were hitch-hiking their way back from the front, changing from one vehicle to another*

Сове́тский космона́вт е́хал по А́нглии сквозь лес приве́тственно ма́шущих рук (*Krok.*)	*The Soviet spaceman drove through England through a forest of hands waving welcome*

Here, in spite of the fact that Gagarin obviously moved in various directions and, moreover, on separate occasions, his tour is presented as a motion in a single direction, though no goal is mentioned or implied. The observed moment in his progress is any moment, standing for all moments, and his progress is brought vividly before the reader's eyes.

Е́здила она́ . . . в высоче́нным шараба́не (Babaev.)	*She travelled about . . . in a very tall charabanc*
Я к ним че́рез воскресе́нье е́зжу, тут ведь бли́зко (Arb.)	*I go to their place every other Sunday—it's not far from here, you see*

The motion is apparently in a single direction—'to their place'. However, not only is the motion repeated and thus not presented as observed at a particular moment but also the journey is a return journey—he goes *and* comes back (see below).

бежа́ть—бе́гать

Бежа́вший ря́дом со мной бое́ц так и лежи́т, раски́нув ру́ки (Nekr.)	*The soldier who had been running alongside me just lay there, his arms outflung*
Лю́ди бежа́ли чёрными фигу́рками по снéгу (A. N. Tol.)	*The little, dark figures of people were running across the snow*
По всем направле́ниям я́рко освещённого насти́ла бегу́т фигу́ры с та́чками (Kat.)	*Figures are running in all directions over the brilliantly illuminated planking*

9+

In the last two examples, and especially the very last, different people are moving in different directions but the individual unidirectional motion of each person takes precedence over the general picture of multidirectional motion.

До неё я люби́л . . . футбо́л и автомоби́ли — бе́гал в кино́ и гоня́л на конька́х (Klen.)	*Before her I loved . . . football and cars—used to dash off to the cinema and race around on skates*
Все пя́тки прошмы́гаешь, бе́гавши[1] открыва́ть (Rom.)	*You could wear all your shoes* (lit. '*heels*') *out with all this running back and forth to open the door*

ползти́–по́лзать

По лени́во теку́щей Во́лге бегу́т пассажи́рские парохо́ды и ползу́т букси́ры с карава́нами барж (A. N. Tol.)	*Along the lazily flowing Volga passenger-steamers race and tugs with trains of barges crawl*
По бри́тым щека́м его́ полз пот (A. N. Tol.)	*Sweat crawled down his shaven cheeks*

The motion is in a single direction—the sweat obviously did not crawl back again![2] Similarly

. . . и на чёрную . . . кры́шу полз по стене́ незате́йливый вьюно́к (Klen.)	*. . . and along the wall an ordinary bindweed crawled up on to the black . . . roof*
При ка́ждом движе́нии его́ холщо́вая руба́ха . . . ползла́ к плеча́м (Chekh.)	*With every movement his denim shirt . . . slid towards his shoulders*

1 N.B.—past imperfective gerund—see p. 246.
2 Compare Слеза́ кати́лась по её щеке́ *A tear rolled down her cheek* (кати́лась would be impossible here) and the remarks on 'idiomatic' uses below.

The motion is repeated but it is always in one direction: the shirt, like the drops of sweat in the example above, does not move back again.

Он не́ был уби́т — не́сколько раз пыта́лся подня́ться, ползти́, протя́гивал ру́ки, крича́л что́-то неслы́шное (Fad.)	*He was not dead—several times he tried to get up, to crawl—he stretched out his arms and shouted out something that could not be heard*

The use of the determinate verb here (compare the examples below) must be justified on the grounds that the author is expressing almost the idea of crawling away, i.e. in a particular direction. If this is not so, then this is an example of the distinction between determinate and indeterminate being blurred and may presage the kind of restriction mentioned above.

Его́ по́дняли на́ ноги, но он упа́л опя́ть; по́лзал в нога́х казако́в (Shol.)	*They lifted him on to his feet but he fell down again and crawled about at the Cossacks' feet*
Тогда́, по́лзая по земле́, я стал собира́ть ру́кописи и дыря́вые мои́ обно́ски (Bab.)	*Then, crawling about on the ground, I began to collect my manuscripts and my ragged old clothes*

It should be borne in mind that the determinate-indeterminate opposition constitutes an aspect system and, just as in the imperfective-aspect system, the speaker or writer often has a choice: it is he who decides how the action shall be presented. Some of the examples above show this exercise of choice on the part of the writer. The exercise of choice is very clear in the following sentence:

Мы ча́сто броди́ли по вече́р- ней Москве́, но ре́дко ходи́- ли под руку: шли ря́дом (Klen.)	*We often wandered about Moscow in the evenings but rarely walked arm in arm: we went side by side*

Here, after the more or less obligatory indeterminate броди́ли, indicating distributed motion, the author chooses another indeterminate verb, indicating repeated or habitual motion or even the 'abstract' idea of motion, and then chooses the determinate verb шли, presenting us with an observed moment and thus evoking a picture of the couple walking along at a particular moment in a single direction.

As far as the choice between determinate and indeterminate verb is concerned, the case of repeated motion in the same direction may appear to be 'marginal'. In fact it is usually the unidirectional motion which takes precedence and in instances where the indeterminate verb appears it can usually be shown that the motion is not unidirectional: it is a case of movement there and back. In the following sentences there is an example of what may in fact be a truly marginal case:

На сле́дующий день Пе́тя Ер- мако́в шёл домо́й без своего́ лу́шего дру́га . . .	*The next day Petya Yer- makov went home with- out his best friend . . .*
Пе́тя ходи́л домо́й оди́н всю неде́лю	*Petya went home alone all week . . .*
На э́тот раз Пе́тя шёл домо́й со свои́м лу́чшим дру́гом (*Krok.*)	*This time Petya went home with his best friend*

In the second sentence the repeated journeys homewards

are expressed by the indeterminate verb ходи́л, so that repetition appears to take precedence over unidirectionality. However, it may be argued that what is being expressed here is *not* unidirectionality but repeated journeys to *and from* home during the course of the week.

Many so-called 'idiomatic' (i.e. inexplicable, unexpected) uses of either the determinate or the indeterminate aspect are not in fact idiomatic at all (we have seen above how носи́ть and ходи́ть в come to mean *to wear*, while нести́ and идти́ в cannot have this meaning). For instance, time moves in one direction only, therefore вре́мя идёт, бежи́т, ползёт *time passes, races by, crawls*, часы́ бегу́т *the hours fly by*, дни та́щатся *the days drag by*, etc. The use of the indeterminate verbs is impossible here. Similarly, any action which is essentially a passage through time must necessarily be presented as unidirectional, hence: Иду́т перегово́ры *Negotiations are proceeding*, Он вёл распу́тную жизнь *He led a dissolute life*, Она́ ведёт себя́ хорошо́ *She behaves well*, Мы с ним вели́ перепи́ску *He and I used to carry on a correspondence*, Жесто́кая борьба́ с ним вела́сь, ведётся сего́дня и бу́дет вести́сь за́втра (Arb.) *A fierce struggle has been waged against this, is being waged today and will continue to be waged tomorrow*. Conversely, in such an expression as води́ть за́ нос *to lead by the nose, to make a fool of*, the notion is not one of passage through time but of 'leading about in various directions' and hence the indeterminate verb is used. Similarly, in such expressions as носи́ть следы́, отпеча́ток, etc., *to bear the traces, imprint*, etc., the obligatory use of the indeterminate verb has arisen because the subject is perceived as 'carrying about' the traces, the imprint, etc., wherever he goes. Marginal cases, showing the possibility of visualizing the action either unidirectionally (as a passage through time) or non-unidirectionally, are found in the choice between вести́ дру́жбу, знако́мство and води́ть дру́жбу, знако́мство *to keep up a friendship*,

9*

though theoretically one would expect only the determinate verb here.

Rain and snow proceed in one direction, hence Дождь/ Снег идёт *It is raining/snowing*, Часто шёл дождь *It often rained*. When one has paid a visit somewhere one has gone and come back, hence the indeterminate verb is used: Я ходил в театр вчера *I went to the theatre yesterday*, В прошлом году она ездила во Францию *She went to France last year*. But if one has simply been on the way somewhere and therefore moving in one direction the determinate verb is used: Я шёл в театр, когда вы меня видели *I was going to the theatre when you saw me*. What *may* be considered idiomatic is the Russian concept that when, for example, one 'climbs up the wall' in rage, or is spoiling for a fight ('climbs into a fight'), or reaches into one's pocket ('climbs into one's pocket'), one moves in one direction and does not return, hence: лезть на стену *to 'climb up the wall'*, лезть в драку *to be spoiling for a fight*, лезть в карман за платком *to reach into one's pocket for a handkerchief*. Even here, however, it is arguable that the unidirectional motion is the logically essential basis of the idiom.

It is true that the determinate verb often has a more 'concrete' or 'actual' connotation than the indeterminate verb but this difference arises, as we have seen above, from the fundamental differences between unidirectional and non-unidirectional motion. Thus, in the sentence quoted above— Думал лететь дальше — самолёты на Москву не шли, etc., the determinate infinitive лететь is used because of the clearly unidirectional motion implied. In the sentence При морозной погоде автобусы не идут[1] the use of the determinate verb arises from the motion 'do not go forward', hence *In frosty weather the buses will not go*, whereas in При морозной погоде автобусы не ходят[1] the use of the in-

1 Quoted from Borras and Christian, *op. cit.*, p. 165.

determinate verb arises from the motion 'do not go in general'—*In frosty weather the buses do not run.*

All other things being equal, the negated indeterminate verb may supplant the negated determinate verb because of its frequently less 'actual' and hence more 'generalized' connotation (cf. the use of the negative imperfective above),[1] as in

Váля: Ларíска, ты кудá вéчером идтí хотéла?

Valya: Lariska, where were you going to go this evening?

Ларíса: В кинó. На послéдний сеáнс.

Larisa: To the cinema. To the last house.

Váля: Не ходí (Arb.)

Valya: Don't go

— Ты кудá кáтишь? — В лес поéхал — остановíлся тот . . . — Ты б не éздил — крíкнул Лызлов (Leon.)

'Where are you going?—'I was going to the wood'. He stopped . . . 'I wouldn't go if I were you!' shouted Lyzlov

When pairs of indeterminate-determinate verbs are provided with the same prefix with the same meaning, the verb derived from the indeterminate verb remains imperfective while the one derived from the determinate verb becomes perfective. One then has an imperfective-perfective pair in which there is no longer the indeterminate-determinate contrast, as in выходíть–выйти *to go out*, улетáть–улетéть *to fly away*, etc. Some indeterminate verbs are replaced by related forms when entering into such pairs: уезжáть (cf. éздить)—уéхать *to leave*, вытáскивать (cf. таскáть)—вытащить *to pull out*, отплывáть (cf. плáвать)—отплыть

1 There is—as is pointed out by A. Mazon in his *Emplois des aspects du verbe russe*—an underlying psychological connection between, on the one hand, imperfective and indeterminate and, on the other hand, between perfective and determinate (in spite of the fact that determinate verbs are imperfective).

to sail off, etc., and the determinate идти́ is replaced by -йти in forming perfectives.

An indeterminate verb which is prefixed but does not form a pair with a similarly prefixed determinate verb[1] *becomes perfective*. If the resulting verb retains the meaning of movement, the indeterminate (non-unidirectional) motion is still clearly perceptible. Thus: Хо́чется слета́ть к Вене́ре, к Ма́рсу, по-настоя́щему полета́ть (Gagarin) *I'd like to fly to Venus, to Mars, to do some real flying*. Here both слета́ть and полета́ть are perfectives, слета́ть being perfective to лета́ть in the meaning *to fly there and back*, полета́ть being an 'attenuative' perfective—*to do a bit of flying (about)*. Such perfectives as сходи́ть, съе́здить, свози́ть, etc., mean 'to go/take somewhere and come back', usually with the additional connotation of 'without staying long at the destination'—Он сходи́л в библиоте́ку *He popped round to the library*, Я съе́зжу в го́род *I'll just pop down into town* (and come back almost at once). Some prefixed indeterminate verbs have imperfectives formed by means of the suffix -ыва-/-ива-. Thus, giving the perfective first, налета́ть–налётывать *to fly* (a specified distance or number of hours), облета́ть–облётывать *to visit* (a number of places) *in flying* or *to 'fly in', to test-fly* (an aeroplane). In some such verbs the indeterminate meaning is no longer immediately clear but has been present nevertheless in the original formation of the prefixed indeterminate verb—износи́ть–изна́шивать *to wear out*, исходи́ть–исха́живать *to walk all over*, etc.

Determinates may also be prefixed with по- but they do not then form pairs with indeterminates prefixed with по-. The latter, as we have just seen, are attenuative perfectives, retaining the non-unidirectional notion. The determinates

---

1 The determinate verb then retains its basic form. The verb разъезжа́ть is imperfective but does not pair with any other verb—and note that the basic form е́здить is replaced by -езжа́ть.

prefixed with по- are either plain perfectives presenting an act of going as delimited, or inceptive perfectives. Он пошёл, for example, means either *he went* or *he set off*. In the latter case the unidirectional notion of шёл is still discernible: he set off and at any moment thereafter he could be observed in the performance of the action—going in a particular direction. Even in the meaning *went* the unidirectional notion of пошёл is present, for Он пошёл в театр means *He went/has gone to the theatre* but makes no implication about his coming back. If on the other hand the visit to the theatre is completed and the subject has come back, then Он ходил в театр *He went* (not 'has gone') *to the theatre* is obligatory. A nice illustration of the differences between пойти and походить is Пойду по берегу похожу (Arb.) *I am going for a walk on the shore* ('I shall go/set off and I shall walk about on the shore').

Changes of direction and speed are also expressed by the determinates prefixed with по-, for such changes imply the beginning of a new phase of unidirectional movement. Thus[1]:

Он пошёл к другу,	*He set off for his friend's* —and at any moment thereafter could be observed, proceeding in one direction:
он шёл по улице Герцена, а на Невском он пошёл налево.	*he went along Herzen Street and on Nevsky Prospekt he went to the left—* a delimited act of going or setting off to the left, during which he could have been observed going or turning to the left:

1 The idea of this illustration was suggested to me by J. Forsyth.

Я ви́дел, как он шёл нале́во.

I saw him turning left.

Он шёл о́чень ме́дленно, пото́м пошёл быстре́е,

He walked very slowly, then he went faster— he began a new phase of motion in a particular direction, during which he could again have been observed:

и по́сле э́того он всё шёл бы́стро

and after that he kept on walking fast

Conclusion
The Russian Language Tomorrow

This brief concluding chapter might well have been entitled 'a foregone conclusion', for it is largely a summary of some of the tendencies that have been mentioned in previous chapters. These 'prognostications' are made with—and should be taken with—the utmost caution. Prognostication is not impossible in linguistics, but the only reliable prognostication is that based on large collections of data covering long periods of time and made in very general terms.

As far as phonetics is concerned, it seems likely that the palatalization of adjacent consonants will become less extensive. In some styles of pronunciation the persistence of an unstressed /e/, at least in some positions, is probable. Some of the old Moscow norms, such as [ʃʃ] instead of [ʃtʃ], and the pronunciation of жалéть, etc., as [ʒtˈleṭ], etc., the pronunciation of hard [s] in the reflexive particle, may disappear altogether from the literary language (Chapter 1). There will undoubtedly be eradication of some stress 'anomalies' and the number of substantives in some of the stress-patterns may be reduced still further, leading perhaps to the disappearance of the least common patterns. The conflicting influences on the location of the stress, however, make it likely that other 'anomalies' will arise (Chapter 2).

The rules for the writing of the vowel letters o and e after ш, ж, ч and щ may be simplified by a further regularization of the orthography. Such a regularization would also have to consider the writing as one word of certain adverbs written at present as two words (Chapter 3).

Some new word-forming elements which are no more than peripheral at present will probably become more productive, some older word-forming elements which are now weakly productive will cease to be productive (Chapter 5). It is possible that abutted compounds may become commoner. Stump-compounds of all types will continue to be formed and the most productive types will continue to be type (a) and type (b), more particularly perhaps type (b) (Chapter 6). A further reduction in the number of substantives having special case-forms (partitive genitive, locative) is certain, but it is unlikely that these special case-forms will disappear entirely for a long time to come. Some eradication of anomalies in the declensions of certain substantives is probable (Chapter 7).

There is some evidence of a very slow tendency towards the loss of flexion in some of the nominal parts of speech. In spoken usage only the last element of long compound numbers is declined (Chapter 9), and one may have here the first steps in a process leading to a situation similar to that in Serbo-Croat, for instance, where the numbers beyond 'four' are invariable. Although proper names ending in -енко and -ко (of Ukrainian origin, e.g. Шевче́нко, Франко́) *may* be declined in the manner of substantives ending in -a (gen. Шевче́нки, dat. Шевче́нке, etc.) it is not now customary to decline them at all. Proper names which are in origin genitive singular or plural (e.g. Живаго, Черны́х) do not decline, nor do foreign names ending in a vowel (e.g. Гюго́, Шо́у) and feminine names ending in a consonant (e.g. Ги́нзбург, Шмидт). Non-Russian place-names ending in a vowel other than unstressed a are not declined (e.g. в Алма-Ата́, в Баку́, в Тбили́си, в То́кио, but в Гватема́ле). Initial-words which are pronounced as the names of the constituent letters (e.g. СССР, ООН) are no longer declined. Those initial-words which are not pronounced as the names of the constituent letters but which end in a vowel (e.g. ОНО́,

НАТО́) and those words which are composed partly of initials and partly of syllables and which also end in a vowel (e.g. РОСТА́, облоно́) do not decline either. Finally, there are several score common substantives, all of foreign origin and all ending in a vowel, which do not decline. Some of these are of old standing, others are more recent. They include such words as арго́, ателье́, атташе́, буржуа́, депо́, дина́мо, жюри́, интервью́, кабаре́, кафе́, кило́, коммюнике́, ко́фе, метро́, пальто́, пиани́но, плато́, ра́дио, такси́, трико́, шасси́, шимпанзе́. All these facts lead one to the conclusion that, if flexion does begin to disappear from the substantive, it is likely to be neuter substantives which undergo the loss first, because the great majority of words which are already indeclinable are neuter in gender.

The distinctive paradigm of relative adjectives has already undergone some modifications and the colloquial language is making further modifications: this paradigm may ultimately give way to the standard adjectival paradigm. The use of the short form will become less common, and it may be that the short form will become restricted to a few adjectives only and to some fixed expressions (Chapter 8).

There will be some slight reduction of the number of verbs in anomalous or unproductive groups, i.e. some verbs will take on a 'normal' conjugation. The ramifications of the modes of action (*Aktionsarten*) may well be reduced. This would be part of the centuries-long progress towards the establishment of a simple bi-aspectual system without further sub-aspectual categories. At present the past imperfective active participle stands outside the four-participle system, but it is nevertheless fairly common, at least in the literary language. It is in fact commoner than the present passive (imperfective passive) participle. Passivity can be and frequently is expressed by means of reflexive participles. These facts suggest the possibility of some shift in the participial system which is at present difficult to foresee. A

10

further reduction in the number of determinate-indeterminate pairs is likely: the less common of these verbs will tend to become restricted to certain fixed expressions or to association with a restricted range of items (Chapter 10).

Bibliography

This bibliography lists all the works mentioned in the book as well as a few works which are not mentioned in the book but which have been consulted or read as background material.

(a) In Russian

Alekseyev, M. P., etc. (Eds.), *Словарь русского языка* ('Academy Dictionary'), Государственное издательство иностранных и национальных словарей, 4 vols., Moscow, 1957–1961

Avanesov, R. I., 'О нормах русского литературного произношения', *Русский язык в школе*, 1961, no. 6, Учпедгиз, Moscow, 1961

Avanesov, R. I., *Очерки русской диалектологии, ч. 1ая*, Учпедгиз, Moscow, 1949

Avanesov, R. I., *Русское литературное призношение*, Учпедгиз, Moscow, 1954

Avanesov, R. I., *Фонетика современного русского литературного языка*, Издательство московского университета, Moscow, 1956

Avanesov, R. I., and Ozhegov, S. I., *Русское литературное произношение и ударение*, Государственное издательство иностранных и национальных словарей, Moscow, 1960

Bogusławski, A., 'О кратких и полных формах прилагательного в сказуемом', *Русский язык в школе*, 1964, no. 1, Просвещение, Moscow, 1964

Bulakhovsky, L. A., *Исторический комментарий к русскому литературному языку*, Радянська школа, Kiev, 5th edition, 1958

Bulakhovsky, L. A., *Русский литературный язык первой половины XIX века*, Учпедгиз, Moscow, 1954

Chernykh, P. Ya., *Историческая грамматика русского языка*, Учпедгиз, Moscow, 1954

Chernykh, P. Ya., *Очерк русской исторической лексикологии — древнерусский период*, Издательство московского университета, Moscow, 1956

Chernyshev, V., *Упрощеніе русскаго правописанія*, Академия наук, St Petersburg, 1904

Chukovsky, K., *Живой как жизнь*, Молодая гвардия, Moscow, 1963

Chukovsky, K., 'О соразмерности и сообразности', *Новый мир*, 1961, no. 5, Известия, Moscow, 1961

Chukovsky, K., *От двух до пяти*, Детгиз, Moscow, 11th edition, 1956

Dal, V. I. (Даль, В. И.), *Толковый словарь живаго великорускаго языка*, 4 vols., Moscow, 1st edition, 1863–1866

Fesenko, A. and T., *Русский язык при советах*, New York, 1955

Filin, F. P., 'О двух значениях глаголов, образованных посредством префикса *на-* и суффикса *-ся*', *Вопросы грамматики — сборник статей к 75-летию Академика И. И. Мещанинова*, Академия наук, Moscow-Leningrad, 1960

Galkina-Fedoruk, Ye. M., *Современный русский язык — лексика*, Издательство московского университета, Moscow, 1954

Galkina-Fedoruk, Ye. M., Gorshkova, K. V., and Shansky, N. M., *Современный русский язык*, Moscow, 1957

Gvozdev, A. N. *Основы русской орфографии*, Учпедгиз, Moscow, 1951

Hingley, R. (Ed.), *Soviet Prose*, Allen & Unwin, London, 1959

Isačenko, A. V., 'Глаголы движения в русском языке', *Русский язык в школе*, 1961, no. 4, Учпедгиз, Moscow, 1961

Ivanov, V. V., *Краткий очерк исторической фонетики русского языка*, Учпедгиз, Moscow, 1959

Ivanov, V. V., *Развитие грамматического строя русского языка*, Учпедгиз, Moscow, 1960

Jakobson, R., 'Избыточные буквы в русском письме', in *Selected Writings, I—Phonological Studies*, Mouton, 'S-Gravenhage, 1962

Kuznetsov, P. S., *Историческая грамматика русского языка — морфология*, Издательство московского университета, Moscow, 1953

Lomtev, T. P., *Основы синтаксиса современного русского языка*, Учпедгиз, Moscow, 1958

Maslov, Yu. S., *Роль так называемой перфективации и имперфективации в процессе возникновения славянского глагольного вида* (Contribution to the Fourth International Congress of Slavists), Академия наук, Moscow, 1958

Obnorsky, S. P., *Очерки по морфологии русского глагола*, Академия наук, Moscow, 1953

Obnorsky, S. P., Review of R. I. Avanesov, *Русское литературное произношение*, in *Русский язык в школе*, XII, 1, Moscow, 1951

Ozhegov, S. I., and Shapiro, A. B. (Eds.), *Орфографический словарь русского языка*, Государственное издательство иностранных и национальных словарей, Moscow, 1957

Panov, M. V., 'Некоторые тенденции в развитии русского литературного языка XX века', *Вопросы языкознания*, 1963, 1, Академия наук, Moscow, 1963

Peshkovsky, A. M., *Русский синтаксис в научном освещении*, Учпедгиз, Moscow, 7th edition, 1956

Pospelov, N. S., 'Соотношение между грамматическими категориями и частями речи в современном русском языке', *Вопросы языкознания*, 1956, no. 6, Академия наук, Moscow, 1953

Shapiro, A. B., Review of R. I. Avanesov, *Русское литературное произношение*, in *Русский язык в школе*, XII, 1, Moscow, 1951

Shcherba, L. V., 'Основные принципы орфографии и их социальное значение', in *Избранные работы по русскому языку*, Учпедгиз, Moscow, 1957

Shcherba, L. V., 'О частях речи в русском языке', *Русская речь*, New Series, Moscow, 1928. Reprinted in L. V. Shcherba, *Избранные работы по русскому языку*, Учпедгиз, Moscow, 1957

Shcherba, L. V., 'Теория русского письма', in *Избранные работы по русскому языку*, Учпедгиз, Moscow, 1957

Spagis, A. A. *Образование и употребление видов глагола в русском языке*, Учпедгиз, Moscow, 1961

Torsuev, G. P., *Вопросы акцентологии современного английского языка*, Академия наук, Moscow, 1960

Trediakovsky, V. K., *Разговор между чужестранным человеком и российским об орфографии старинной и новой и о всем что принадлежит к этой материи*, St Petersburg, 1748

Trofimov, V. A., *Современный русский литературный язык — фонетика, графика*, Издательство ленинградского университета, Leningrad, 1957

Ushakov, D. N., etc., *Толковый словарь русского языка*, 4 vols., Огиз, Moscow, 1935–40

Vinogradov, V. V., *Из истории изучения русского синтаксиса*, Издательство московского университета, Moscow, 1958

Vinogradov, V. V., *Русский язык*, Учпедгиз, Moscow, 1947

Vinogradov, V. V., Istrina, Ye. S., Barkhudarov, S. G. (Eds.), *Грамматика русского языка* ('Academy Grammar'), 3 vols., Академия наук, Moscow, 1952–54, revised reprint 1960

Yakubinsky, L. P., *История древнерусского языка*, Уч-педгиз, Moscow, 1953

—— *Правила русской орфографии и пунктуации*, Учпедгиз, Moscow, 1957

(b) In English

Albrow, K. H., 'The phonology of the personal forms of the verb in Russian', *Archivum Linguisticum*, XIV, 2, Glasgow, 1963

Borras, F. M., and Christian, R. F., *Russian Syntax*, University Press, Oxford, 1959

Boyanus, S. C., *A Manual of Russian Pronunciation*, Sidgwick & Jackson, 2nd edition, London, 1944

Boyanus, S. C., *Russian Pronunciation* and *Russian Phonetic Reader*, Lund Humphries, London, 1955

Browder, R. P., and Kerensky, A. F., *The Russian Provisional Government* 1917—*Documents*, vol. II, University Press, Stanford, 1961

Carlsen, I. M., and Edwards, P. M. H., *A Numericon of Russian Inflections and Stress Patterns*, University of British Columbia, Vancouver, 1955

Cherry, E. C., Halle, M., and Jakobson, R., 'Toward the logical description of languages in their phonemic aspect', *Language*, 29, Baltimore, 1953

Ebeling, C. L., *Subject and Predicate, especially in Russian* (Contribution to the Fourth International Congress of Slavists), Mouton, 'S-Gravenhage, 1958

Entwistle, W. J., and Morison, W. A., *Russian and the Slavonic Languages*, Faber, 1949

Forsyth, J., *A Practical Guide to Russian Stress*, Oliver & Boyd, Edinburgh, 1963

Forsyth, J., 'The Russian Verbs of Motion', *Modern Languages*, XLIV, 4, London, 1963

Halliday, M. A. K., 'Categories of the Theory of Grammar', *Word*, vol. 17, no. 3, New York,, 1961

Jakobson, R., Review of G. L. Trager, *Introduction to Russian, a course for college students*, in *Slavonic Review*, XXII, part 3, Menasha, Wisconsin, October, 1944

Jones, D., *An Outline of English Phonetics*, Heffer, Cambridge, 8th edition, 1956

Jones, D., *The Pronunciation of English*, University Press, Cambridge, 4th edition, 1956

Klepko, V., *A Practical Handbook on Stress in Russian*, Foreign Languages Publishing House, Moscow, 1963

Langer, Susanne K., *An Introduction to Symbolic Logic*, Dover, New York, 2nd edition, 1953

Matthews, W. K., 'Russian Grammatical Design', *Slavonic Review*, XXIX, no. 72, London, 1950

Matthews, W. K., *Russian Historical Grammar*, Athlone, London, 1960

Matthews, W. K., *The Structure and Development of Russian*, University Press, Cambridge, 1953

Morison, W. A., *Studies in Russian Forms and Uses—the Present Gerund and Active Participle*, Faber, London, 1959

Olmsted, D. L., 'The so-called inserted vowels in Russian', *Language Learning*, vol. III, Ann Arbor, 1950

Partridge, M., 'The stress of long compounded words in Russian', *Le Maître phonétique*, no. 114, London, 1960

Pulkina, I. M., *A Short Russian Reference Grammar*, Foreign Languages Publishing House, Moscow, 1960

Restan, P. A., 'The objective case in negative clauses in Russian—the genitive or the accusative?' *Scandoslavica*, VI, Copenhagen, 1960

Rozental', D. E., *Modern Russian Usage*, Pergamon, Oxford, 1963

Sapir, E., *Language*, Harvest Books, New York, 1960

Stilman, L., *Russian Alphabet and Phonetics*, Columbia University Slavic Studies, New York, 1949

Struve, G., 'Some observations on past imperfective gerunds in Russian', *Slavic Word*, no. 2, New York, 1953

Sturtevant, E. H., *An Introduction to Linguistic Science*, Yale University Press, New Haven, 1960

Trager, G., 'The phonemes of Russian', *Language*, no. 10, Baltimore, 1934

Trofimov, M. V., *Handbook of Russian, II—Accidence and Syntax*, Sherratt & Hughes, Manchester, 1939

Trofimov, M. V., and Jones, D., *The Pronunciation of Russian*, University Press, Cambridge, 1923

Uglitsky, Z., 'Accusative and genitive with transitive verbs preceded by a negative in contemporary Russian', *Slavonic Review*, XXXIV, 83, London, 1956

Unbegaun, B. O., *Russian Grammar*, University Press, Oxford, 1960

Ward, D., 'A critique of Russian orthography', *In Honour of Daniel Jones*, Longmans, London, 1964

Ward, D., 'Double-stressed words—interpretation, terminology, notation', *Le Maître Phonétique*, no. 116, London, 1961

Ward, D., 'Is there a phoneme ɣ in Russian?' *Le Maître Phonétique*, no. 112, London, 1959

Ward, D., 'Russian ʃ and ʒ', *Le Maître Phonétique*, no. 110, London, 1958

Ward, D., 'Some remarks on the e-phoneme in Russian', *Archivum Linguisticum*, VI, 1, Glasgow, 1954

(c) *In other languages*

Baecklund, A., *Die univerbierenden Verkürzungen der russischen Sprache*, Uppsala, 1940

Bielfeldt, H. H., (Ed.), *Rückläufiges Wörterbuch der russischen Sprache der Gegenwart*, Akademie-Verlag, Berlin, 1958

Braun, M., *Grundzüge der slawischen Sprachen*, Vandenhoeck & Ruprecht, Göttingen, 1947

Broch, O., *Slavische Phonetik*, Winter, Heidelberg, 1911

Dox, G., 'Zum heutigen russischen Wortschatz', *Österreichische Osthefte*, vol. 2, 1960, Arbeitsgemeinschaft Ost, Vienna, 1960

Kiparsky, V., *Der Wortakzent der russischen Schriftsprache*, Winter, Heidelberg, 1962

Mahnken, I., and Braun, M., 'Zum "expiratorischen Akzent" im Russischen', *Zeitschrift für Phonetik*, VI, Akademie-Verlag, Berlin, 1952

Mahnken, I., and Braun, M., 'Zur Vokalquantität im Russischen', *Zeitschrift für Phonetik*, V, Akademie-Verlag, Berlin, 1951

Mazon, A., *Emplois des aspects du verbe russe*, Champion, Paris, 1914

Mazon, A., *Grammaire de la langue russe*, Librairie Droz, Paris, 2nd edition, 1945

Mazon, A., *L'aspect des verbes slaves (principes et problèmes)*/Вид в славянских языках (принципы и проблемы) (Contribution to the Fourth International Congress of Slavists), Академия наук, Moscow, 1958

Mazon, A., *Lexique de la guerre et de la révolution en Russie (1914–1918)*, Champion, Paris, 1920

Mazon, A., *Morphologie des aspects du verbe russe*, Champion, Paris, 1908

Nachtigall, R., *Akzentbewegung in der russischen Formen- und Wortbildung*, Winter, Heidelberg, 1922

Scheitz, E., *Russische Abkürzungen und Kurzwörter*, VEB Verlag, Berlin, 1961

Shcherba, L. V., *Court exposé de la prononciation russe*, supplement to *Le Maître Phonétique*, Nov.–Dec., 1911

Sørensen, H. C., *Aspect et temps en slave*, Universitetsforlaget, Aarhus, 1949

Steinitz, W., *Russische Lautlehre*, Akademie Verlag, Berlin, 2nd edition, 1957

Trubetzkoy, N., *Das morphonologische System der russischen Sprache*, Travaux du Cercle Linguistique de Prague, no. 52, Prague, 1934

Živković, S., 'Podjela glagolu po vidu (aspektu)', *Jezik*, 1959–60, nos. 1 and 2, Zagreb, 1959

Index

1. *English*

Authors' names are included in this index if they are mentioned in the text and, in some instances, if they are mentioned in footnotes. The names (in brackets) of the authors of the illustrative sentences in certain chapters are not included.

The items marked with an asterisk are to be consulted in connection with the item 'productivity of word-forming processes'.

281

/t/, 26, 34
/t/ & /ţ/, 26–27
technical jargon, 20
'technicization', 20
tense, 103, 106; in gerunds, 106, 245–246; in participles, 246–247, 249–250
terminative verbs, 229, 231
Tolstoy, A. N., 22, 238
'too . . .', 197
*transference, 115
Trediakovsky, V., 78
Trofimov, M. V., 60 (note 1), 61 (note 3), 192, 209 (note 1), 211, 221
/ts/, 35
/tʃ/, 35
typographical reform, 77

/u/, 28–29
ultra-short vowels, 83
Unbegaun, B. O., 62 (note 2), 63, 112 (note 1), 131–2, 214, 216, 221
unidirectional, 252 *et seq.*
unit, 91, 92
Ushakov, D. N., 61 (note 2), 63, 191

Value-judgements of language, 19
velar consonants, 34, 85
verbal parts of speech, 106–107
*verbs, Ch. 10; compound, see 'compound verbs'
verbs of motion, 250–252; 'idiomatic' uses of, 261–262; meaning of, 252–254; prefixed, 250, 263–266
Vinogradov, V. V., 192
vocabulary, see 'words, sources of'; changes in, 17, 19

voice, 39, 103, 106
voiced consonants, 38, 39, 76
voiceless consonants, 38, 39, 76, 77
voicelessness, 39
voicing, 38, 40
Vostokov, A. Kh., 108
vowel letters, 69–72
vowels, 27–34; substitution of, 29–32, 76, 77
vulgarisms, 21, 23

Weak position, 74
weak stress, 46
West European alphabets, 77
*whole compounds, 142–156
word, 91, 92; structure of, 111
*word-formation, 111; by affixation & de-affixation, 119–140; by borrowing, 113–115; by coalescing, 136–137, 138, 141–142; by compounding, 142–156; by phonetic processes, 113, 117–118, 118–119; by recategorization or transference, 115 116; by resemanticization or polysemanticization, 115; by stump-compounding, 156–163
words, sources of, Ch. 5 & 6

/x/, 34

Yazykov, D. I., 78
Yefimov, A., 146 (note 2)
Yesenin, 140
Yevtushenko, Ye., 114 (note 1)

Zero-ending, 104
zero predicator, 95
Zoshchenko, 23
/ʒ/, 35
/ʒ/, 35

2. *Russian*

This index includes roots, prefixes, suffixes and endings and also whole words which are singled out in the text for particular comment. Except in the case of verbs, it does not in general include words which are quoted in the text merely as examples of classes. Where necessary, a brief indication of the subject-matter is given in English.